The complete
illustrated
book of
CARD
GAMES

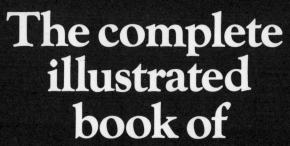

The complete
illustrated
book of
CARD
GAMES

George F Hervey

Doubleday & Company, Inc.
Garden City, New York.

Published by
The Hamlyn Publishing Group Limited
London · New York · Sydney · Toronto
Astronaut House, Feltham, Middlesex, England
© The Hamlyn Publishing Group Limited 1973
ISBN 0 600 31281 X
ISBN 0 385 0 3251 X Doubleday

Library of Congress Catalog Card Number 73-78145

Printed in Great Britain by
Butler and Tanner Ltd.,
Frome, England

Contents

Introduction

Books that describe an appreciable number of card games are sometimes given the adjective of comprehensive or complete. Such a description must be taken with the proverbial grain of salt, because altogether so many card games are known–and there is ample room for more–that to place a description of every one between the two covers of a book is virtually impossible. The most that can be done is to describe firstly those games that are so well known that they have an indefeasible right to be included; and secondly those that a competent authority has a right to include because their lack of popularity is, in his opinion, due to their having never been properly advertised. It is a perilous path and one that is apt to betray the idiosyncracies of the writer, because all the time he has to face difficulties and make reservations. Games that are well known in one country are not always so in another; even in the same country a game that is popular in one locality may not be in another. Like dog racing and off-the-peg clothes, quite a number of card games are the victims of snobbery.

In treading this rather perilous path, the present writer hopes that those who come to this book will either know the games described, or will have heard of them and wish to know more about them, and that they will have some knowledge of how card games in general are played and will not be disappointed to find that limitations of space have forbidden the dotting of every I and the crossing of every T. He cannot hope for more.

Every man has his cross to bear. If that of Sir Winston Churchill was the Cross of Lorraine, that of the present writer is the nomenclature of card games, because this book is addressed as much to card players in the English-speaking nations across the Atlantic as to those in the Mother Country. There are many differences of language that can be reconciled only with give-and-take. He is preferring the American *jack* to the English *knave* because it is extensively used by English card players; on the other hand, he is preferring the English *pack* to the American *deck* for no better reason, he must confess, than that to English ears it has an archaic ring. It is much the same with the *deuce* and *trey* of American card players, although in the article on poker he has had to retain the term deuces-wild because to write twos-wild is surely unthinkable. To balance the account, American card players must accept the fact that the game that goes by the name of knaves could hardly be altered to jacks. Many differences occur in the names that are given to card games, and some have attracted to themselves several names. This difficulty has been overcome, satisfactorily he hopes, by cross-indexing; some inconsistency, however, is inevitable.

Card games do not admit of a precise arrangement. In this book they have been arranged according to the number of players who may take part at one table; as, however, most card games can be played, in one form or another, by a varying number of players, it is more correct to say that the games have been arranged according to the number of players for which they are best suited; but party games and banking games are grouped separately, and among the party games some will be found suitable for members of the younger generation who may find that playing a game of cards is a less noisy pastime than playing an electric guitar. It is not an ideal arrangement, but it has the merit of convenience, and is less arbitrary than arranging the games in alphabetical order, and more practical than arranging them by their family resemblances. Most card games have a number of variations. Only the more popular ones have been given a place in this book, and, with some rare and inevitable exceptions, descriptions of them follow the description of the parent game.

The aim of the present writer is nothing higher than to explain how the various games are played; and when no authoritative organisation has laid down the scoring, rules of play and appropriate penalties for breaking them, the practice that he recommends is that of the majority of experienced players. If here and there he has broken form and given a few hints on skilful play, it is not to compete with the text books, but because without them the bare bones would be unreadable.

In conclusion he thanks the editor of *The Field* (of which newspaper he has been cards correspondent since January 1940) and the managing editor of Teach Yourself Books, for giving him permission to reprint—with necessary revisions, alterations and modifications—some material that has already appeared under his name in *The Field* and *Card Games for One*.

George F. Hervey
Bagshot 1973

The Publishers wish to acknowledge the kindness of Waddingtons Playing Card Co Ltd, which supplied the cards for the illustrations.

Games for
One player

Patiences
Solitaires

Bisley

SINGLE-PACK

Remove the four Aces from the pack and place them face upwards
in a row on the table. Deal nine cards in a row to the right of
them, and the rest of the pack in three rows of thirteen cards each,
below them (see illustration). When the four Kings become
available they are placed above their respective Aces.

The Aces are built on upwards and the Kings downwards in
suit-sequences. It does not matter where the two sequences meet.

Only the bottom card of a column is available for play. It
may be built either on its Ace- or King-foundation, packed on the
bottom card of another column, or itself be packed on. Packing

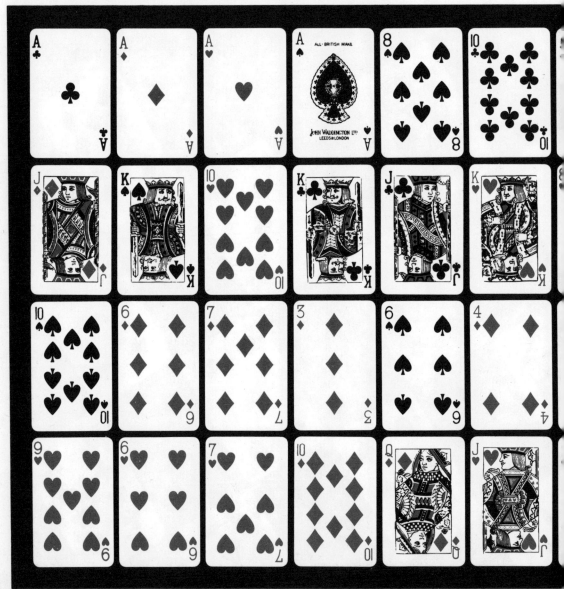

may be either upwards or downwards in suit-sequence, and the player may change this at his convenience. A space left vacant in the layout, by the removal of a card, is not filled.

In the layout below, the **K ♦** is played above the **A ♦**, the **2 ♠** is built on the **A ♠**, and the **2 ♥** on the **A ♥**. This exposes the **3 ♠** which is built on the **2 ♠**. The **Q ♦** is built on the **K ♦**. The **9 ♦** is packed on the **10 ♦**, and the **8 ♦** on the **9 ♦**. Now the **8 ♣** is packed on the **9 ♣**, exposing the **2 ♣** which is built on the **A ♣**. And so on.

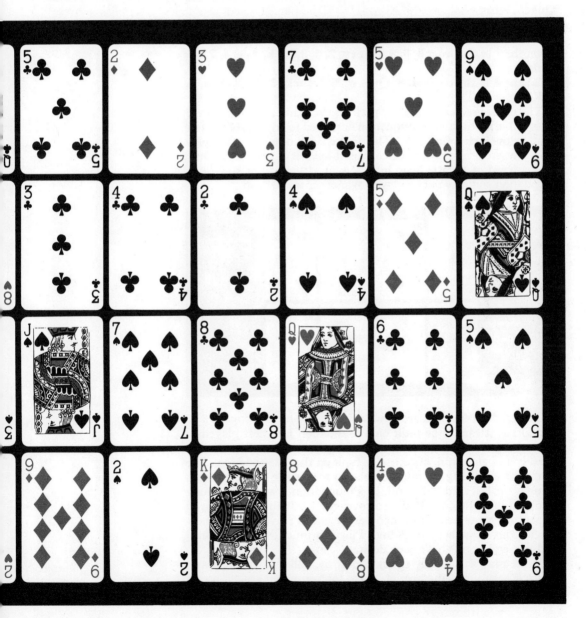

Calculation

SINGLE-PACK

Calculation, or Broken Intervals, is a one-pack patience that is well-named, because it is necessary to calculate at the turn of every card, and it offers more scope for skilful play than any other patience.

Any **Ace**, any **2**, any **3** and any **4** are placed in a row on the table to form four foundations. The object of the game is to build, regardless of suits, the remaining forty-eight cards on them, as follows:

On the **Ace** in the order **Ace, 2, 3, 4, 5, 6, 7, 8, 9, 10, Jack, Queen, King**.

On the **2** in the order **2, 4, 6, 8, 10, Queen, Ace, 3, 5, 7, 9, Jack, King**.

On the **3** in the order **3, 6, 9, Queen, 2, 5, 8, Jack, Ace, 4, 7, 10, King**.

On the **4** in the order **4, 8, Queen, 3, 7, Jack, 2, 6, 10, Ace, 5, 9, King**.

The cards are dealt from the pack one at a time, and every card must either be built on a foundation or played to any one of a waste heap below each foundation. The pack is dealt only once, but play from a waste heap may continue after it has been exhausted. Only the top card of a waste heap may be played; it may be built on a foundation and may not be played to another waste heap.

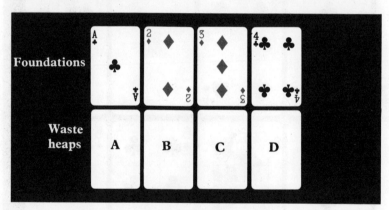

The cards in the pack are now dealt one at a time. Suppose a **10** is dealt, as it cannot be built on a foundation it is best played to waste heap **B**. Next a **6** is dealt; it is built on the 3-foundation. Next comes an **8**, and, of course, is built on the 4-foundation. The next card is a **King**. It must be played to a waste heap, but as a **King** is the last card to be built on a foundation it would be wrong to play it to waste heap **B** and so cover the **10**. It should be played to another waste heap, and many experienced players would now reserve this waste heap for Kings. Play continues in this way until all forty-eight cards have been dealt.

If the play is carefully thought out, by building on the waste heaps descending sequences of two to four or more cards, towards the end of a game excellent progress will be made.

Crossword

SINGLE-PACK

The twelve court cards are removed from the pack and temporarily put aside, leaving the player with a pack of forty cards. The top card of the pack is placed, face upwards, anywhere on the table, and the remaining cards are dealt one by one and each, as it is dealt, is placed on the table to touch – either at top or bottom, either side or at one of the four corners – a card already played. Once played a card must not be moved.

The object of the game is to form a square of seven cards each way whose pips add up to an even number. The court cards do not count; they are brought in when necessary to serve as stops in the same way as the black squares in crossword puzzles. The pips of the cards between the court cards must, of course, also add up to an even number. When forty-eight cards have been played there will be one space to fill and four cards left in the player's hand. He may choose which of these cards he likes to fill the vacant space. A game in progress is shown below and a completed game in Plate 1.

Demon

SINGLE-PACK

Demon is probably the best known of all the many one-pack patiences. It is sometimes known as Fascination, sometimes as Thirteen, and, in America, as Canfield, because it was reputedly invented by Richard A. Canfield, a well-known gambler of the late 19th century, whose practice it was to sell the pack for $52.00 and pay $5.00 for every card in the foundation row when the game came to an end. It was not altogether as profitable as it may seem, because for every player he had to employ a croupier to keep an eye on him during the play.

Thirteen cards are dealt face downwards in a pile and the top card is faced. The pile is known as the heel, and four cards are dealt face upwards in a row to the right of it. The next card of the pack is dealt face upwards and placed above the first card of the row. It indicates the foundations.

The 10 ♦ is the first of the four foundations, and the 3 ♦ is the top card of the heel. As they become available, the other three 10s are played to the right of the 10 ♦, and the object of the game is to build on them round-the-corner suit-sequences up to the 9s. The four cards to the right of the heel are packed in descending sequences of alternate colours. As a start, therefore, the J ♦ is built on its foundation-card; the 4 ♣ is packed on the 5 ♥ and the 3 ♦ on the 4 ♣. The card in the heel below the 3 ♦ is turned and, if it cannot be built on a foundation or packed on a card in the layout, is played to the space left vacant by the J ♦. The next card in the heel is then exposed.

The bottom card of the four columns may be built on a foundation, but a sequence may be moved from one column to another only as a whole, and then only if the sequence can be packed on the next higher card of a different colour.

The stock is dealt to a waste pile in batches of three cards at a time, but if there is less than three cards at the end of the stock they are dealt singly. The stock is dealt and redealt until the game is won, or lost because no further move can be made.

When all the cards in a column have been played, the space that is left must be filled at once with the top card of the heel and the next card of the heel exposed. A space must not be filled from the cards in hand, and when the heel is exhausted, spaces are filled from the waste heap, and the player need no longer fill a space at once, but leave it vacant until a suitable card is available.

PLATE 1 *(opposite)*
A completed game of crossword

Flower Garden

SINGLE-PACK

The Flower Garden, sometimes called the Bouquet and sometimes the Garden, is a fascinating one-pack patience with the added merit that success is not entirely the result of the fortuitous order of the cards.

Six packets of six cards each are fanned on the table. They are known as the beds (see Plate 2). The remaining sixteen cards are retained in hand. They are known as the bouquet.

The object of the game is to release the four Aces, play them to a row above the beds, and build on them ascending suit-sequences to the Kings.

All the cards in the bouquet are exposed cards and may either be built on the Ace-foundations or packed on the outer card of a bed in descending sequence irrespective of suit and colour. A sequence may be moved from one bed to another provided the sequence is retained. When a bed has been cleared, the vacant space may be filled either with a card from the bouquet, or by an exposed card or sequence from another bed.

If the layout is as on Plate 2 the bouquet in hand is:

The play is: play the A♣ to the foundation row, and build the 2♣ on it, followed by the 3♣ from the bouquet. Pack the Q♦ on the K♦, and the J♦ on the Q♦. Pack the 10♦ from the bouquet on the J♦, and the 9♥, 8♠ and 7♠ on it. Now the 6♠ is packed on the 7♠ and the A♦ played to the foundation row. The 5♦ is packed on the 6♠, the 6♣ on the 7♦ and the 2♠ on the 3♠. And so on.

At the best of times the patience is not an easy game, and the player will have difficulty in winning this one owing to the high cards in the bouquet and on top of the beds. If an alternative play is available, it is to be preferred to packing a card from the bouquet on a bed, because reducing the number of cards in the bouquet reduces the number of cards that may be played at one time. For the same reason an empty bed is not always advantageous, and it is unwise to pack too many cards on one bed in order to empty another. The main aim of the player should be to release the Aces, 2s and 3s, because a game may well be lost if even one low card is immobilized, and certainly if two are.

PLATE 2 *(opposite, above)* **The layout for flower garden**
PLATE 3 *(opposite, below)* **The layout for klondike**

Klondike

SINGLE-PACK

The demon (see page 16) and the Klondike are probably the two best-known and most popular of the one-pack patience games. In England the name of Canfield is sometimes attached to the Klondike. This name, however, is a misnomer, and to be corrected, because Canfield is the name that in America is given to the patience that we in England call the demon.

Twenty-eight cards are dealt face downwards in slightly over-lapping rows of seven cards, six cards, five cards, four cards, three cards, two cards and one card. The bottom card of each row is turned face upwards (see Plate 3).

As they become available, Aces are played as foundations to a row above the layout; the object of the game is to build on the Aces ascending suit-sequences to the Kings.

An exposed card at the bottom of a column is available to be built on a foundation, or it may be packed in a descending sequence of alternate colour. A sequence may be moved from one column to another, but only as a whole and when the highest card of the sequence may be placed on the next higher card of another colour. When an exposed card is played, the face-downwards card immediately above it is turned face upwards; when a whole column is moved, the space must be filled by a King which may or may not have a sequence attached to it.

The stock is dealt one card at a time to a waste heap, of which the top card is available for building on a foundation or packing on a column in the layout. Only one deal is allowed.

An Ace must be played to the foundation row as soon as it becomes available, but all other cards may be left in position if the player prefers to wait on the prospect of finding a better move later in the game.

In the layout on Plate 3 the 5 ♦ is packed on the 6 ♣, and the card under the 5 ♦ is turned face upwards. The J ♣ is packed on the Q ♥, and the K ♦ moved to fill the space vacated by the J ♣. The card under the K ♦ is now turned face upwards. And so on.

Klondike has been the subject of several variations. One of the best is *Joker Klondike*. It is played in the same way as the parent game, but with the Joker added to the pack. Whenever the Joker becomes available for play it must be built on a foundation as the next card in sequence. Other cards, if in correct sequence, are built on it, but when the natural card that it replaces becomes available it is substituted for the Joker which is built on another foundation.

A player may choose on which foundation he will build the Joker. If it becomes available for play before a foundation has been started it must remain in its position until an Ace turns up and a foundation started.

La Belle Lucie

SINGLE-PACK

La Belle Lucie, or the Fan, is one of the classical one-pack patiences; it has a very pleasing layout. The entire pack is spread on the table in seventeen fans of three cards each and one of a single card, as illustrated.

As the Aces become available they are placed above the layout as foundations, to be built on in ascending suit-sequences to the Kings. Only the end card of each fan and the single card are available for play. They may be built on a foundation, packed on the end card of another fan in descending suit-sequence, or themselves be packed on in descending suit-sequences. A space made by playing off a complete fan is not filled.

When all possible moves have been made, all the cards except those played to the foundations, are picked up, shuffled, and redealt in fans of three. If one or two cards are left over they make separate fans. Two redeals are allowed.

In the layout illustrated the A ♥ and A ♣ are played to the foundation row. The 2 ♥ is built on the A ♥, and the 7 ♣ is packed on the 8 ♣. This releases the 2 ♣ that is built on the A ♣. The J ♦ is packed on the Q ♦, the J ♥ on the Q ♥, and the A ♠ followed by the 2 ♠ go to the foundation row. And so on.

Little Spider

SINGLE-PACK

The two red Aces and the two black Kings (or the two black Aces and the two red Kings) are placed in a row on the table to serve as foundations. The remaining forty-eight cards are dealt, face upwards, in two rows of four cards each, one above the foundation cards, the other below them.

The object of the game is to build ascending suit-sequences on the Aces to Kings, and descending suit-sequences on the Kings to Aces.

During the deal a card may be built from the upper row on any of the four foundation cards, but from the lower row only on the foundation card directly above it.

After every batch of eight cards has been dealt, the top cards of all eight piles are playable and may be built on any foundation cards or packed on any other pile in the layout. The piles are packed in ascending or descending, continuous sequences (an Ace ranks below a 2 and above a King) regardless of suit. A space made by removing an entire pile is not filled.

In the layout illustrated, the **Q ♣** may be built on the **K ♣** and the **2 ♥** on the **A ♥**. The **10 ♣** may be packed on the **J ♠**, and the **5 ♣** on the **6 ♠**. And so on.

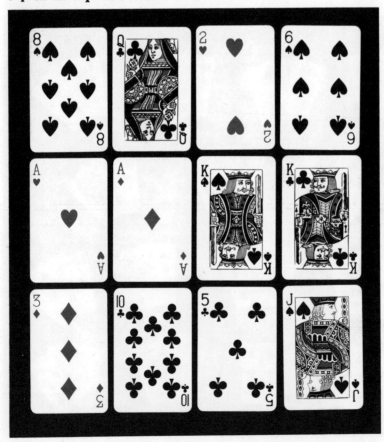

Maze

SINGLE-PACK

Maze is an excellent patience because some skill is necessary if it is
to be successful.

The fifty-two cards of the pack are dealt face upwards in two
rows of eight cards each, and four of nine cards each. The four
Kings are then discarded. This leaves four spaces, or six in all,
because as well as the spaces left by the discard of the Kings, the
spaces at the end of the first and second rows are taken into the
layout for the play (see illustration).

The object of the game is to arrange the forty-eight cards in four ascending suit-sequences, from Aces to Queens, beginning with an Ace at the extreme left of the top row and ending with a Queen at the extreme right of the bottom row. The sequences follow on, from the end of one row to the beginning of the next, as in reading and writing. Only one card may be moved at a time.

The rules for moving a card into a space are:

1. The card must be in suit-sequence one higher than the card on the left of the space or one lower than the card on the right of the space, and it is to be assumed that not only are the rows continuous but that the bottom row is continuous with the top row.

2. When a space occurs on the right of a Queen it may be filled with any Ace, as an alternative to the card one lower in suit-sequence than the card on the right of the space.

Suppose the layout is as in the illustration. After the four Kings have been discarded, the space left vacant by the **K** may be filled by any Ace, or with the **9 ♠** (by reason of the **10 ♠** on the right of the space) or the **8 ♠** (by reason of the **7 ♠** at the end of the bottom row). The space at the extreme right of the top row may be filled either with the **2 ♥** or **4 ♥**, that at the extreme right of the second row either with the **10 ♥** or **10 ♠**. The space left vacant by the **K ♦** may be filled either with the **Q ♣** or **5 ♠**.

To begin the game. Play the **A ♠** to the top left corner of the layout, and the **10 ♥** to its vacant place. Play the **5 ♦** to the left of the **6 ♦** in the top row, and the **J ♦** to the left of the **Q ♦** in the bottom row. Play the **10 ♠** to the extreme right of the second row, and the **2 ♠** followed by the **3 ♠** to the right of the **A ♠** in the top row. Play the **5 ♠** to the left of the **6 ♠**, the **J ♣** to the left of the **Q ♣** and the **4 ♠** to the left of the **5 ♠**. The **5 ♥** is played to the left of the **6 ♥**, the **9 ♥** to the left of the **10 ♥** and the **9 ♠** to the left of the **10 ♠**. Now the **5 ♦** in the top row may be played to the right of the **4 ♦** and the **4 ♠** to the right of the **3 ♠** in the top row. With the **A ♠, 2 ♠, 3 ♠** and **4 ♠** in position, the game progresses well.

Raglan

SINGLE-PACK

The four Aces are placed in a row in the centre of the table as foundations. Below them forty-two cards are dealt, face upwards, in seven, slightly overlapping, rows; the first of nine cards, the second of eight, and so on down to a row of three cards. The remaining six cards (the stock) are placed face upwards in a row below the layout (see Plate 4).

The object of the game is to build ascending suit-sequences on the Aces, to the Kings.

The bottom cards of the columns, and the six cards in the stock are exposed. They may be built on a foundation, and those at the bottom of a column (but not those in the stock) may be packed in descending sequences of alternate colour. All cards must be moved singly; sequences must not be moved. When all the cards of a column have been removed, the player, if he wishes, may fill the space with any exposed card.

In the layout on Plate 4, the **5 ♦** is packed on the **6 ♠**, and the **3 ♠** on the **4 ♥** that has been left exposed by the play of the **5 ♦**. The **Q ♥**, in the stock, may be packed on the **K ♠**, and the **10 ♠** on the **J ♦**. Now the **9 ♥** may be packed on the **10 ♠**. The **4 ♠** in the stock is packed on the **5 ♦**, the **3 ♦** on the **4 ♠** and the **6 ♥** on the **7 ♣**. The space is filled by the **Q ♣**, the **2 ♣** is played to its foundation, the **J ♠** is packed on the **Q ♥**, the **8 ♠** on the **9 ♥** and the **10 ♦** on the **J ♠**. The **9 ♠** is packed on the **10 ♦**, the **8 ♥** on the **9 ♠**, the **6 ♦** is played to the space and the **2 ♠** followed by the **3 ♠** are built on their foundation. The space is filled with the **4 ♥**, the **5 ♣** is packed on the **6 ♦** and the **4 ♥** on the **5 ♣**. The **7 ♦** and the **6 ♣** from the stock are packed on the **8 ♠**, the **5 ♥** on the **6 ♣** and the space is filled with the **9 ♦**. Now the **2 ♥**, **3 ♥**, **4 ♥**, **5 ♥**, **6 ♥** and **7 ♥** are built on their foundation. The **7 ♣** is packed on the **8 ♥**, the space is filled with the **7 ♠**, and the **2 ♦** and **3 ♦** are built on their foundation, followed by the **4 ♠** and **5 ♠** on theirs. Although the **3 ♣** and **4 ♣** are badly placed the game has progressed well, and there is every chance that it will succeed.

Scorpion

SINGLE-PACK

Seven cards, four face downwards and three face upwards, are dealt in a row. Two more rows are dealt in the same way, and then four rows of face-upwards cards. For convenience the rows may overlap slightly (see illustration). The remaining three cards are temporarily set aside.

Leaving the four Kings within the layout, the object of the game is to build on them descending suit-sequence to the Aces.

The cards at the bottom of the columns are exposed, and they may be packed with the next lower cards in suit-sequence. To do this a card may be taken from anywhere in the layout, but if a card is not taken from the bottom of a column, all the cards below it in the column must be taken with it.

In the layout shown, the 3 ♦ may be packed on the 4 ♦, but the 2 ♣ must go with it. In the same way, the 5 ♠ may be packed on the 6 ♠, but the 7 ♠, 6 ♥, A ♣ and 10 ♦ must be moved with it. And so on. Nothing, of course, is packed on an Ace.

When a face-downwards card is cleared, it is turned face upwards, and when a whole column is cleared the space is filled by a King, together with any cards below it in the column from which it is taken.

When no further moves can be made, the three cards, temporarily set aside, are now dealt face upwards, one to the foot of each of the three columns at the extreme left of the layout.

The game is by no means an easy one and calls for some care and forethought if it is to succeed.

As a start, the layout should be inspected closely. If there is a reverse sequence, such as Q ♦, J ♦, K ♦, in one column the game can never be won; nor can it if there is a criss-cross, such as the 9 ♠ on the 6 ♦ in one column and the 5 ♦ on the 10 ♠ in another. In such cases as these it is a waste of time not to redeal.

If the layout offers promise of success, the first move should be an attempt to uncover the face-downwards cards. In the layout illustrated, for example, it will be seen that the 4 ♣, together with the 9 ♦, 3 ♠ and Q ♣, will free a face-downwards card if the combination is packed on the 5 ♣. The first move, therefore, is to pack the 5 ♠, together with the 7 ♠, 6 ♥, A ♣ and 10 ♦, on the 6 ♠.

Careful thought should always be given to a situation before a move is made. Carelessness may well end by the player blocking the game.

Fourteens

DOUBLE-PACK

Fourteens is one of several two-pack patience games composed by Mr Charles Jewell. Forty-eight cards are dealt in the form of an open cross (see Plate 5). To win the game the table must be cleared of every card in the pack. Counting the Jacks as 11, the Queens as 12 and the Kings as 13, any two cards that touch each other, either at the sides, the corners or at top and bottom (either within the same quarter of the cross or, so to speak, across its upright and arms) are discarded if together they have a pip total of fourteen. There is, however, no compulsion to discard a touching pair. When two cards have been discarded, those that remain on the table are closed up towards the centre of the cross, but not across its upright or arms. When all discards have been made, and the cards that remain on the table have been closed up, the layout is filled with cards from the stock.

In the layout on Plate 5, the J ♥ and 3 ♠ in the fourth quarter are discarded and the 5 ♠ and 8 ♦ moved to the left. Now the Q ♦ may be moved either upwards or to the left and very clearly it should be moved to the left in order that it may be paired and discarded with the 2 ♦. The 4 ♣ and 9 ♠ are moved upwards, the K ♠ and A ♥ are discarded, and the 6 ♠ is moved upwards. In the second quarter the 3 ♠ and J ♦ are discarded, and the 6 ♣ and K ♠ moved downwards. This allows the 6 ♣ (in the second quarter) to be paired and discarded with the 8 ♦ (in the fourth quarter) and the K ♠ (in the second quarter) to be moved to the left. The layout is very favourable to success, because in the first quarter the J ♠ may be discarded with the 3 ♥, the 6 ♥ and 3 ♣ moved to the right, and the 8 ♥ and 6 ♠ discarded. In the second quarter the J ♠ and 3 ♣ may be discarded and the 7 ♦ moved downwards. In the third quarter there is the choice of discarding the 3 ♦ either with the J ♦ or with the J ♣. And so on.

The game calls for considerable foresight, and a watchful eye must be kept on the four cards at the centre of the cross, because unless they can be paired, and discarded, the movement of the layout towards the centre is obstructed. Very often it is unwise to discard a pair and the better play to keep it in reserve. Judicious pairing and discarding, coupled with skilful movements in closing up, helps towards getting the right card into position to get rid of a card that is holding up the game at the centre of the cross. The end game calls for exact play, because it usually contains a number of traps into which it is very easy for the thoughtless player to get caught.

Indian Carpet

DOUBLE-PACK

Indian Carpet, Crazy Quilt, Japanese Rug or Quilt, is a two-pack patience with a very attractive layout (see Plate 6). An Ace and a King of each suit are played to the centre as foundations. Below them, sixty-four cards are dealt face upwards in eight rows of eight cards each; they are laid vertically and horizontally in turn.

The Ace-foundations are built on in ascending suit-sequences to the Kings, and the King-foundations in descending suit-sequences to the Aces.

Any card in the layout is available for play, provided that either of its shorter sides does not touch another card. Thus in the layout on Plate 6 the **2♠** in the top row may be built on its Ace-foundation, but the **2♥** may not. The play of the **2♠** leaves the **5♦** and **J♠** free to be played later.

Spaces in the layout are not filled, and the cards in the layout are not packed. The remaining thirty-two cards are turned one at a time, and any card that cannot be built on a foundation is played to a waste heap. Available cards in the layout may be packed on the top card of the waste heap either in ascending or descending round-the-corner suit-sequences.

The waste heap may be redealt once.

Miss Milligan

DOUBLE-PACK

Miss Milligan is a very popular two-pack patience, and by no means an easy one.

Eight cards are dealt in a row. Any Aces are played to the centre of the table, to be built on in ascending suit-sequences to the Kings. The cards in the layout are packed in descending sequences of alternate colour. A space may be filled only by a King, with or without a sequence. When all moves have been made in the first row, a further eight cards are dealt, one card to each column, slightly overlapping the cards in the first row, and filling any spaces. No packing or building of a card on a foundation may be made until all eight cards have been dealt. Play continues in this way, making moves after each row of eight cards has been dealt, until the pack is exhausted. Sequences must be moved intact.

When the whole pack has been dealt, but not before, if a card at the bottom of a column blocks the run of a sequence, it may be taken into the hand and held in reserve until further moves enable the player to find a place for it in the layout. This is known as waiving, and though it may be repeated as often as the player wishes, only one card at a time may be waived.

Paganini

DOUBLE-PACK

Paganini is a double-pack patience game, similar in principle to but more interesting than, the single-pack game known as spaces. It was composed by Mr Charles Jewell.

The entire pack is dealt face upwards on the table in eight rows of thirteen cards each, as shown in the accompanying illustration.

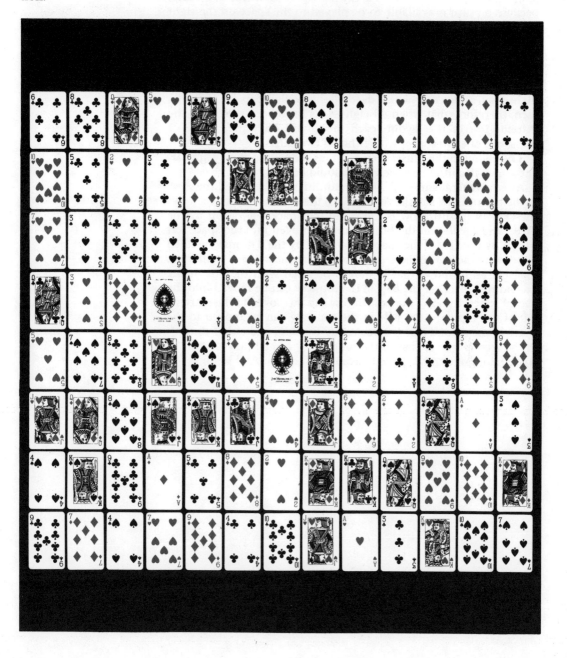

The object of the game is so to arrange the cards that each row consists of one suit beginning with an Ace (on the left) and ending with a King (on the right). No row is singled out for any particular suit; the player makes his own decision but, having made it, must not alter it.

Play begins by moving one of the Aces to the extreme left of a row. It will be appreciated, therefore, that as the game proceeds the whole of the layout is moved one space to the left so to speak. When a card is moved it leaves a space in the layout which is filled with the next higher card of the same suit as the card on the left of the space. Filling a space leaves another space in the layout. In turn this is filled in the same way, and so on, until a run is brought to an end by removing a card from the right-hand side of a King, because no card is available to be played to the space on the right of a King.

The game calls for a show of skill. To begin, a player has to decide which of the eight Aces he will move first and to the extreme left of which of the eight rows he will move it to. Then, whenever a card is moved in the layout, there is, at all events early in the play, a choice of two cards to fill the available space. It will be seen, therefore, that when all eight Aces have been moved to the extreme left of the layout, each move will offer the choice of filling one of eight spaces with either of two cards.

The layout in the illustration is not as difficult as it may appear. Indeed, with a little care the game should be won.

After a general survey of the possibilities in the game, the **A ♥** in the bottom row should be moved to the extreme left of the row; the **Q ♥** in the fifth row is moved to the space left vacant by the **A ♥**; and the **9 ♣** in the bottom row is moved into the space left vacant by the **Q ♥**. The space left vacant by the **9 ♣** may be filled either with the **2 ♥** in the second row or the one in the seventh row. Consideration shows that it should be filled with the one in the second row, because the **6 ♣** in the top row can be moved into the vacant space, the **A ♣** in the fifth row can be moved to the extreme left of the top row, the **6 ♣** in the top row can be moved to the space in the second row left vacant by the **2 ♥**, and either the **2 ♣** in the second row or that in the fourth row can be moved into the space (alongside the **A ♣**) left vacant by the **6 ♣**. And so on.

Robin Post

DOUBLE-PACK

Robin Post is a 2-pack patience composed by Colonel G. H. Latham, R.E. It is one that calls for considerable thought and skill, not only because so many moves are available but because every move opens the door to a number of variations.

Fifty-two cards are dealt face upwards in rows of four, five, six, seven, eight, seven, six, five, four, with a space of one card's width between each card so that the cards only touch each other corner to corner. In Plate 7, the cards are laid out in a smaller area, but it is to be imagined that the 2 ♦ on the extreme right, for instance, has its left hand corners touching the 3 ♦ and 6 ♠, while its right hand corners are free.

The object of the game is to release one Ace and one King of each suit, play them to the centre as foundations, and build on the Aces ascending suit-sequence to the Kings, and on the Kings descending suit-sequences to the Aces. At any stage of the play, if the top cards of two foundation-piles of the same suit are in sequence, any or all of the cards of one pile (with the exception of the original Ace- or King-foundation card) may be reversed onto the other.

The cards in the layout are subject to the following four rules:
1. A card which has two or more corners free may be lifted and played. In Plate 7, the cards with two or more corners free are the 6 ♠ and 2 ♦ on the extreme edges of the layout, and those in the top and bottom rows.
2. A card which has only one corner free may not be lifted and played, but may be packed on either in ascending or descending sequence of alternate colour.
3. A card that has no corner free may neither be lifted and played nor packed on.
4. A movable sequence must be moved as a whole, not as a part, and may be reversed only onto a single card.

The remaining fifty-two cards of the pack are turned one at a time and played to a waste heap if they cannot be built on the foundation cards or packed on the cards in the layout. At any stage of the game, however, the layout may be completed with cards from the stock. The cards must be dealt to the original top row of the layout, from left to right, and, provided there are enough cards left in the stock, the layout must be filled before further moves are made either to the foundations or within the layout.

In Plate 7 the Q ♣ in the top row can be packed on the J ♦ at the left of the fourth row. Similarly the 10 ♦ in the top row can be packed on the 9 ♠ at the left of the second row. This will provide both the A ♣ and 5 ♠ with two free corners and the A ♣ can be played to the centre as a foundation.

Royal Cotillion

DOUBLE-PACK

Arrange one Ace and one 2 of each suit in two columns, the 2s to the right of the Aces. To the left of the Aces deal twelve cards in three rows of four cards each – it is called the left wing; and to the right of the 2s sixteen cards in four rows of four cards each – it is known as the right wing (see illustration).

The object of the game is to build on the Aces suit-sequences in the order: **A 3 5 7 9 J K 2 4 6 8 10 Q**, and on the 2s in the order: **2 4 6 8 10 Q A 3 5 7 9 J K**.

From the left wing only the bottom card of a column may be built on a foundation and the space is not filled; from the right wing any card may be built on a foundation and the space must be filled either with the top card of the waste heap or that of the stock.

The stock is turned once and any card that cannot be built on a foundation, or is not needed to fill a space in the right wing, is played to a waste heap.

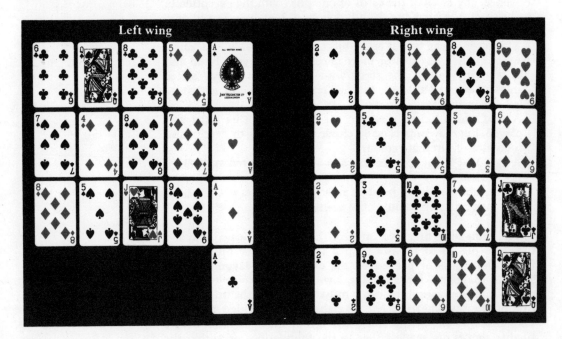

Left wing   Right wing

PLATE 4 *(opposite)*
The layout for raglan
PLATE 5 *(overleaf, left)* **The layout for fourteens**
PLATE 6 *(overleaf, right)* **The layout for Indian carpet**

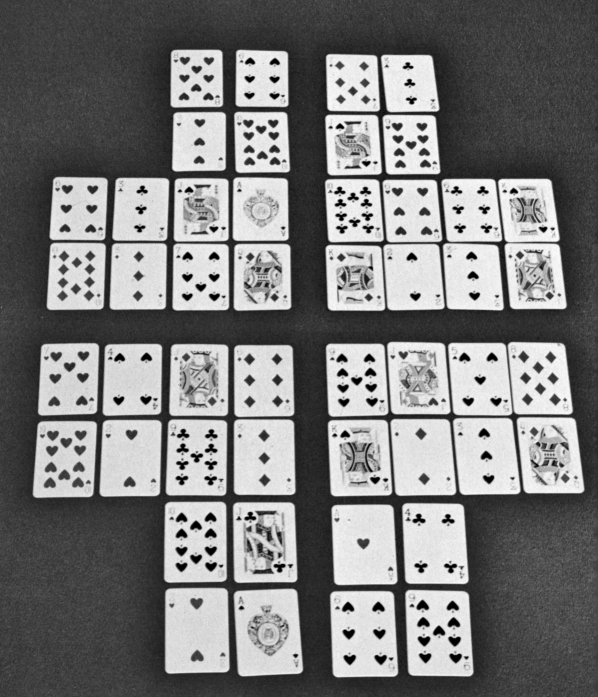

Royal Parade

DOUBLE-PACK

PLATE 7 *(opposite)*
The layout for robin post

Royal Parade is a popular two-pack patience with the alternative names of Financier, Hussars and Three Up.

Twenty-four cards are dealt in three rows of eight cards each (see illustration). Aces take no part in the game and are discarded. The cards in the layout must be arranged so that the top row consists of eight 2s, the middle row of eight 3s, and the bottom row of eight 4s, and these cards must be built on in suit-sequences at intervals of three cards, namely:

2	3	4
5	6	7
8	9	10
J	Q	K

In the layout illustrated the **A ♦**, in the top row, and the **A ♣**, in the bottom row, are discarded: the **4 ♠**, in the middle row, is moved to the space in the bottom row left vacant by the discard of the **A ♣**, and the **7 ♠**, in the top row, built on it. Either the **3 ♥** or **3 ♣**, both in the top row, may be moved to fill the space in the middle row left vacant by the **4 ♠**, and clearly the **3 ♥** should be chosen because the **6 ♥**, in the bottom row may be built on it. And so on.

When all moves have been made, eight cards are dealt to waste heaps below the layout. Aces, as they are dealt, are discarded; other cards are used to build on the foundations or to fill spaces in the layout. Play continues in this way, making moves after each deal of eight cards to the waste-heaps, until the pack is exhausted. Only the top cards of the waste heaps may be moved to the layout.

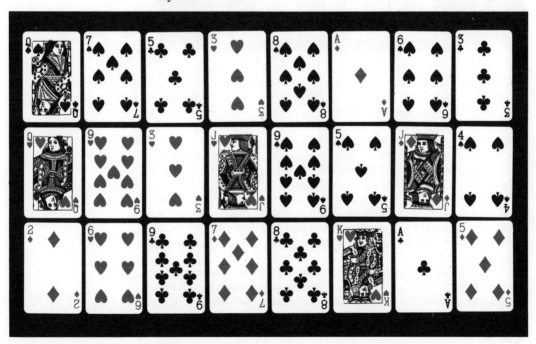

Saint Helena

DOUBLE-PACK

Saint Helena, or Napoleon's Favourite, is a two-pack patience in which the packs are not shuffled together but used one after the other. Although the game gives a player some scope for ingenuity and the exercise of his memory, it is such a simple game that one rather doubts that it received its name because it was Napoleon's chief amusement during his last years.

An Ace and a King of each suit are arranged in two rows, the Kings above the Aces. Twelve cards are then dealt, clockwise, beginning above the left-hand King, as shown in the diagram:

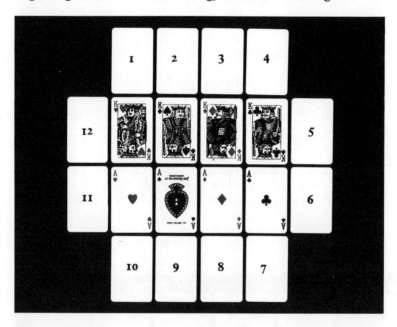

The Kings are built on in descending suit-sequence to the Aces, and the Aces in ascending suit-sequences to the Kings; with the restriction that cards dealt to spaces 1, 2, 3, 4 may be built only on the Kings, cards dealt to spaces 7, 8, 9, 10 only to the Aces, and cards dealt to spaces 5, 6, 11, 12 to either.

When all moves have been made the spaces are filled from the pack, and when no further moves are to be made, another twelve cards are dealt to cover the cards in position.

When the pack has been exhausted, the restriction of play is lifted, and cards may be built on any foundation from any one of the twelve surrounding waste heaps. Also, the top card of each waste heap may now be packed on either in ascending or descending suit-sequence.

Three deals in all are allowed. The waste heaps are picked up in reverse order 12 . . . . 1, and turned face downwards, so that the bottom card of the twelfth waste heap becomes the top card of the re-made stock. No shuffling is allowed.

Shah

DOUBLE-PACK

The Shah, sometimes known as the Star, is a two-pack patience that derives both its names from its layout. The King of Hearts is placed in the centre of the table, the other seven Kings are discarded (they take no part in the game) and the eight Aces are arranged about the King of Hearts, as illustrated on Plate 8.

The object of the game is to build suit-sequences on the Aces to the Queens, so that if the game succeeds, the King of Hearts (the Shah) will be surrounded by the eight Queens (his harem).

A card is dealt to the outside of each Ace. If a **2** is dealt it is played to its foundation and another card is dealt to fill the vacancy. In the same way, if a **2** has been played to a foundation and a **3** is dealt it is played to the foundation and another card dealt from the pack to fill the vacancy.

The deal to the outside of the Aces, or points of the stars, is made three times. After this the outside cards are packed in descending suit-sequences.

In the layout on Plate 8, the **4 ♦** may be packed on the **5 ♦**, the **8 ♥** on the **9 ♥**, the **4 ♣** on the **5 ♣**, the **8 ♠** on the **9 ♠**, and so on.

The stock is turned one card at a time, and those cards that cannot be built on a foundation or packed on the layout are played to a waste heap.

If all the cards of a ray are played, the space may be filled by one card from the outer circle.

Spider

DOUBLE-PACK

There are several variations of Spider. The one described in this article is deservedly considered the best, and, indeed, among the best of all patiences, because it frequently calls for deep analysis. According to *Redbook Magazine* it was the favourite patience of the late President Franklin D. Roosevelt.

Forty cards are dealt to the table in four overlapping rows of ten cards each: the first, second and third rows face downwards, the fourth row face upwards, as in the diagram.

Foundation cards are not played to the centre. The game is to build within the layout, descending suit-sequences on the eight

Kings to the Aces. A completed sequence is discarded, so that the game is won when the table is cleared of all cards.

The cards at the bottom of the columns may be packed in descending sequences irrespective of suit and colour, and when a card is moved from one column to another the face-downwards card immediately above it is turned face upwards and becomes available for play.

In the diagram any of the three sixes may be packed on the **7 ♠** and the **9 ♦** may be packed on either of the tens. Two cards will thus be exposed.

When all the cards have been moved from a column, the space may be filled by any exposed card or sequence of cards.

After all possible moves have been made, and spaces filled, ten cards are dealt from the stock, face upwards, one to the bottom of each column, overlapping the cards in position.

Play is continued in this way until the stock is exhausted. The last deal from the stock will, of course, be of only four cards.

Sultan

DOUBLE-PACK

Sultan, sometimes, but rarely, known as Emperor of Germany, is a two-pack patience that calls for some skill if it is to be successful.

The eight Kings and one Ace of Hearts are removed from the pack and arranged on the table as shown in the diagram. With the exception of the central King of Hearts they serve as foundations to be built up in suit-sequences to the Queens, the Aces ranking between the Kings and the 2s.

On each side of the foundations, deal a column of four cards, as shown in the diagram. It is known as the divan, and the cards dealt to it are available to be built on the foundations. When one is played, the space is filled either from the stock or from the waste heap, but need not be filled immediately.

The pack is turned one card at a time to a waste heap, and may be dealt three times.

Management of the divan is of great importance. The general rule is not to fill a space with a card that is unlikely to be wanted during the immediate deal. If, for example, a foundation is built up to a 7, and both 8s are already buried, the 9s and higher cards should be played to the waste heap, because if used to fill a space in the divan they would be wasted.

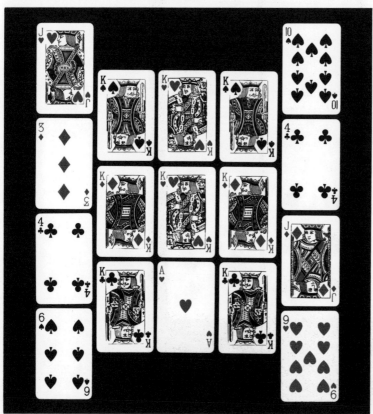

Windmill

DOUBLE-PACK

Like shah (see page 41) Windmill or Propeller gets its name from the layout. Any King is placed face upwards on the table, and two cards are dealt above it, two below it, and two on each side of it, to form a cross (see illustration). The first four Aces that are dealt, whether to the layout or as the stock is turned, are played to the angles of the cross.

The object of the game is to build on the central King a descending, round-the-corner, sequence of fifty-two cards, regardless of suit and colour, and ascending suit-sequences, regardless of suit and colour, on the four Aces to the Kings.

In the layout shown, the **A ♦** is played to an angle of the cross, the **Q ♦** is built on the **K ♠**, and the **J ♥** on the **Q ♦**. At any time a card may be taken from an Ace-foundation and played to the King-foundation, but only one card may be taken from each Ace-foundation during the building of any one sequence on the King-foundation.

The stock is turned to a waste heap, and a space in the layout must be filled from the waste heap, or from the stock if there is no waste heap.

There is no second deal, but when the stock is exhausted, the waste heap may be taken up and the first card dealt. If it can be played to a foundation, the next card is dealt, and so on. The game, however, comes to an end when a card can no longer be played to a foundation.

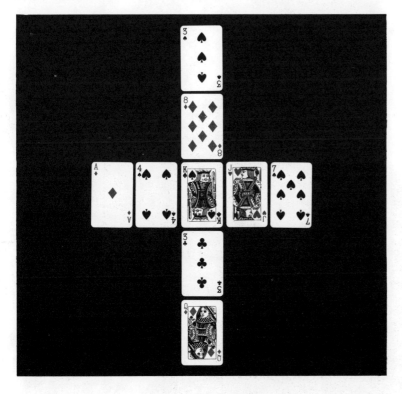

Games for Two players

48

All Fours

All Fours is known in America as Old Sledge. It is a game for two players played with the full pack of fifty-two cards, which rank from Ace (high) to 2 (low). The game is won by he who first scores 7 points. The points are scored as follows:

High. The player who is dealt the highest trump in play scores 1 point.

Low. The player who is dealt the lowest trump in play scores 1 point.

Jack. The player who wins the Jack of trumps (if it is in play) scores 1 point.

Game. Each player counts the honours among the tricks he has won, and, counting the Ace as 4, the King as 3, the Queen as 2, the Jack as 1 and the Ten as 10, the player with the highest total scores 1 point. If there is equality the non-dealer scores the point.

The points are not counted until the end of the deal, but they should be understood from the start because they illustrate the object of the game.

Six cards are dealt in bundles of three to both players, and the thirteenth card is turned up to determine the trump suit.

The non-dealer now declares whether he will stand or beg. If he says 'I stand' he accepts the turned-up card as the trump suit and play begins. If he says 'I beg' he rejects the turned-up card as the trump suit, and the dealer must either accept or refuse the proposal to make another suit trumps. To refuse he says 'Take one'. The non-dealer then scores 1 point for gift and play begins. To accept he says 'I run the cards'. He deals three more cards to his opponent and three to himself, and turns up the next card to determine the trump suit. If this is the same suit as the original trump suit, he runs the cards again, and continues to run them until a different trump suit is turned up. In the rare, but not impossible, event of the pack being exhausted without a different trump suit being turned up, there is a redeal by the same player. If the turned-up card is a Jack, the dealer scores 1 point, and if, when the cards are run, the turned-up card is again a Jack, the dealer again scores 1 point.

Play begins when the trump suit has been determined, and if the cards have been run, the players first discard from their hands enough cards to reduce the cards held to six. The non-dealer leads to the first trick. His opponent must follow suit or trump. Unlike at most games, however, a player may trump even though he is able to follow suit, but he must not discard if he holds either a card of the suit led or a trump. If he does he has revoked and his opponent scores 1 point.

The winner of a trick leads to the next, and so on until all six tricks have been played. The players then turn up their tricks and score for High, Low, Jack and Game.

These four scoring features are fundamental to the game and are counted whenever it is possible to do so. If, for example, there is only one trump in play it counts 2 points, because it is both High and Low.

The deal passes in rotation.

ALL FOURS FOR FOUR PLAYERS is played with two players playing in partnership against the other two in partnership.

The method of play is the same as in the parent game, except that only the dealer and the opponent on his left (eldest hand) look at their cards to determine the trump suit. When they have done this, but not before, the other two players look at their cards and come into the game for play.

If a player exposes a card it is liable to be called by an opponent.

SEVEN UP is a variation of the parent game that receives its name from the method of scoring.

Both players (or both sides if four are playing) begin with seven counters each. Every time that a point is scored the player (or side) that wins it puts a counter aside, and the player (or side) who first gets rid of his counters wins the game. If both go out in the same deal, the winner is the one who first counts out when the points are scored for High, Low, Jack and Game.

ALL FIVES is a variation of the parent game that is played for 61 points up. For convenience the score is best kept on a cribbage board (see Plate 11).

The mechanics of the game are the same as those of the parent game, and points are pegged when the following trumps are won in a trick: Ace 4 points, King 3 points, Queen 2 points, Jack 1 point, Ten 10 points and Five 5 points. After the hand has been played, the honours are counted as in the parent game, to determine the point for Game, with the addition that the player who has won the 5 of trumps scores 5 points for it.

Bezique

The standard game of Bezique is played by two players, with two packs of cards from which the 6s, 5s, 4s, 3s and 2s have been removed. The cards rank in the order: **A 10 K Q J 9 8 7**.

Eight cards are dealt to each player in packets of three, two, three. The remaining forty-eight cards (the stock) are placed face downwards on the table, and the dealer exposes the top card to denote the trump suit. It is placed alongside the stock, and if it is a **7** he scores 10 points.

The non-dealer leads to the first trick. As at most games the winner of a trick leads to the next, but it is a feature of bezique that a player is under no obligation to follow suit to the card led. The object of the game is to score points for declaring certain cards and combinations of cards. The declarations, and the points that may be scored for them, are as follows:

Double Bezique = 500 points. Two **Q ♠** (or **Q ♣** if Spades or Diamonds are trumps) and two **J ♦** (or **J ♥** if Spades or Diamonds are trumps).

Sequence in Trumps = 250 points. **A 10 K Q J** of the trump suit.

Any Four Aces = 100 points.

Any Four Kings = 80 points.

Any Four Queens = 60 points.

Any Four Jacks = 40 points.

Bezique = 40 points. **Q ♠** (or **Q ♣** if Spades or Diamonds are trumps) and **J ♦** (or **J ♥** if Spades or Diamonds are trumps).

Royal Marriage = 40 points. **King** and **Queen** of the trump suit.

Common Marriage = 20 points. **King** and **Queen** of the same plain suit.

A player scores 10 points if he holds a **7** of the trump suit and exchanges it for the turn-up card; and 10 points are scored for playing a **7** of the trump suit.

When a player has won a trick he may declare by placing the appropriate cards face upwards on the table. He may make as many declarations as he chooses, always provided that the declarations do not involve the same cards. If the exposed cards show more than one declaration the player must announce which declaration he intends to score, and leave the other to be scored when he wins another trick. A card that has once scored cannot again be used to form part of a similar declaration. As an example, a player may expose **K ♠ Q ♠ J ♦** score 40 for bezique and announce 'Twenty to come' meaning that the next time he wins a trick he will score 20 points for the common marriage of the King and Queen of Spades. He may not expose a second Jack of Diamonds and score bezique with the Queen of Spades. The cards that have been declared, and so exposed on the table, remain a part of the player's hand and he may play them to later tricks.

Tricks should be gathered and kept by the player who wins them, because at the end of a deal a player scores 10 points for every Ace and every 10 that he has won. They are known as brisques.

When both players have played to a trick they replenish their hands from the stock: winner takes the top card, loser the next.

When the stock is exhausted the last eight tricks are played, and the game takes on a rather different character. Now, if a player has a card of the suit that has been led he must play it, and he must win a trick if he is able to. No further declarations may be made, and the aim of the player is to win brisques and the last trick for which 10 points are scored.

The deal passes to the other player, and so alternately, until one of them has reached an agreed number of points, usually 2,000.

The score cannot be kept satisfactorily with pencil on paper. It is best to use the special bezique markers that take the form of indicators marked as clocks on thin cardboard.

The following hand, played by two experienced players, illustrates many of the finer points of good play.

South dealt, and the hands were:

Clubs were trumps, the 10 of Clubs having been turned up.

The turn-up card is important because it is a sequence card, and a high one at that since it ranks immediately below the Ace.

The main features of North's hand are that he holds two sequence cards (the Queen and Jack of Clubs), a 7 of trumps to exchange for the valuable 10, and three Queens, which put him well on the way to a declaration of four Queens.

The main features of South's hand are a bezique Queen (the Queen of Spades) and three low trumps, including the 7; but, of course, as yet South does not know that North holds both the Queens of trumps, so that a sequence for him is impossible. It is South's lead, and it is necessary for him to win a trick to exchange the 7 of Clubs for the 10. An inexperienced player might be tempted to lead an indifferent card, such as the 7 of Hearts, hoping that North will have nothing to declare and will refuse to win the trick. This, however, is very artless play, and the better play is for South to lead his highest trump because it compels North to use a sequence card if he wants to take the trick and make a declaration. So . . .

Trick 1 South led the 9 of Clubs. North, who appreciated the importance of the turn-up card, won with the Queen of Clubs. This was North's best play, although it suffers from the defect that it reduces North's chance of declaring four Queens, and it informs South that virtually he has no hope of a sequence because North would hardly play a sequence card if he lacked a duplicate. North exchanged the 7 of Clubs for the turn-up card, and scored 10 points. He drew the King of Clubs (giving him no less than four of the five sequence cards), and South the 9 of Hearts.

Trick 2 North led the 9 of Diamonds, and South played the 7 of Hearts. North declared the royal marriage and scored 40 points, making his total 50 points. North drew the King of Hearts, and South the Ace of Hearts.

Trick 3 North led the 7 of Hearts, and South played the 9 of Diamonds. North declared the common marriage in Hearts and scored 20 points, making his total 70 points. North drew the Ace of Clubs, and South the Jack of Hearts.

Trick 4 North now held a sequence, but, in order to declare it, he had first to win a trick. A Heart must be led, and he chose the Queen. Undoubtedly it was the best lead. The Ace of Hearts is not a good lead, because, if trumped, it will cost North a brisque; and it is better for North to save for four Kings, instead of for four Queens, because not only does it gain 20 more points, but North had already played a Queen so the chance of drawing a Queen was slightly less than that of drawing a King. South played the 9 of Hearts. North declared his Ace, 10 and Jack of Clubs, and scored 250 points for the sequence, giving him a total of 320 points. South had not yet scored. North drew the 10 of Spades, and South the Jack of Diamonds.

At this point the hands were:

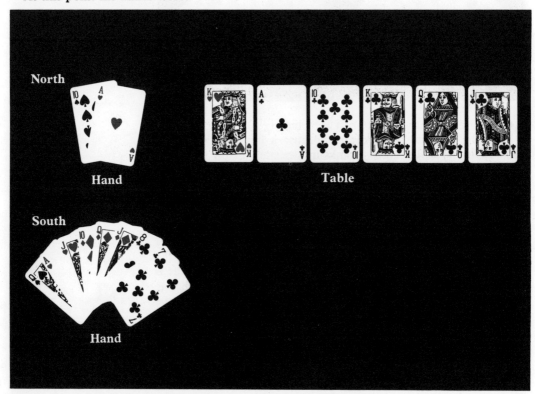

Trick 5 North's trumps were no longer of vital importance to him, and could be played if desired. The two Kings were important because North had made up his mind to save for Kings, and it is an error of tactics to change one's mind during the game. The Aces and 10s were important, because they furnish brisques. So North led the Jack of Clubs. South had a bezique in his hand, but unfortunately he could not win the trick and declare it. The best he could do was to play the Jack of Hearts. North drew the 8 of Diamonds, and South the Queen of Diamonds.

Trick 6 North led the 8 of Diamonds. South won with the 10 of Diamonds, putting away a brisque for himself, and declared bezique. South's 40 points for bezique was his first score, and he was a long way behind North's 320 points. South drew the 10 of Hearts, and North the Ace of Clubs.

Trick 7 South now had the lead. He chose the 7 of Clubs and scored 10 points, making his total 50. It was the best lead, because the lead of either Heart would probably be trumped and a brisque lost. He had to save for four Queens, and the Jack of Diamonds was out of the question since there was always the possibility of declaring double bezique. North was more or less compelled to win with the Queen of Clubs. North drew the 8 of Diamonds, and South the Queen of Spades.

Trick 8 North led the 8 of Diamonds, and South won with the 8 of Clubs and declared four Queens (60 points) giving him a total of 110. North, with a total of 320 points, was still well ahead, but he noted with some concern that South would be able to declare double bezique if he was lucky enough to draw the other Jack of Diamonds. South drew the 9 of Spades, and North the 8 of Spades.

Trick 9 South led the 9 of Spades, and North won with the 10 of Spades. North drew the Jack of Spades, and South the 8 of Spades.

Trick 10 North led the 8 of Spades, and South played the other 8 of Spades. North drew the 8 of Hearts, and South the Jack of Hearts.

Trick 11 North led the 8 of Hearts, and South won with the 10 of Hearts. South drew the King of Diamonds, and North the 8 of Hearts.

At this point the hands were:

The score was North 320 points, South 110 points.

Trick 12 South led the Jack of Hearts, and North played the 8. It would not have been good play for North to win with the Ace of Hearts because, though this would have given him a brisque, it is better for North to save for four Aces now that he held three. South laid down his King of Diamonds and scored a common marriage (20 points), giving him a total of 130 points. South drew the 7 of Spades, and North the Ace of Spades.

Trick 13 South led the 7 of Spades. North won with the Jack of Spades, and declared four Aces (100 points). This raised his total to 420, and he had a good lead on South, whose score was only 130 points. North drew the Jack of Clubs, and South the 9 of Spades.

The hands were now:

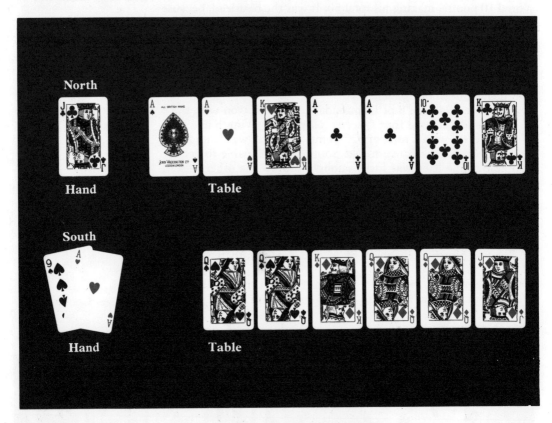

and South's hand with its three bezique cards was not without possibilities.

Trick 14 North led the Jack of Clubs, and South played the 9 of Spades. North drew the Jack of Spades, and South the 9 of Hearts.

Trick 15 North led the Jack of Spades, and South played the 9 of Hearts. North drew the King of Clubs, and South the Jack of Diamonds.

Trick 16 Now, of course, the whole game changed, because South held a double bezique, though he had to win a trick before he could declare it. If the stock is nearly exhausted it is proper for North to lead trumps in an attempt to prevent South from winning a trick. It was, however, too early in the game for these tactics, so North led the Ace of Spades, hoping that it would not be trumped, and South, who had no trump in his hand, discarded the married Queen of Diamonds. North drew the 10 of Diamonds, and South the 10 of Clubs, a vital card.

Trick 17 North, who by this time suspected that South held double bezique, led the Ace of Hearts, hoping that South would still not be able to trump. This time, however, he was doomed to disappointment, because, of course, South was able to win with the 10 of Clubs and declare double bezique. The score of 500

PLATE 8 *(opposite)*
The layout for shah

PLATE 9 *(opposite, above)* **The layout for competitive golf patience**
PLATE 10 *(opposite, below)* **A game of stop! in progress**

points for double bezique raised South's total to 630 and gave him a lead of 210 points because North's score was only 420 points. South drew the Ace of Spades, and North the King.

Trick 18 South, who had no further use for his bezique Jacks, led a Jack of Diamonds. North won with the 10 of Diamonds and declared four Kings (80 points), raising his score to 500 points. North drew the 9 of Clubs, and South the Ace of Diamonds.

Trick 19 North led the 9 of Clubs, and South played the Jack of Diamonds. North drew the 8 of Clubs, and South the Ace of Diamonds.

The hands were now:

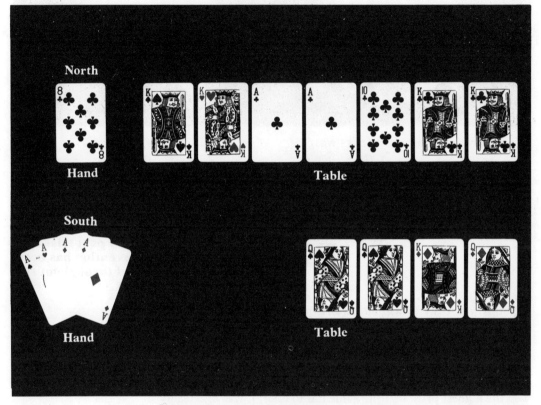

Trick 20 North now suspected that South was on the point of declaring four Aces. His tactics, therefore, had to be aggressive, and, since the other 10 of Clubs had been played, his trumps were all winners, and he played them to prevent South from declaring. North led the Ace of Clubs, and South played the Queen of Spades. North drew one 7 of Diamonds and South the other.

Trick 21 North led the Ace of Clubs, and South played the 7 of Diamonds. North drew the Queen of Hearts, and South the 10 of Spades.

Trick 22 North led the 10 of Clubs, and South played the Queen of Spades. North declàred the common marriage in Hearts (20 points) raising his total to 520 points. North drew the King of Spades, and South the 7.

Trick 23 North led the King of Clubs, and South played the 7 of Spades. North drew the King of Diamonds, and South the 10 of Hearts.

Trick 24 (last trick) North led the King of Clubs, and South played the Queen of Diamonds. North scored 10 points for the last trick bringing his total to 530 points. South's score was 630 points, and from the time that he declared double bezique North had little chance to overtake him. He did well, however, to prevent South from declaring four Aces and so adding another 100 points to his score. North drew the King of Hearts, and South picked up the 7 of Clubs exposed on the table.

After picking up their cards from the table, the hands of the two players were:

North   South

The play to the last eight tricks was:

North	South
K ♥	<u>A ♥</u>
7 ♦	<u>A ♦</u>
K ♦	<u>A ♦</u>
K ♠	<u>A ♠</u>
<u>Q ♥</u>	10 ♥
<u>K ♠</u>	10 ♠
8 ♣	<u>K ♦</u>
<u>K ♥</u>	7 ♣

In the summary of play, the underlined card is the card which wins the trick, and its player leads to the next trick. This convention has been used throughout this book

South was lucky to win all his brisques, giving him a score of 100 points: North won six brisques for a total of 60 points. The final score, therefore, was: South 730 points; North 590 points.

Altogether a fine deal, and one worth studying, because it illustrates the importance of playing for double bezique. For the first half of the deal North was well ahead, but after South had won the highest prize that the game has to offer, it was practically impossible for North to win the deal, and all his efforts had to be directed towards preventing South from gaining an even bigger lead. North played well to reduce South's lead of 210 points (gained at the seventeenth trick) to 140.

RUBICON BEZIQUE has the advantage over the parent game that, as long ago as 1887, a committee of the Portland Club drew up a code of laws under which it should be played.

It is very similar to the parent game, and, like it, is a game for two players, but four packs of cards, not two, are used, and there are some differences in the preliminaries, the scoring and the routine of the game.

In the preliminaries, nine cards (not eight) are dealt to each player, either singly or in packets of three, and there is no turn up of the top card of the stock, so that the peculiar value of the 7 of trumps is lost.

The scoring is the same as in the parent game, with the following additions:

Carte Blanche = 50 points. If either player is dealt a hand without a court card he is entitled to score for carte blanche. Both players are entitled to score it. Before a player can score, however, he must show his hand to his opponent. Thereafter, each time that he draws a card from the stock he may show it to his opponent and score 50 points if it is not a court card.

Ordinary Sequence = 150 points. **A 10 K Q J** of any suit other than the trump suit.

Triple Bezique = 1,500 points. Three **Q ♠** and three **J ♦** (or **Q ♣** and **J ♥** if either Spades or Diamonds are trumps).

Quadruple Bezique = 4,500 points. Four **Q ♠** and four **J ♦** (or **Q ♣** and **J ♥** if either Spades or Diamonds are trumps).

Last Trick = 50 points.

The routine differs from that of the parent game in the following essentials:

1. A game is complete in one deal.
2. Trumps are determined by the first marriage or sequence declared by either player.
3. The tricks are left exposed on the table until such time as a brisque is played. After this the tricks are gathered and turned in the usual way.
4. If a card is played from a declared combination, subsequently the combination may be filled by adding an appropriate card and the declaration scored again.
5. If a player has declared two marriages in the same suit, he may rearrange the Kings and Queens on the table and declare two more marriages.
6. Brisques are disregarded for scoring except to break a tie or to save a player from being rubiconed.
7. If a player fails to score 1,000 points he is rubiconed. His score is added to (not subtracted from) that of his opponent, who adds a further 1,300 points (not 500) for the game. Further, if a player fails to score 100 points, the winner adds an extra 100 points to his score.

BEZIQUE FOR THREE PLAYERS is played with three packs of cards, and the players compete all against all. The play is the same as in the parent game with the addition of a score of 1,500 points for triple bezique.

BEZIQUE FOR FOUR PLAYERS is played with six packs of cards, or 192 cards in all. Two play in partnership against the other two.

The dealer places twenty-four cards face downwards in a pile on the table, and on this he places a marker so that the players will be warned when the stock is nearing exhaustion. He deals nine cards to each of the four players and places the remainder of the pack (132 cards in all) face downwards on top of the marker.

In general, the play follows that described under rubicon bezique (above) but there are some differences in the scoring and in declaring.

Carte Blanche = 100 points.

Double Carte Blanche = 500. Both partners being dealt hands without a court card.

Quintuple Bezique = 13,500 points. Five **Q**♠ and **J**♦ (or **Q**♣ and **J**♥ if either Spades or Diamonds are trumps).

Sextuple Bezique is so unlikely that no score has been alloted to it. Should it occur, the correct score is 40,500 points.

Any Four Aces = 1,000 points.

Any Four Tens = 900 points.

Any Four Kings = 800 points.

Any Four Queens = 600 points.

Any Four Jacks = 400 points.

The game bonus is 1,000 points, the rubicon 2,500 points and brisques are disregarded.

In all other essentials the scoring is the same as in rubicon bezique. The partnership principle, however, introduces two new features in the methods of declaring combinations. First, after winning a trick, a player may either declare or leave it to his partner to do so. Secondly, a player may declare a combination either with his own cards (including those on the table already declared by him) or with one or more of his own cards and one or more of his partner's declared cards. Indeed, since a player holds only nine cards, quintuple bezique (and sextuple bezique if it occurs) can only be declared with the help of partner.

The player on the left of the dealer leads to the first trick.

Beyond these additions, the play follows that of rubicon bezique.

SIX-PACK BEZIQUE, sometimes, but rarely, known as Chinese Bezique, is a game for two players, and generally considered the most popular variation of the family. Sir Winston Churchill was a keen player and an able exponent of the game.

Six packs are shuffled together and both players lift a part of the pack and show the bottom cards to determine choice of seat and deal. The one who shows the higher card has the choice, and would be advised to pass the deal to his opponent because there is a slight disadvantage in dealing. If equal cards are shown the players cut again.

The dealer takes a number of cards at random off the top of the pack, and the non-dealer estimates how many have been taken. If his estimate proves correct he scores 150 points. The dealer deals twelve cards, one by one, to his opponent and himself, and scores 250 points if he has taken exactly twenty-four cards from the top of the pack.

There is no turn-up to determine the trump suit. It is determined, as in rubicon bezique (above), by the first declared marriage or sequence by either player.

The declarations are scored for as follows:

Sequence in Trumps = 250 points.

Sequence in a Plain Suit = 150 points.

Royal Marriage = 40 points.

Common Marriage = 20 points.

Bezique = 40 points | If Spades are trumps bezique is **Q** ♠ and
Double Bezique = | **J** ♦ ; if Diamonds are trumps **Q** ♦ and
 500 points | **J** ♠ ; if Hearts are trumps **Q** ♥ and **J** ♣ ;
Triple Bezique = | and if Clubs are trumps **Q** ♣ and **J** ♥.
 1,500 points |
Quadruple Bezique = |
 4,500 points |

Four Aces in Trumps = 1,000 points.
Four Tens in Trumps = 900 points.
Four Kings in Trumps = 800 points.
Four Queens in Trumps = 600 points.
Four Jacks in Trumps = 400 points.
Any Four Aces = 100 points.
Any Four Kings = 80 points.
Any Four Queens = 60 points.
Any Four Jacks = 40 points.
Carte Blanche = 250 points.

The non-dealer leads to the first trick. It is not compulsory to follow suit, and the card that is led holds the trick unless a higher card of the same suit is played or a trump is played to the lead of a plain suit. As points are not scored for brisques, nor for winning tricks, the tricks are not gathered and turned but left face upwards on the table in a pile. The winner of a trick may score for a declaration. He takes the top card of the stock (the loser takes the next card of the stock) and leads to the next trick.

A declaration is made by placing the appropriate cards face upwards on the table. They are left there and are available for play as though in the hand of the player. Declarations are scored when made, and the same card may be counted in a declaration more than once.

No declaration may be made after the last two cards of the stock have been drawn. The players then pick up any cards they have on the table and play off the last twelve tricks. As in the parent game, a player must now follow suit to the card led, and must win a trick if he is able to.

Every deal constitutes a game, and the player with the higher score wins. He adds 1,000 points to his score, and rubicons his opponent if he has failed to score 3,000 points.

EIGHT-PACK BEZIQUE is identical with six-pack bezique (above) except for the increased number of cards and the following differences in the routine and scoring:

1. Each player is dealt fifteen cards.
2. The scores for beziques are:
    Bezique = 50 points.
    Double Bezique = 500 points.
    Triple Bezique = 1,500 points.
    Quadruple Bezique = 4,500 points.
    Quintuple Bezique = = 9,000 points.
3. In the trump suit the scores are for:
    Five Aces = 2,000 points.
    Five Tens = 1,800 points.
    Five Kings = 1,600 points.
    Five Queens = 1,200 points.
    Five Jacks = 800 points.
4. A player who fails to score 5,000 points is rubiconed.

California Jack

California Jack is played with the full pack of fifty-two cards, the Ace ranking high the 2 low. It is a game for two players that derives from all fours (see page 48) but is generally considered an improvement on it.

The non-dealer cuts the pack and exposes the bottom card to decide the trump suit. The dealer deals six cards, one at a time, to each player, and places the remainder of the pack face upwards on the table, taking the precaution to square it up so that only the top card can be seen.

The non-dealer leads to the first trick. The winner of a trick takes the top card of the stock, the loser the next card. A player must follow suit if he can, and he loses 1 point if he revokes.

When the stock is exhausted and the last six cards have been played, the tricks won by each player are examined, and 1 point is scored for winning High (Ace of trumps), Low (2 of trumps), Jack (Jack of trumps) and Game (majority of points, counting each Ace won as 4 points, each King as 3 points, each Queen as 2 points, each Jack as 1 point, and each Ten as 10 points).

The game is won by the player who first scores 10 points.

The player should aim to keep both winning and losing cards in his hand because if the exposed card of the stock is valuable he will wish to win it, but if it is not, he will wish to lose the trick on the chance of the next card of the stock being a more valuable one. The Tens, of course, are the cards to go for.

A good California Jack hand. There are two good cards for trick-winning and three for losing

SHASTA SAM is a variation of the game in which the stock is placed face downwards on the table instead of face upwards. It is a less skilful game as, of course, the winner of a trick does not know what card he will draw.

Casino

Although Casino (sometimes erroneously spelt cassino) is essentially a game for two, played with the full pack of fifty-two cards, it may be played by three or four. The only difference is that if three players take part they play all against all, and if four take part two play in partnership against the other two.

The dealer deals two cards face downwards to his opponent, then two face upwards to the table, and then two face downwards to himself. This is repeated, so that both players end with four cards each, and there are four exposed cards (the layout) on the table. The remaining forty cards (the stock) are placed face downwards on the table.

The numeral cards count at their pip values. The Ace counts as 1, and the court cards are used only for pairing: they have no pip value.

The object of the game is to take in cards which score as follows:

The 10 ♦ (Great Casino) = 2 points.
The 2 ♠ (Little Casino) = 1 point.
The majority of cards (27 or more) = 3 points.
The majority of Spades (7 or more) = 1 point.
Each Ace = 1 point.
All cards in the layout (the Sweep) = 1 point.

Each player in turn, beginning with the non-dealer, plays a card until both players have exhausted their four cards. When this occurs, the same dealer deals four more cards to his opponent and four to himself, but none to the layout. Play continues in this way until the stock has been exhausted. In all, therefore, there are six deals to complete the game, and before making the final deal the dealer must announce it. If he does not, his opponent has a right to cancel the deal.

When a player plays a card from his hand he has the choice of several plays.

He may *Pair*. If, for example, there are one or more 5s in the layout, he may play a 5 from his hand and take it up as a trick with all the other 5s in the layout. A court card, however, may be paired with only one card of the same rank at a time.

He may *Combine*. It is an extension of pairing that allows a player to pick up cards from the layout of the total pip value of a card in his hand. Thus a player playing a 9 may take up a 7 and a 2, or a 6 and a 3 from the layout, or all four cards if they are in the layout.

He may *Build*. He may play a card to a card in the layout to make up a total that he is in a position to take with another card in his hand. If, for example, a player holds a 9 and a 2, and there is a 7 in the layout, he may build the 2 on the 7, so that the next time he plays (provided his opponent has not forestalled him) he may play the 9 and take all three cards as a trick. The build may be continued by either player up to a maximum of five cards, but a build can be taken only as a unit. The player who has built must take up the combination when next it is his turn to play, unless he prefers to win something else, or he decides to make another build.

He may *Call*. It is an extension of building that allows a player to earmark one or more combinations for subsequent capture. Suppose, for example, a player holds in his hand two 8s and that there is a 5 and a 3 in the layout (see illustration). He could, of

Layout

Hand

course, combine one of his 8s with the 5 and 3 in the layout, but this would only give him three cards in the trick. The better play, therefore, is for him to play one of his 8s to the layout and announce 'Eight'. Then, when next it is his turn to play, provided his opponent has not forestalled him, he may play his other 8 and pick up all four cards in the trick.

When a player cannot pair, combine, build or call, he must play one of his cards to the layout. It is known as trailing. It is advisable to play a low card, but not an Ace, little casino or a Spade.

When the last eight cards have been played any left in the layout are the property of the winner of the final trick, but it does not count as a sweep.

This ends the game, except for the formality of the players examining their tricks and counting their scores.

There is no penalty for making a build incorrectly, or for capturing cards to which a player is not entitled, because his opponent has the opportunity to see the error and demand that it is corrected. If, however, a player makes a build when he has no card in his hand to capture it or trails when he has a build in the layout, he automatically forfeits the game. If a card is faced in the pack, or if the dealer when dealing exposes a card, other than when dealing cards to the layout, the exposed card is played to the layout and the dealer plays the hand with fewer than four cards.

Casino is sometimes considered a game for children. It is, however, very far from being so. Among card players it is widely spoken of as one of the best of all two-handed games and it is often played for high stakes. To be successful a player needs an elephantine memory, and the capacity to deduce from the card played by an opponent what cards he is most likely to be holding in his hand.

ROYAL CASINO is an improvement on the parent game because the court cards play a more important part. The Aces count 1 or 14 (at the option of the player), the Kings 13, the Queens 12 and the Jacks 11, and they may be used for combining and building. Thus an 8 and a 4 may be taken with a Queen, a 6, a 4 and a 3 with a King, and so on.

Twenty-one points constitute the game.

In **DRAW CASINO**, after the first round of a deal, the forty undealt cards are placed face downwards on the table to form a stock. Then each player, after playing, draws a card from the stock to bring the number of cards in his hand up to four. When the stock is exhausted the hands are played out and the count made as in the parent game.

SPADE CASINO may be played either as royal casino (above) or as the parent game, with the addition that the Ace, Jack and 2 of Spades count 2 points each, and all the other Spades 1 point each.

Game is 61 points, and it is convenient and customary to keep the score on a cribbage board (see Plate 11).

Colonel

Colonel is a version of coon-can (see page 183) for two players. The full pack of fifty-two cards is used, and each player is dealt ten cards, one at a time. The rest of the pack is placed face downwards on the table, between the players, and the top card (known as the optional card) is turned face upwards and placed alongside the stock.

The object of the game is to make sequences of the same suit, threes and fours of a kind, and declare them by placing them face upwards on the table. The hand ends when one of the players has declared all his cards. A sequence must be of at least three cards, but once it has been declared either player, in his turn, may add to it. In the same way, if three of a kind has been declared, either player in his turn may add the fourth card to it.

The non-dealer plays first. He takes into his hand either the optional card or the top card of the stock. He declares any sequences, threes or fours of a kind that he holds, and discards a card from his hand. The discard is placed on top of the optional card, or in its place if the optional card has been taken up. The dealer plays next. He has the choice of taking the card that the non-dealer has discarded or the top card of the stock.

It will be seen, therefore, that the routine of the play is very simple. Each player in turn takes into his hand either the top card of the stock or the card his opponent has discarded, he then declares any sequences, three or fours that he holds, or adds to those already declared either by himself or his opponent, and then discards a card from his hand. In a sequence the Ace is high. A player is not under compulsion to declare: indeed it is good play to refuse to declare for as long as possible in an attempt to declare one's hand all at once. This way one's opponent has less chance to declare all his cards, but it is to be borne in mind that a player who fails to declare when he can runs the risk that his opponent will go out before him.

When a player has declared all his cards, his opponent loses points for every card remaining in his hand, the Ace, King, Queen and Jack counting as 10 points each, the remaining cards their pip values.

If the stock is exhausted before either player has declared all his cards, both players show the cards remaining in their hands and the player with the lower total wins the hand. He adds to the score the total of his opponent's hand less that of his own.

A refinement of the game is that before the stock is exhausted either player may challenge. If the challenge is rejected by the opponent, the hand continues to be played out. If, however, the challenge is accepted, both players expose their hands and the player with the lower total wins. He adds to his score the total of his opponent's hand without deducting his own. If the right cards to make sequences and threes of a kind are not coming to a player, it is good play for him to fill his hand with low cards and then challenge.

67

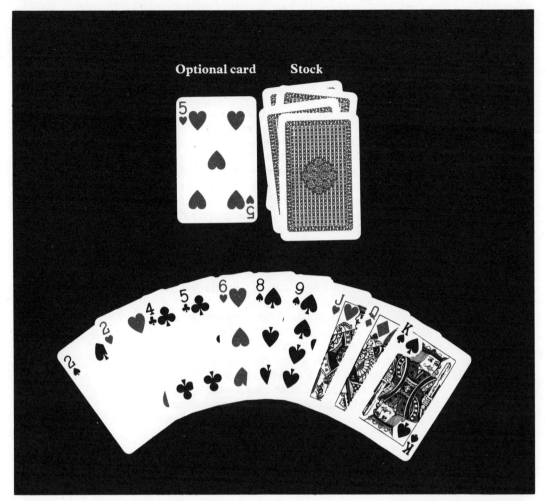

Optional card   Stock

It would be good play
to take the Five of
Hearts, as it gives
chances of a set of
Fives or a sequence
in Hearts. The King
of Spades might be
discarded

Comet

Two 52-card packs, with the same design on their backs, are used alternately. The packs must be prepared by rejecting all the Aces, putting all the red cards into one pack and all the black cards into another, and interchanging a red and a black 9.

Eighteen cards are dealt to each player, one at a time, and the remaining twelve cards are put aside; they play no part in the game. The non-dealer begins the game by playing one of his cards, face upwards, to the centre of the table. The players then, alternately, build up on it by rank only. Suits are disregarded. Any number of cards, provided they are of the proper rank, may be played in one turn. The four 8s, for example, may be built on a 7, the four Jacks on a 10, and so on. When a player is unable to build it is a stop, and his opponent begins a new sequence by playing any card he chooses. Obviously a King is always a stop.

The 9 of the opposite colour is called the comet. It may represent any card that the holder chooses, but may be played only in turn. It is a stop, and the player who plays it begins a new sequence.

The player who is first to get rid of all the cards in his hand is the winner. He scores the total of pips left in his opponent's hand, the court cards counting as 10 each. If both players are stopped and both are left with cards in their hands, both hands are counted. The lower hand wins and scores the value of his opponent's hand less the value of his own. If a player wins the hand while the comet is in the hand of his opponent he scores double. If a player wins by playing the comet, he doubles his score, and if he wins the hand by playing the comet as a 9 he quadruples his score.

COMMIT is a variation of the parent game that is suitable for more than two players. It is played with the standard pack of fifty-two cards from which the 8 of Diamonds has been removed, and as many other 8s and 7s as may be necessary for the players to be dealt an equal number of cards.

The players place an equal number of units into a pool.

The player on the left of the dealer begins by playing any card to the centre of the table. The others play cards on it as able, and not necessarily in rotation. The cards played must follow in sequence. Only the 6 of Spades may be played on the 5 of Spades, the 8 of Clubs on the 7 of Clubs, and so on.

The 9 of Diamonds is the comet and may be played either when all the players are stopped or when the holder of it has played regularly and is unable to continue the sequence. After it has been played, any player in rotation may either continue by playing the 10 of Diamonds on it, or the card next above that for which the comet has been substituted.

The player who plays the comet receives 2 units from each of the other players, and any player who plays a King receives 1 unit from each of the other players. The player who is first to get rid of his cards wins the pool, and receives 2 units from a player who has been left with the comet in his hand, and 1 unit for each King.

Competitive Patiences

GOLF PATIENCE, like golf itself, is best played by two, but three-ball matches and foursomes are not difficult to arrange.

Each player has a pack of fifty-two cards. He deals the top thirty-five face upwards in five overlapping rows of seven cards each (see Plate 9). This forms the links.

The remaining seventeen cards are dealt one at a time to a waste heap. Every time that a card is dealt the bottom card of one of the columns of the links may be packed on it in ascending or descending sequence irrespective of suit and colour. In the links on Plate 9 if the first card that is dealt to the waste heap is the **7 ♥**, the **8 ♦** may be packed on it, the **9 ♦** on the **8 ♦**, the **10 ♠** on the **9 ♦**, the **9 ♥** on the **10 ♠**, and so on. Play continues in this way until the run is brought to an end either by a King or because no further packing can be made. The next card is dealt to the waste heap, and the game continues until all seventeen cards have been turned. The number of cards left in the links represents the number of strokes for the hole. Nine or eighteen holes are played.

Occasionally a player will clear the links before dealing all seventeen cards to the waste heap. When this occurs, the number of cards left in hand count as a plus score in the player's favour, and, at the end of the game, are deducted from his total score.

The players play each hole simultaneously.

POKER PATIENCE is suitable for any number of players. Each has a pack of fifty-two cards. One player takes a card from the top of the pack and places it face upwards anywhere on the table. He continues with a second card, a third, a fourth, and so on until twenty-five cards in all have been played. A card is placed on the table anywhere that the player chooses but it must touch a card (either at the top or bottom, either side or at any corner) previously played. The object of the game is to form a square of five cards each way, making poker combinations in each row and column.

As the player takes a card from the pack he announces it, and the other players take the same card from their packs and arrange them on the table.

When all twenty-five cards have been arranged in a square, the players total their scores and the highest wins. There are several methods of scoring. The one below is to be recommended. It gives the fairest result because it is based on the relative difficulty of forming the combinations in poker patience, and not on the relative likelihood of the hands in the regular game of poker.

Royal Straight Flush = 50 points.   *Straight* = 7 points.
Straight Flush = 37 points.   *Threes* = 5 points.
Fours = 25 points.   *Two pairs* = 3 points.
Full House = 12 points.   *Pair* = 1 point.
Flush = 10 points.

---

*Poker hands are defined on page 190

The game lends itself to considerable skill. One player's layout might be:

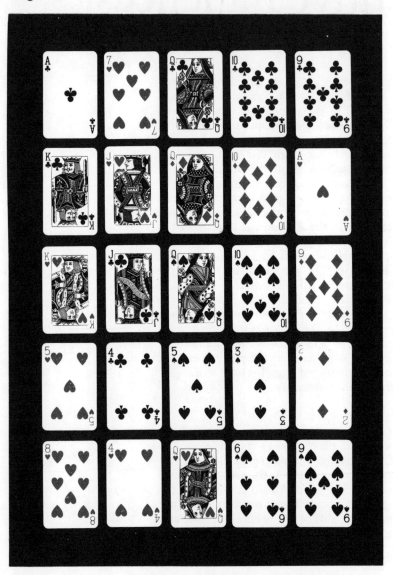

For this he scores:

Row 2	Straight	7 points
Row 3	Straight	7 points
Row 4	Pair	1 point
Column 1	Pair	1 point
Column 2	Two Pairs	3 points
Column 3	Fours	25 points
Column 4	Threes	5 points
Column 5	Threes	5 points
		54 points

With the same cards another player's layout might be:

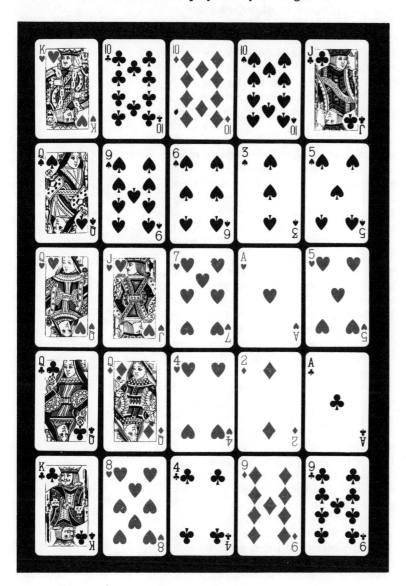

For this he scores:

Row 1	Threes	5 points
Row 2	Flush	10 points
Row 3	Flush	10 points
Row 4	Pair	1 point
Row 5	Pair	1 point
Column 1	Full House	12 points
Column 2	Straight	7 points
Column 3	Pair	1 point
Column 5	Pair	1 point
		48 points

Whether poker players will prefer the shadow to the substance is at least doubtful, but before the First World War the game attracted a big following: matches were played, tournaments arranged and even leagues were formed.

STOP! which is also known as Crapette and Russian Bank, is a game for two players. They sit facing each other (see Plate 10) and each has a pack of fifty-two cards which, for convenience in sorting, should be of different colour or design.

The first player (determined by cutting a pack) plays twelve cards face downwards in a pile on his right, and covers it with the thirteenth card face upwards. This is his depot. Alongside it he deals four cards face upwards in a column. This is his file. Aces, as they occur, are placed in a row in front of the player. They serve as foundations and are built on in ascending suit-sequences to the Kings. The cards in the file are packed in descending suit-sequences of alternate colour. A space in the file is filled from the depot, and the next card in it is turned face upwards. When all moves have been made from the file and the depot, the player turns a card from the stock. If he can build it on an Ace-foundation or pack it on a card in the file, he turns up the next card of the stock, and so on. If he cannot play the card to an Ace-foundation or to a file, he plays it to a waste heap, and covers it with the next card from the stock.

The second player lays out his cards in exactly the same way, and when he has made all possible moves, the first player once more takes up the game, and so on.

A player is allowed to build on his opponent's Ace-foundation, and pack on his file, and he may play cards from his depot and file (but not from his stock and waste heap) to his opponent's waste heap packing the top card in ascending or descending sequence irrespective of suit and colour.

When a player's stock is exhausted he takes up the waste heap and redeals it without shuffling.

The game is won by the player who first gets rid of all the cards in his stock and waste heap, together with the cards that his opponent may have played to the waste heap.

The game is governed by ten rules and it is a feature of the game that if a player breaks any one of them, his opponent may call 'Stop!', point out which rule has been broken and himself take up the game, first making the move that his opponent has failed to make. A player is not compelled to call 'Stop!' if his opponent breaks a rule, but if the call of 'Stop!' is to be operative it must be made before the offender makes a further play.

1. A player must prefer to play a card to an Ace-foundation than to a file.
2. A player must prefer to play a card to a file than to his waste heap.
3. A player must prefer to play from his depot than from a file or his waste heap.
4. A space in a file must be filled from the depot before any other play is made.
5. When a card has been played from the depot, the next card must be turned before making a further play.
6. The top card of the depot must be used to fill a space in the file in preference to playing it elsewhere.
7. A card in a file may be packed only in a descending suit-sequence of alternate colour.
8. An Ace-foundation may be built on only in an ascending suit-sequence to a King.
9. A player must not play a card from his opponent's file.
10. A player must make a play when he can.

Cribbage

Cribbage is believed to have been developed out of the older card game of Noddy, by Sir John Suckling in the reign of Charles I. Originally it was a two-handed game, but variations for three and four players are now known.

The two-handed game is the most popular, and of it there are three variations: 5-card, 6-card and 7-card. Points won are marked with a peg on what is known as a noddy board (one is being used in Plate 11). It is oblong in shape, has a double row of holes, thirty in each row, and is divided, for convenience in scoring, into groups of five holes. The board is placed between the two players; both start from the same end of the board and peg their scores first along the outer row of holes and then along the inner row—once round the board at the 5-card game, twice round at the 6-card game and three times round at the 7-card game. In each case the game ends when one player reaches the game hole from which he started. Thus, at 5-card cribbage the game is 61 holes, at 6-card 121 holes, and at 7-card 181 holes.

FIVE-CARD CRIBBAGE FOR TWO PLAYERS, which is the original game, is generally considered the most scientific of the variations. In the manner of scoring it is unique, and the play is different to that of most card games, because it calls for no effort of memory. Good judgement and concentration are the chief qualities that lead to success.

The full pack of fifty-two cards is used. The players cut for deal; the lower deals first. When cutting for deal, and for scoring sequences, the cards rank in order from Ace (low) to King (high), but, for counting, the King, Queen and Jack count 10 each and the other cards at their pip values. Five cards are dealt to each player, and the non-dealer pegs 3 holes (Three for Last) as compensation against the advantage of the first deal of a game.

The players look at their cards, and then place two of them face downwards on the right of the dealer. These four cards are known as the *Crib*. The non-dealer then cuts the pack, and the dealer turns up the top card of the cut and places it on top of the pack. The card is known as the *Start*, and if it is a Jack the dealer pegs 2 holes (Two for his Heels).

Scores are made partly in play and partly by the scoring values of the cards in hand. The latter, however, are not pegged until the play ends.

During the play of the hand, scores are made as follows:

If a player plays a card of the same rank as the previous one played, he pegs 2 for a *Pair*, but court cards pair only rank with rank—that is to say King with King, Queen with Queen and Jack with Jack.

If a player plays a third card of the same rank as a pair he pegs 6 for *Pair-Royal*.

If a player plays a fourth card of the same rank as a pair-royal he pegs 12 for a *Double Pair-Royal*.

A *Sequence* (or *Run*) is pegged at 1 for each card with a minimum of three cards and a maximum of seven. The cards need not be of the same suit, nor need they be played in sequential order, but, as the Ace is low, **A K Q** is not a sequence, and a sequence is destroyed by a pair or an intervening card. If the dealer plays a 7 and the non-dealer a 5, the dealer may now play a 6 and peg 3, and the non-dealer may continue either with a 4 or an 8 and peg 4.

If a player plays a card which, with those already played, adds up to *Fifteen* he pegs 2, and, again, if they total *Thirty-one* he pegs 2.

Out of this an important point arises. If, when the player whose turn it is to play cannot do so without exceeding thirty-one, he says 'Go'. His opponent then plays a card or cards up to the limit. If the cards that he plays bring the total up to exactly thirty-one he pegs 2; if not he pegs 1 (One for Last).

This ends the play, and the players, beginning with the non-dealer, count their scores by combining their own cards with the start. The dealer then exposes the crib (it is his exclusive property) and any values that he finds in it (making full use of the start) he pegs to his score. Should either player hold the Jack of the same suit as the start he pegs 1 (One for his Nob). If a player holds in his hand three cards all of the same suit he pegs 3 for a *Flush*, and 4 if the start is of the same suit. In the crib, however, nothing is scored for a flush unless, with the start, it is a flush of five; if it is the dealer pegs 5.

Two other features of the scoring call for special mention. First, a player must count his hand aloud, and if he overlooks any score, either in play or otherwise, his opponent may call 'Muggins', point out the omission, and peg the score for himself. Secondly, if a player reaches the game hole before his opponent has gone halfway round the board a *Lurch* is scored, that is to say the winner scores two games instead of only one.

Points are scored during the play by a player adding the value of the card played by the opponent to a card played from his own hand. Thus if a 10 or court card is led, and a player plays a 5, he scores fifteen and pegs 2 holes (Fifteen-Two as it is called for short). If a 6 is led, and he plays another 6, he scores for a pair and pegs 2. Again, a 4 is led, he plays a 6, and the opponent plays a 5: he pegs 3 for a sequence and 2 for fifteen. And so on.

The general principles of play may be illustrated in an elementary deal.

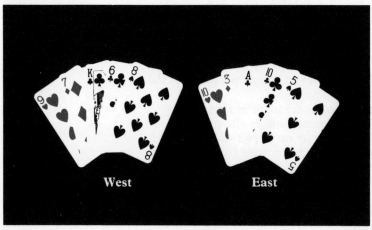

West　　　　　East

East is the dealer.

West holds a sequence of four. As a result the King of Clubs will go to the crib, and for his other card he must choose between the 6 of Clubs and the 9 of Hearts. There is not much in it, but as the 6 of Clubs is of the same suit as the King, there is a slight advantage in discarding the 9 of Hearts, because the 6 of Clubs (along with the King) might help to give East a flush in his crib.

East has an easy choice of discards. Indeed, it is obvious that he will discard the Ace of Clubs and 3 of Diamonds.

West cuts the cards, and East turns up the King of Spades.

The position is now:

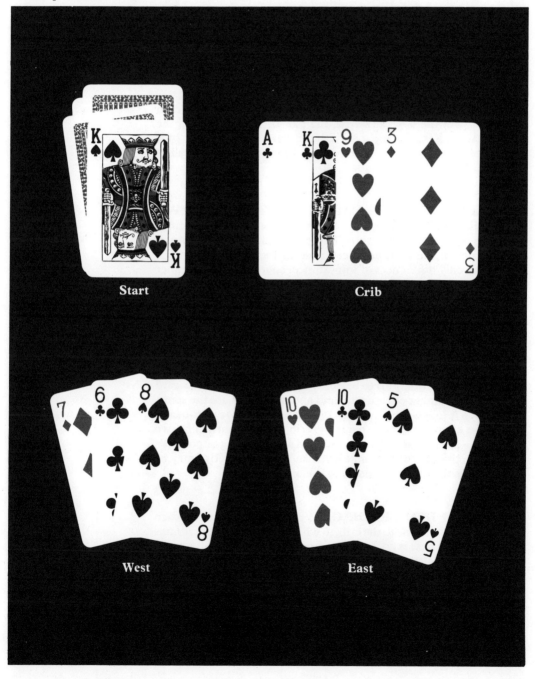

Start

Crib

West

East

West leads the **7** ♦ and says 'Seven'. It is his best lead because if East plays an 8 and pegs 2 for fifteen, West can play the **6** ♣ and peg 3 for sequence. He will not, of course, play the **8** ♠, because if East holds another 8 he will play it and not only peg for a pair-royal but for thirty-one as well.

In the event, East cannot play an 8 and score for fifteen. His best play, therefore, is the **10** ♣ announcing 'Seventeen'. This makes it impossible for a fifteen to be scored against him.

West has no better play than the **8** ♠ announcing 'Twenty-five', because the closer the total to 31 the better is the chance that East will be unable to play.

East plays the **5** ♠ announcing 'Thirty'.

West says 'Go' and as East has not got an Ace he pegs One for Last.

The hands are now counted.

West is not helped by the start. All he can score is 2 for fifteen and 3 for sequence. This with his Three for Last gives him a score of 8.

East pegs 6 for fifteen (two 10s and the **K** ♠ in the start, each combined with the **5** ♠) and 2 for the pair of 10s. In the crib he finds an Ace, a King a 9 and a 3. With the start this gives him 2 for the pair of Kings. He, therefore pegs 10 holes, making 11 in all as he has already pegged One for Last.

SIX-CARD and SEVEN-CARD CRIBBAGE FOR TWO PLAYERS.

The 6-card and 7-card variations of cribbage differ very little from the 5-card game. There is, in fact, no difference in the play nor in the crib, and very little in the mechanics of the game. The only differences of importance, apart from the number of cards, are that the non-dealer does not receive Three for Last, that the cards are played out to the end (the player failing to score for go leading again, thus giving his opponent the chance of making a pair or fifteen) and that in the 6-card variation the play is twice round the board (121 holes) and in the 7-card three times round (181 holes).

The general principles explained for the parent game hold good at the 6-card variation. It is to be noted, however, that in the 6-card variation the number of cards in hand and in the crib are the same, from which it follows that it is not so important for the non-dealer to make an effort of trying to baulk the crib by his discard. The two objectives – preserving any values in hand and baulking opponent's crib – are in this case on the same level, and either objective may be preferred, as the nature of the hand dictates.

THREE-HANDED CRIBBAGE.

Five cards are dealt to each player, and an extra one to the crib, to which each player contributes one card only. There is no Three for Last. The start is cut for in the usual way. The player on the left of the dealer plays first, and has first Show. He deals the succeeding hand. The score may be pegged on a triangular board open in the centre, or on the regular board furnished with a pivotted arm that permits a third player to peg. The game is once round the board.

FOUR-HANDED CRIBBAGE. Two play as partners against the other two, the partners sitting facing each other. Each player is dealt five cards and discards one to the crib, which is the property of the dealer. The player on the left of the dealer plays first. The others follow in clockwise rotation. Consultation between partners is not allowed, nor may they prompt each other, but a player may help his partner in the count of the hand or crib. The cards are played out to the end, as in the 6-card and 7-card variations. Game is usually twice round the board (121 holes).

Écarté

Écarté is played with a 32-card pack; that is to say with a pack from which the 2s, 3s, 4s, 5s, and 6s have been removed. The cards rank in the order: King (high), Queen, Jack, Ace, 10, 9, 8, 7 (low).

The two players are deal five cards each, either in packets of three and two, or two and three, and the rest of the pack is placed face downwards on the table, between them. To determine the trump suit the top card of the pack is turned face upwards. After looking at his cards, the non-dealer either plays or proposes. If he proposes, the dealer has the choice of either accepting or playing, and if he accepts both players may exchange any or all of their cards for others from the pack. By agreement the exchange of cards may continue until the pack is exhausted.

The non-dealer has first lead. The object of the game is to win three tricks, called the Trick. The winner scores 1 point for this, and if he wins all five tricks (the Vole) he scores 2 points. The game is won by the player who first wins 5 points, and it is customary to count a treble if a player wins the game and his opponent has failed to score; a double if his opponent has scored only 1 or 2 points, and a single if his opponent has scored 3 or 4 points.

So far, then, écarté appears to be childishly simple. The game, however, lends itself to a number of refinements that raise it to the level of an adult game. If the non-dealer does not propose, but plays, and fails to make the Trick, the dealer scores 2 points instead of only 1. In the same way, if the dealer refuses a proposal, and plays, and fails to make the Trick, the non-dealer scores 2 points. The value of the Vole (2 points) is not affected by playing without proposing.

Another important feature of the game is that if the dealer turns up a King as trumps, or if a player is dealt the King of the trump suit, he scores 1 point. The point can be scored by the non-dealer only if he declares the King before he makes the opening lead, and by the dealer only if he declares it before he plays to the first trick. A player is under no compulsion to declare the King, and, indeed, sometimes it is better to sacrifice the point for declaring the King than to declare it and so disclose to the opponent that this important card is held against him.

With the score West 3 points, East 4 points, East deals and the 8 ♠ is turned up.

West   East

East decides to play and must win the game if he handles his cards correctly. In the event he loses the game by incautious play. He leads **K ♣** on which West plays **7 ♣**. West does not declare the **K ♠** because East has played without proposing and, therefore, will lose 2 points if he fails to win the Trick. On the other hand, if he wins the Trick, declaring the King will be of no help to West.

East is lulled into a false sense of security, and unaware that the **K ♠** is against him he assumes that it is safe to lead **Q ♠**. West wins with **K ♠**, leads **Q ♦** to force East to win with **J ♠**, and comes to the last two tricks, and with them wins the game, with **A ♠** and **A ♥**.

There are a number of stock hands, holding which a player should play and not propose, and equally refuse the opponent's proposal. The more important of them are set out below. In all cases Spades are trumps:

1. Any three trumps supported by two inferior cards in outside suits – ♠ **J 10 7** ♥ **8** ♦ **10**
2. Any two trumps supported by three cards in one outside suit – ♠ **10 8** ♥ **J 8 7**
3. Any two trumps supported by the King and a low card in an outside suit, and one indifferent card in another suit – ♠ **A 8** ♥ **K 7** ♦ **9**
4. Any one trump supported by four cards headed by the King (or Queen) in an outside suit – ♠ **J** ♥ **K 9 8 7** (or **Q J 8 7**)
5. Any one trump supported by three cards headed by a court card in an outside suit, and any high court card in another suit – ♠ **10** ♥ **J 10 7** ♦ **Q**
6. Any hand that contains three queens (or better) and even though it may lack a trump card – ♥ **Q 7** ♦ **Q 7** ♣ **K**
7. Any hand that contains four high cards (King, Queen, Jack) and even though it may lack a trump card – ♥ **K** ♦ **Q J** ♣ **Q 7**

These stock hands are based on the Law of Probability, supported by the experience of the best players, who set great store on them. So far as the dealer is concerned, they are the minimum types of hands for him to play on. In a number of cases he may do better if he follows his luck, or decides to play on what is called a hunch, but the non-dealer should never propose when holding a hand similar to one of the above types. The reason is that he has the opening lead, and, at écarté, the opening lead is of vital importance.

East deals and the **10 ♠** is turned up.

West   East

West plays and if he leads **Q ♥** he wins the Trick no matter how East plays.

If, however, West had dealt, East would be on lead and if he led the **K ♦** he would win the Trick no matter how West played. In fact, West would be hard put to save the Vole, and, indeed, would do so only if he retained the **J ♣** and not the **Q ♥**. An experienced player would, of course, retain the **J ♣** (although the **Q ♥** is a higher card) because he holds three Hearts and only one Club, and since there are only eight cards in a suit it is about seven to five on that East's last card is a Club and not a Heart.

The deal is of some interest because it illustrates the danger of leading the Queen of trumps, unless the King has been turned up as trumps. It will be seen that if West decides to lead the **Q ♠**, East wins with the **K ♠**, runs his Diamonds (scoring the Trick) and West will save the Vole only if he retains the **J ♣**. On the other hand, it is to be noted that the lead of the singleton King of trumps is nearly always a good lead, and rarely damages the leader's hand.

As a general rule it is best for a player to play when he cannot see his way to discarding more than two cards; but if a player's hand guarantees him the Trick, or virtually so, he should propose or accept, because if the proposal is refused he is on easy street (since the Trick is more or less in his pocket) and if the proposal is accepted he has the opportunity to convert his hand into one on which he may win the Vole.

Stock   West

German Whist

German Whist is a very simple game. Each player is dealt thirteen cards. The remaining twenty-six cards are placed face downwards between the players and the top card is turned face upwards to denote the trump suit.

The non-dealer leads to the first trick. Thereafter the player who wins a trick leads to the next, and so on. A player must follow suit if he can. If he cannot he may either trump or discard. The winner of a trick takes into his hand the exposed card from the top of the stock: the loser takes the next card from the stock (he does not show it to his opponent) and turns up the next card of the stock.

When the stock is exhausted, the players play out the remaining thirteen cards, and at this stage of the game the player with a good memory will know exactly which cards his opponent holds.

The game is complete in one deal, and the player who wins the majority of tricks receives an agreed number of points per trick for all in excess of those won by his opponent. If both players win thirteen tricks, there is, of course, no score.

Although German whist is a simple game it offers good memory training for those who aspire to succeed at more advanced games, and, at the same time, gives exercise in the technique of card play.

If a player holds a strong trump suit he should lead his trumps early in the game so as to command the game in the later stages of the play, and if the exposed card is a trump it is always good play to make an effort to win it.

On the other hand, it is not always good play to win a trick. Much depends on the value of the exposed card. The 9 ♦ is exposed. West leads the **7 ♦** and East holds **♦ Q 6 3**. East should play **3 ♦**, and allow West to win the trick. It is not worth while wasting the **Q ♦** which should be kept in hand for better things later in the game. By contrary, if the **J ♦** is the exposed card, East should win the trick with the **Q ♦**, because now he is exchanging the **Q ♦** for an equivalent card and adding a trick to his total.

It is advisable to hold command of as many suits as possible, because it enables one to take a trick whenever the exposed card is worth winning, without losing control of the suit.

West holds the hand opposite.

Spades are trumps, and the exposed card is **K ♣**.

The **K ♣** is worth winning, but leading the **A ♣** is not the best play. West will win the trick, but the value of his hand will remain unchanged. West should prefer to lead the **K ♦**, because if it wins the trick his hand will be that much better, and if East is able to win the trick with the **A ♦**, West's **Q ♦** has been promoted to top Diamond.

Gin Rummy

Many variations of rummy (see page 197) are known, but for two players the one generally preferred is Gin Rummy with the Hollywood scoring, so called because during the war it was taken up with much publicity by the cinema stars.

The game is played with a full pack of fifty-two cards that rank from King (high) to Ace (low). The players cut to determine who deals first, but, thereafter, the player who wins a hand deals for the next one.

Ten cards are dealt to each player and the next card is turned face upwards and placed on the table between the players; it is known as the up-card. The rest of the pack is placed faced downwards alongside it.

The object of the game is to meld one's cards into sets of three or four of the same suit, and into sequences of three or more of the same suit. Sets and sequences must be independent of each other: a player is not allowed to meld the same card into a sequence and a set.

The non-dealer has first choice of taking the up-card into his hand. If he does not, he must offer it to the dealer. If either player takes the up-card, he discards a card from his hand face upwards on the table. If neither player takes the up-card, the non-dealer takes the top card of the stock and discards a card from his hand to cover the up-card. The dealer then has the option of taking into his hand either the card that the non-dealer has discarded or the top card of the stock. When he has taken one of them into his hand, he, too, discards a card from his hand. The discards are placed one on top of the other, so that only the card immediately discarded can be seen, and the discard pile must not be examined by the players while the hand is in play.

Play continues in this way—each player in turn either taking the top card of the discard pile or the top card of the stock—until one of them elects to go down (called knocking) or there are only two cards left in the stock. Neither may be drawn, and if the player who draws the fiftieth card discards without knocking, the hand is declared a draw; neither player scores and the same dealer deals again.

The player who knocks must do so after drawing a card and discarding, and his unmelded cards must not exceed a total of 10 points—court cards count 10 points each and the others their pip values.

Unless a player has declared gin (*i.e.* knocked with all his cards melded) his opponent can reduce his loss by adding cards from his hand to the melds exposed by his opponent.

North, who has not declared gin, knocks with the melds on the right.

South holds in his hand:

♠ J 6 3 2   ♥ Q A   ♦ Q J   ♣ K 6

and reduces his loss by adding J♠, 6♠, A♥ to North's sequences, and the K♣ to his set of Kings.

Play now ceases, and the score is made up as follows:

1. The unmelded cards of the players are totalled to determine their respective point-counts.
2. A player who has declared gin scores 25 points plus his opponent's point-count.
3. If gin has not been declared: if the knocker's point-count is less than that of his opponent's, the knocker wins the hand and scores the difference between the two point-counts; if the opponent's point-count is less than that of the knocker or if the two point-counts are equal, the opponent wins the hand and scores 20 points for undercutting plus the difference (if any) between the two point-counts.

The scores are recorded on a sheet of paper ruled as follows:

	Jack	Sam	Jack	Sam	Jack	Sam
Box 1						
Box 2						
Box 3						
Box 4						
Box 5						

Every hand won and score entered is known as a box. The first time that a player scores he enters the points in the first column only. The second time that he scores he enters them in the second column and adds them to his score in the first column. The third time that he scores he enters them in the third column and adds them to the scores last entered in the first and second columns. Thereafter, every time that a player scores he adds his score to the scores last entered in all three columns.

When the score of a player in a column reaches a total of 100 points or more, the column is closed. The winner of a column scores 100 points for winning it, and a further 20 points for each box that he has won in excess of those won by his opponent. If, however, the opponent has won more boxes than the winner of the column, the opponent scores 20 points for each box that he has won in excess of those won by the winner of the column, and this score is deducted from that of the winner of the column.

If a player fails to score in any column he is blitzed, and the total score of the winner of the column is doubled. The player who has been blitzed in any column makes his first, or second, score in the next column which has not been won.

The game ends when all three columns have been won.

If a player wins all three columns, his final score is determined by adding together the total scores of all three columns. If a player wins two columns (his opponent one column) the final score is determined by adding together the total scores of the winner of the two columns, and subtracting the lower score from the higher.

Honeymoon Bridge

Thirteen cards are dealt to each player and the remaining twenty-six cards are placed face downwards between them.

The non-dealer leads to the first trick. Thereafter the player who wins a trick leads to the next. A player must follow suit if he can. The winner of a trick takes the top card of the stock, the loser takes the next card. The first thirteen tricks are played without a trump suit, and the tricks do not count in the final score.

When the stock is exhausted, the two players bid as in bridge (see page 125) the dealer first; bidding continues until one player passes a bid, double or redouble. The player who does not make the final bid leads to the first trick, and the play continues as in the regular game except that only two, instead of four, players are competing. The players score as in bridge.

If a player revokes during the play of the first thirteen tricks, or if he draws a card out of turn, or sees more than one card when drawing from the stock, his opponent, when it is his turn to draw from the stock, may look at the two top cards and take either. Other irregularities are governed by the laws of bridge.

In **HONEYMOON BRIDGE WITH A WIDOW** the players sit in adjacent seats and the cards are dealt into four hands (as in the regular game) of twelve cards each. The remaining four cards (the widow) are placed face downwards in the centre of the table.

The players bid as in the regular game (the dealer bids first) and when a bid has been passed, doubled or redoubled, the player who has won the declaration takes up the widow hand and, without showing it to his opponent, takes one card into his own hand, one into his dummy, and gives the other two cards to his opponent to take one into his hand and the other into his dummy.

The player who has won the declaration may demand the opening lead to be made either by his opponent or by his opponent's dummy.

Thereafter the play and scoring proceed as in the regular game.

In **SEMI-EXPOSED HONEYMOON BRIDGE** the players sit in adjacent seats and the cards are dealt as in the regular game, except that the first six cards to the dummies are dealt face downwards in a row, the remaining cards, six face upwards on top of them and one face upwards by itself.

The dealer bids first, and the bidding ends when a bid has been passed, doubled or redoubled. The hand on the left of the player who has won the declaration leads to the first trick. The play and scoring are as in the regular game, except that a player may play from his dummy only a face-upwards card. When a face-upwards card has been played, the card under it is turned face upwards, and becomes available for play.

Jo-jotte

Although Jo-jotte was invented by Ely Culbertson in 1937, it is not altogether a modern game, but a variation of the old French game of belotte in itself very similar to klaberjass (see page 89) and its several variations.

It is a game for two players, and played with the short pack, namely a pack from which all cards below the rank of 7 have been removed.

The rank of the cards varies. If there is a trump suit, the cards of the suit rank in the order: **J 9 A 10 K Q 8 7**. In plain suits, or if the hand is played in No-Trumps, the order is: **A 10 K Q J 9 8 7**.

Each player is dealt six cards (either singly, or in bundles of two or three) and the thirteenth card of the pack is placed face upwards on the table. It is known as the turned card.

There are two rounds of bidding. The non-dealer bids first. He may either accept the suit of the turned card as trumps, or pass. If he passes, the dealer has the same option. If both players pass, the non-dealer may name any suit, other than that of the turned card, as trumps, or he may declare No-Trumps or he may pass. If he passes for the second time, the dealer has the same option. If both players pass twice the hand is abandoned and the deal passes, but if either player names a suit as trumps, his opponent may overbid it by declaring No-Trumps, but not by naming another suit as trumps. Either player may double his opponent's declaration, and any double may be redoubled.

When the declaration has been determined (doubled, redoubled or passed) the dealer deals three more cards to his opponent and to himself, and he places the bottom card of the pack face upwards on top of the undealt cards of the pack. It has no significance in play but is solely informatory and, therefore, is known as the information card.

The player who has made the final declaration is known as the declarer: his opponent as the defender.

At this stage of the game the defender may announce that instead of defending against the declarer's contract he will himself become declarer at a Nullo contract; a contract, that is, to lose every trick. The declarer may now declare a Slam. It is a contract to win every trick either in the suit originally named by him (he cannot change the suit) or in No-Trumps.

The defender then announces his melds, if he holds any. A meld is four of a kind (except 9s, 8s and 7s at No-Trumps, and 8s and 7s in a suit declaration). A meld carries a score of 100 points and is scored (as at bridge (see page 126)) above the line. Only the player with the highest-ranking meld may score for it, and he may score for a second meld if he holds one.

Next, beginning with the defender, the players score for sequences, and for this purpose the cards take their normal rank of Ace (high), King, Queen, Jack, 10, 9, 8, 7. For a sequence of five cards the holder scores 50 points above the line, for a sequence of four 40 points, and for a sequence of three 20 points. If two sequences are of equal length, that headed by the highest card takes precedence. If both sequences are equal, a sequence in the trump suit wins over one in a plain suit; if both sequences are in plain suits neither is scored for. Only the player with the higher-ranking sequence may score for it, and he may score for any other sequences that he may hold.

Clubs are trumps. Defender scores 200 points above the line for his melds of 10s and Queens, and the declarer cannot score for his meld of Kings because in the trump suit the 10 is higher than the King.

Hearts are trumps. Neither player has a meld. Defender declares his 4-card sequence in Spades but he cannot score for it because the declarer has an equal sequence in the trump suit (Hearts). The declarer, therefore, scores 40 points above the line for his 4-card sequence in Hearts and a further 20 points for his 3-card sequence in Diamonds.

Finally, it is to be noted that if the declarer elects to play the hand in the same suit as the turned card, either player if he holds the 7 of the suit may exchange it for the turned card.

The player who leads to a trick may lead any card that he chooses. The second player is limited in his play; for he must obey the three rules that follow:

1. He must follow suit if he can.
2. If a trump has been led he must not only follow suit if he can, but win the trick by playing a higher trump if he holds one.
3. If a plain suit has been led and he is unable to follow suit, he must win the trick by trumping if he can.

Second player may discard a worthless card only when he is unable to obey one or other of these three rules.

Winning a trick has no value in itself. What counts is winning tricks with certain cards in them: these are scored as follows:

For winning the Jack of trumps   20 points
For winning the 9 of trumps   15 points
For winning any Ace or 10   10 points
For winning any King or Queen   5 points
For winning the last trick (except at Nullo)   10 points

The example that follows is a simple one to illustrate the mechanics of the game.

Defender   Declarer

Hearts are trumps. The turned card is **K ♠**: the information card **Q ♦**.

Defender leads **A ♣**, and the play is:

Defender	Declarer
A ♣	**Q ♣**
10 ♣	**10 ♥**
8 ♦	**A ♦**
J ♦	**7 ♦**
8 ♣	**8 ♥**
9 ♥	**9 ♦**
10 ♠	**9 ♠**
Q ♠	**A ♥**
7 ♥	**J ♥**

Declarer scores for taking:

Jack of trumps (♥)	20 points
A ♥	10 points
A ♦	10 points
10 ♥	10 points
10 ♣	10 points
Q ♠	5 points
Last trick	10 points
	75 points

Defender scores for taking:

9 of trumps (♥)	15 points
A ♣	10 points
10 ♠	10 points
Q ♣	5 points
	40 points

In addition to the above, if a player holds the King and Queen of the trump suit (if there is one) he may score 20 points provided he announces 'Jo' when he plays the King and later 'Jotte' when he plays the Queen. He cannot score for the combination if he plays the Queen before the King.

Game is won by the player who first scores 80 points below the line, which may be made in one hand or in a series of part-scores, and the player who wins the rubber (best out of three games) scores a bonus of 300 points.

The declarer of a Nullo contract scores a bonus of 200 points if he loses every trick; if he takes a trick, however, his opponent scores 200 points for the first and 100 for every subsequent trick.

The declarer of a Slam scores a bonus of 500 points if he wins every trick; and if a player wins every trick but has not bid Slam he scores a bonus of 100 points.

Scoring below the line, towards game, is calculated as follows:

1. If the declarer's total score, including melds, sequences, trick scores and bonuses (if any) is greater than the defender's total score, he scores his trick score below the line, and the defender scores his trick score above the line.

2. If the defender's total score is greater than the declarer's, the two trick scores are added together and scored by the defender below the line.

3. If the contract is doubled or redoubled, the player with the higher total scores both his and his opponent's trick score, doubled or quadrupled, below the line.

4. If there is a tie in total points, the trick scores of both players are put in prison and awarded to the player who obtains the higher total in the following deal.

Klaberjass

Klaberjass is probably better known in America than in England, because under the names of Clabber, Clobber, Clubby, Klab and Klob, it occurs in Damon Runyon's amusing stories, and in 1937 a variation of the game, under the name of jo-jotte (see page 85) was publicized by Ely Culbertson. Despite the similarity of names it is not identical with the Hungarian game of kalabriás, which is a game for three or four players. There may have been a common ancestor, or possibly the game was taken to the New World by Central European immigrants and there adapted as a two-handed game with klaberjass as a bowdlerized version of kalabriás.

The game is played with a pack from which the 6s, 5s, 4s, 3s and 2s have been removed. In the trump suit the cards rank in the order **J 9 A 10 K Q 8 7**; and in the other three suits **A 10 K Q J 9 8 7**.

Six cards are dealt to both players, in two bundles of three cards each. The next card of the pack is turned face upwards on the table (it is known as the turn-up card) and the rest of the pack is placed face downwards so as partly to cover it.

The non-dealer bids first. He may *take-it* (*i.e.* accept the turn-up card as the trump suit); *pass* (*i.e.* refuse to accept the turn-up card as the trump suit); or *schmeiss* (*i.e.* offer to play with the turn-up card as the trump suit or throw in the hand, as his opponent prefers). If the opponent says 'Yes' to a schmeiss there is a fresh deal; if he says 'No' the hand is played with the turn-up card as the trump suit.

If the non-dealer has passed, the dealer may either take-it, pass or schmeiss.

If both players pass there is a second round of bidding. Now the non-dealer may name any one of the other three suits as trumps, or he may schmeiss (*i.e.* offer to name one of the other three suits as trumps or throw in the hand, as his opponent prefers), or he may pass. If he passes, the dealer may name one of the other three suits as trumps, or throw in the hand.

When a player accepts or names a trump suit, the bidding ends, and the player who has accepted or named a suit as trumps is called the maker.

There is never more than two rounds of bidding, and when the trump suit has been settled, the dealer deals three more cards, one at a time, to the two players. He then turns up the bottom card of the pack and places it on top of the pack. It takes no part in the play, and is put where it is only to be seen.

If either player has been dealt the 7 of the trump suit, he may exchange it for the turn-up card.

Only sequences are melded, and for melding the cards rank in the order from Ace (high) to 7 (low). A 3-card sequence counts 20 points, a 4-card or longer one 50 points.

The non-dealer begins by announcing the value of his best sequence. If his best sequence is of three cards he says 'Twenty'; if of four or more cards he says 'Fifty'. If dealer has a better sequence he says 'No good'; if he lacks a better sequence he says 'Good'; if he has an equal sequence he askes 'How high?'. The non-dealer then announces the top card of his sequence. The dealer then says whether it is good, no good, or if he has a sequence headed by an equal card. In this last event neither player scores unless one of the sequences is in the trump suit, which wins over a sequence in a plain suit.

The non-dealer leads to the first trick; thereafter the winner of a trick leads to the next. A player must follow suit if he can, and if he cannot he must play a trump if he holds one. If a trump is led, the second player must win the trick if he can.

After the first trick has been played, the player with the highest meld shows it and scores for all sequences in his hand. His opponent cannot score for any sequences that he may hold.

A player who holds the King and Queen of the trump suit may score 20 points so long as he announces 'Bella' immediately after he has played the second of them to a trick. If a player holds the Jack of the trump suit, as well as the King and Queen, he may score for the sequence as well as for bella.

When all the cards have been played, each player examines his tricks and scores points for winning in his tricks:

Jasz (the Jack of the trump suit)	20 points
Menel (the 9 of the trump suit)	14 points
Any Ace	11 points
Any 10	10 points
Any King	4 points
Any Queen	3 points
Any Jack (except Jasz)	2 points
Last Trick	10 points

If the maker's total, including melds and cards won, is higher than the opponent's, each scores all the points he has won. If the totals of the two players are equal, the opponent scores the points he has won, the maker nothing. If the opponent's total is higher than that of the maker's, the two totals are added together and the opponent scores them.

The player who first reaches 500 points wins the game.

KLABERJASS FOR FOUR PLAYERS is played in partnership, two playing against two. Eight cards are dealt to each player, and the dealer turns up his last card for trumps.

Each player in turn, beginning with the player on the left of the dealer, may either take-it or pass. There is no schmeiss. If all four players pass, there is a second round of bidding during which each player in turn has a right to name the trump suit. If all four players pass the second round of bidding there is a fresh deal.

The player who names the trump suit becomes the maker, and his side must score more than the opposing side.

The player on the left of the dealer leads to the first trick.

Pinocle[*]

Pinocle in its original form is a game for two players similar to bezique (see page 50). It is played with a pack of forty-eight cards, namely a pack that consists of **A 10 K Q J 9** (in this order) in each of the four suits, duplicated.

Twelve cards are dealt to both players, either three or four cards at a time, and the next card is turned face upwards to indicate the trump suit. The rest of the pack is placed face downwards on the table to half cover the exposed card.

The object of the game is to win tricks that include those cards which carry a scoring value when won in a trick, and to meld certain combinations of cards that carry a scoring value.

When taken in a trick each Ace scores 11 points, each 10 scores 10 points, each King 4 points, each Queen 3 points, and each Jack 2 points. The player who wins the last trick scores 10 points.

The values of the melds are:

Class A

A 10 K Q J of the trump suit	150 points
K Q of the trump suit (royal marriage)	40 points
K Q of a plain suit (common marriage)	20 points

Class B

Pinocle (**Q ♠** and **J ♦**)	40 points
Dis (**9** of the trump suit)	10 points

Class C

Four Aces – one of each suit	100 points
Four Kings – one of each suit	80 points
Four Queens – one of each suit	60 points
Four Jacks – one of each suit	40 points

The non-dealer leads to the first trick. Thereafter the winner of a trick leads to the next. It is not necessary for a player to follow suit to a led card. The winner of a trick replenishes his hand by taking the top card of the stock; the loser of the trick takes the next.

After a player has won a trick and before drawing from the stock, he may meld any of the above combinations. To meld he places the cards face upwards on the table in front of him, where they remain until he decides to play them to a trick, or until the stock is exhausted. Melding is subject to the three rules that follow:

1. Only one meld may be made at a turn.
2. For each meld, at least one card must be taken from the hand and placed on the table.
3. A card already melded may be melded again so long as it is in a different class, or in a higher-scoring meld of the same class.

---

*Pinocle is frequently spelt pinochle, but the Oxford Dictionary does not sanction the H.

That is to say, if Hearts are trumps a player may meld ♥ K Q and score for the royal marriage, and later he may add ♥ A 10 J and score for the sequence. He cannot first declare ♥ A 10 K Q J and score for sequence and later declare the royal marriage.

If the dealer turns up a dis as the trump card he scores 10 points. Thereafter a player holding a dis may count it merely by showing it when winning a trick. He may count the dis and make another meld at the same time. After winning a trick, the holder of a dis may exchange it for the trump card.

The player who wins the twelfth trick may meld if he is able to. He then draws the last face-downwards card of the stock and must show it to his opponent. The loser of the trick takes into his hand the card exposed on the table.

The last twelve tricks are now played off. During this period of play a player must follow suit if he can to the card led; if he cannot he must trump the trick if he holds a trump. If a trump is led the second player must win the trick if he can.

Melds are scored when they are declared. The score for cards won in tricks are added after the hand has been played out, a total of 7, 8, or 9 points is counted as 10.

Every deal may constitute a game, or the players may prefer that the winner will be he who first reaches an agreed figure.

At pinocle skill and experience count for much. An ability to remember which cards have been played contributes much towards success. When it comes to playing off the last twelve cards, the experienced player will never be in any doubt about which cards his opponent holds. Thus, when playing to the last trick before the stock is exhausted, a player should be able to weigh up the merits of winning the trick and melding, preventing his opponent from melding, or losing the trick and so obtaining the exposed trump card to add to his trump length in the final play off.

Piquet

Piquet is probably the best known of all card games for two players; there is no doubt that it is more skilful and interesting than any other. It is played with a 32-card pack, namely a pack from which the 6s, 5s, 4s, 3s and 2s have been removed, sometimes called the short or piquet pack. The cards rank from Ace (high) to 7 (low) and he who cuts the higher card has the right of first deal; he would be advised to take it because there is some advantage to be gained from it.

Twelve cards are dealt to both players in packets of either twos or threes, and the remaining eight cards (*talon*) are placed face downwards on the table between the players. The non-dealer may now exchange any five of his cards with the five top cards of the talon. He need not exchange as many as five cards, but he must exchange at least one, and, if he has not exchanged five cards, he may look at those that he was entitled to draw. The dealer may exchange cards up to the number that remain in the talon. He, too, must exchange at least one card. If he does not exchange all the cards, he may look at those that he was entitled to, but he must show them to his opponent if he does. The players place their discards face downwards on the table in front of them. The discards of the players should not be mixed together as, during the play of the hand, the players are entitled to look at their own discards.

The score is made up in three ways: the count of the hand; the count during the play of the cards; the extraordinary scores.

The hand is counted in the following way:

1. The *Point*, which is the number of cards held in the longest suit. The player who holds the longest suit wins the point, and scores 1 point for each card that he holds in it. If the number of cards in the suits held by the players is the same, the player with the highest count (Aces 11, Kings, Queens and Jacks 10 each, and other cards at their pip values) wins the point. If the count is equal neither player scores.
2. *Sequences*, which must not be of less than three cards of the same suit, are won by the player who holds the most cards in one sequence. As between sequences of equal length, the highest wins. For a sequence of three (tierce) 3 points are scored; for a sequence of four (quart) 4 points are scored. For a sequence of five (quint) 15 points are scored; for a sequence of six (sixième) 16 points; for a sequence of seven (septième) and for a sequence of eight (huitième) 18 points.
3. *Quatorzes* and *Trios* are any four or three cards of the same rank higher than the 9. The player who holds the superior quatorze or trio wins. Thus, a player who holds a trio of Aces will win even though his opponent may hold trios of Kings *and* Queens. In the same way, a player who holds trios of Aces, Kings, Queens and Jacks, will score nothing if his opponent holds a quatorze of 10s. Quatorzes are scored at 14 points each; trios at 3 points each.

The count of the hand must be declared in the order: point,

sequence, quatorze and trio, and, on demand, a player must show any combinations of cards for which he has scored. In practice, however, this is rarely necessary, because the opponent is usually able to infer from his own cards what cards are against him.

When counting the hand a player is not compelled to declare all that he holds. It is in order, and sometimes the very best play, to mislead one's opponent by declaring less than one holds in order to conceal one's strength. The practice is known as sinking. The player who holds a quatorze of Aces may declare only a trio. The opponent may inquire which Ace is not being reckoned, and the player may name any Ace he chooses, because the explicit reply: 'I do not count the Ace of Clubs' is not a guarantee that the player does not hold this card.

After the non-dealer has counted his hand he leads a card. The dealer then counts his hand and plays a card to the non-dealer's lead. Two cards constitute a trick, and it is compulsory for the second player to follow suit to the led card if he can do so. If not he may play any card he chooses, because there is no trump suit. The player who leads to a trick scores 1 point, and if his opponent wins it he scores one point for doing so (except in the case of the last trick, when he scores 2 points) and leads to the next trick, scoring 1 point for the lead. After all twelve tricks have been played, the player who has won most tricks scores 10 points for having done so (Ten for the Cards, as it is called). There is no score to either player if they win six tricks each. Plate 12 shows play in progress.

There are four extraordinary scores:

1. *Carte Blanche.* If a player is dealt a hand that contains no court card he may claim carte blanche and score 10 points. It takes precedence over any other scoring combination, but the player must announce his carte blanche as soon as he picks up the cards dealt to him, and he must show his hand, though he need not do so until after his opponent has discarded.

2. *Pique.* If a player scores in hand and play 30 points, before his opponent scores anything, he wins a pique and scores 30 points for it. Only the non-dealer can win a pique, because he scores 1 point for the first lead before the dealer counts his hand; this, of course, automatically rules out the dealer from scoring for a pique.

3. *Repique.* If a player scores in hand alone a total of 30 points, before his opponent scores anything, he wins a repique and scores 60 points for it. Either player may score for a repique, because points in hand are counted in priority to those won in play.

4. *Capot.* If a player wins all twelve tricks he wins a capot and scores 40 points, not 10, for the cards. The capot, however, is not counted towards a pique because the points are not scored until the hand has been played.

The players deal alternately, and a *partie* (game) consists of six deals (three deals each). At the end of the *partie* the player with the higher score deducts from his score that of his opponent, and adds 100 points to the result. If, however, one player fails to score 100 points, he is rubiconed, and the player with the higher score adds the two scores together, and a further 100 points. If the score after six deals is equal, each player has one more deal, and if the score still remains equal the *partie* is a draw.

Most card games are played in silence. Piquet is a continuous dialogue. When a player counts his hand he declares his point, sequences, quartorzes and trios, and his opponent confirms whether they are 'Good', 'Not good' or 'Equal', and, if equal, the player announces the pip total which his opponent declares 'Good', 'Not good' or 'Equal'. Then, during the play of the hand, the two players announce their scores as each trick is played.

At piquet it is customary to call the non-dealer the elder (hand) and the dealer the younger (hand). The deal below (after both players have discarded) illustrates the method of scoring and is not to be accepted as an example of good play.

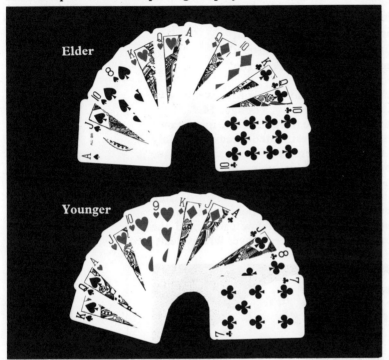

Elder : 'Point of four'.
Younger : 'Making?'
Elder : 'Thirty-nine.'
Younger : 'Not good.'
Elder : 'Queens and Tens—six'. (He counts his score for his trios without waiting for younger to confirm that the count is good. He knows that his trio of Queens is good because, from his own cards, he can see that younger cannot hold a quatorze or a better trio than one of Jacks. His announcement 'Queens and Tens' means that he holds three Queens and three 10s. If he held four Queens and three 10s he would announce 'Fourteen Queens and three Tens'.)

Elder, who has no more to count, leads the Ace of Spades— 'Seven'.

Younger now counts his hand.

Younger : 'Point of four—forty,' (Elder has a right to ask in which suit the point is. In this case, however, he has no need because he knows from his own cards that it can only be in Hearts.) 'and tierce to the Jack—seven.' (Here, again, elder has no need to ask because, from his own cards, he knows that the tierce must be in Hearts.)

Younger plays the Queen of Spades on elder's Ace of Spades, and repeats his score—'Seven'.

The rest of the play is:

Elder		Younger	
J ♠	'Eight'	K ♠	'Eight'
Q ♥	'Eight'	A ♥	'Nine'
K ♥	'Nine'	J ♥	'Ten'
10 ♠	'Ten'	7 ♣	'Ten'
8 ♠	'Eleven'	8 ♣	'Ten'
K ♣	'Twelve'	A ♣	'Eleven'
10 ♦	'Twelve'	10 ♥	'Twelve'
Q ♦	'Twelve'	9 ♥	'Thirteen'
Q ♣	'Thirteen'	J ♣	'Fourteen'
A ♦	'Fourteen'	J ♦	'Fourteen'
10 ♣	'Fifteen'	K ♦	'Fourteen'

Elder, winning the trick–'Sixteen, and the cards twenty-six.'
This ends the deal with the score at Elder 26, Younger 14.

A player's first consideration must be the point. The importance
of scoring for the point cannot be over-estimated, because not only
does it add to a player's score, but it protects him against a pique
or repique, and, of course, scoring for point diminishes the
opponent's score to the same extent. Normally, therefore, a
player should retain his longest suit intact and discard from
shorter suits. This, however, does not always hold good, particularly if the longest suit consists mainly of low cards, and the
shorter suits of high ones. The inexperienced player who is dealt:

will be tempted to retain the Spades, and discard from the other
suits, with a view to scoring for point and sequence. The experienced player will know that the better course is to discard
all five Spades, because the Jack of Spades is the only card that
will raise the suit from a quart to a sixième, and the odds are about
three to one against drawing it. It is likely that retaining the
Spades will win the point, but almost certainly it will result in the
loss of the cards. This will make a big difference to the score, and
always the cards must be considered together with the point. If the
non-dealer holds a long suit headed by top cards, usually it guarantees the point and the cards. The suit, therefore, must be preserved
at all costs, but this is of much less importance for the dealer
because he may never obtain the lead.

A good general rule emerges. The discards of the non-dealer
should be made towards obtaining an attacking hand; that of the
dealer towards obtaining a defensive hand; that is to say a hand
in which there is some strength in as many suits as possible.

Subject to these considerations, it is best to discard from as few
suits as possible, and, once a player has made up his mind to

discard from a suit, he should discard the whole of it, unless it is necessary to retain the suit guarded. Sequence cards should be retained in preference to non-sequence cards, and, of course, cards that help to make up trios and quatorzes should never be discarded if it is to be avoided.

Playing to the score is very important, particularly in the last deal of a *partie*. As an example: If a player is well ahead, and sees the opportunity to gain a rubicon, he should discard cautiously and play so as to prevent his opponent from saving the rubicon by scoring 100 points. By contrary, if a player is in danger of being rubiconed, he should be prepared to take some risks, since only a big score will save him. It must be remembered, however, that if a player is rubiconed his score is added to that of his opponent, so if there is no chance of saving the rubicon he should play to keep his score down. To this end he should declare only equities or those scores that will save pique and repique, and he should aim to divide the cards.

AUCTION PIQUET originated in Oxford, and was developed by some British prisoners of war during the war of 1914.

The bidding takes place before the discard. It is opened by the non-dealer. He may pass, and if he does and the dealer does also, there is a redeal by the same player. The lowest bid that may be made is one of Seven. It is an undertaking to win, or lose, seven of the twelve possible tricks. There is no penalty for a bid out of turn nor for an underbid, because these irregularities merely give information to the opponent.

The most interesting feature of the game is the minus bid. It is an undertaking to lose the stated number of tricks. It ranks neither above nor below a normal (plus) bid. In a minus deal the player scores everything good in his opponent's hand. A player may double a bid made by his opponent, and the player who has been doubled may redouble or shift to a higher bid.

After bidding, the players discard. The routine is the same as at the parent game except that there is no compulsion for the players to discard at least one card.

The declarations follow, and the players may declare the point, sequences, trios and quatorzes in any order they choose. Sinking is allowed in plus deals but not in minus ones.

The scoring is as follows:

The value of point, sequences, trios, quatorzes, cards and capot, are the same as in the parent game.

In plus deals pique (30 points) is obtained on the score of 29 and repique (60 points) on the score of 30. In minus deals both pique and repique are obtained on the score of 21.

The *partie* (six deals) is worth 150 points, and rubicon is under 150 points. In the event of a tie a seventh deal is played and the *partie* ends if it is tied.

A player scores 10 points for every trick won in a plus deal (or lost in a minus deal above (or below) the declared contract.

If a player fails to make his contract the opponent scores 10 points for every trick by which he is short.

Overtricks and undertricks are effected by doubling and redoubling, but scores in hand and play are not.

Although a player scores 1 point for winning a trick he does not score for leading a losing card, nor an additional 1 point for winning the last trick.

Tablanette

Tablanette is a game for two players that is easy to learn and worth learning because it is remarkably fascinating to play.

From a full pack of fifty-two cards, six cards are dealt face downwards to the two players, and four cards face upwards to the table between them. The rest of the pack is temporarily set aside. If any Jacks are dealt to the table they are removed, placed at the bottom of the pack, and the spaces filled with cards from the top of the pack.

The non-dealer plays first. If he plays a card of the same rank as any of the four cards on the table, he takes the card; or, if there are any two or three cards on the table whose values if added together equal that of the card played, he takes these cards. For this purpose a King counts 14, a Queen 13, and an Ace either 11 or 1. The Jack plays a special part in the game and its function will be explained later. The other cards count at their pip values.

If the cards on the table and the player's hand are:

he will play the **K ♥** and take the **K ♠** from the table. If he holds:

he will play the **A ♥** and take the **2 ♥** and **9 ♣** from the table, because together they total 11, a value of an Ace.

The card played and those taken from the table are kept in a pile, face downwards, on the table by the player who took them.

If at any time a player is able to take all the cards on the table (there may be only one, or there may be more than four) he announces 'Tablanette' and scores the total value of all the cards taken plus the value of the card he has played. If, for example, the cards on the table are:

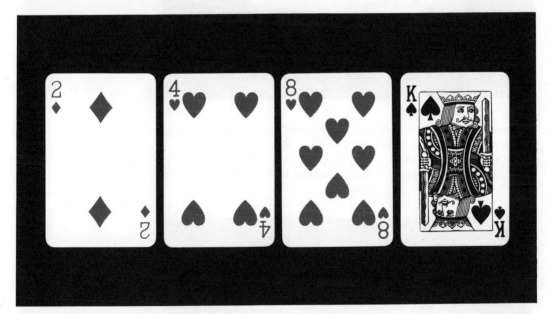

and a player holds any of the other three Kings, he will be able to announce 'Tablanette', because his King will take the **K ♠** and the other three cards whose values total 14. The score for this will be 42 points (*i.e.* 14 × 3).

The special function of the Jack is that playing it allows the player to take all the cards on the table, but it does not allow him to score for a tablanette. Obviously, therefore, a Jack is an excellent card to hold, because playing it compels the opponent to play a lone card to the table and when there is only one card on the table the player whose turn it is to play is in a good position to score a tablanette.

The players play in rotation until they have exhausted their six cards. The dealer then deals another six cards to each, and so on until the pack is exhausted.

When the last batch of six cards has been played, any cards left on the table are taken by the player who last took a card from the table.

The players examine the cards they have taken, and score 1 point for the 2 ♣ and for every Ace, King, Queen, Jack and 10 (except the 10 ♦ which scores 2 points). Finally, if a player has taken 27 or more cards he scores 3 points.

The deal passes in rotation, and the game is won by the player who first scores a total of 251 points.

There is more skill in the game than may be apparent at first sight. If, for example, there is only an 8 on the table and the player holds:

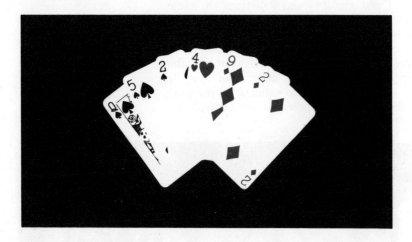

his best play is the 4 ♥, because no one card has a value of 12 and the opponent, therefore, cannot score a tablanette.

As at all card games it is very important to keep in mind the cards that have been played. The opponent has scored a tablanette and the player holds:

He has to play a card to the table, and the natural tendency is to play the **3 ♥**, because this will give the opponent a minimum score if he can again announce 'Tablanette'. But if no 3s have been played, but a 10 has, then it is better to play one of the 10s, because the chances are against the opponent holding the remaining 10, and there is a possibility that he holds one of the remaining three 3s.

TABLANETTE FOR THREE PLAYERS is played in the same way as the parent game, except that the players are dealt four cards (instead of six) at a time.

Games for
Three players

Black Maria

Black Maria, sometimes known as Black Lady and sometimes as Slippery Anne, is very similar to hearts and its several variations. (see page 157). It is considered best played as a game for three, but may be played by more.

The 2 of Clubs is removed from the pack, and seventeen cards are dealt to each player. The cards rank in the normal order from Ace (high) to 2 (low) and, after a player has looked at his cards, he passes three of them to his right-hand opponent and receives three from his left-hand opponent, which he must not look at until he has passed three on.

When the exchanges of cards have been made, the player on the left of the dealer leads to the first trick. Thereafter, the player who wins a trick leads to the next. A player must follow suit to the led card provided he can do so. Otherwise he may discard any card he chooses. There is no trump suit.

The object of the game is to avoid winning a trick which contains a penalty card. These cards, and the penalties that go with them, are:

Every card in the Heart suit—1 point each.
The Ace of Spades—7 points.
The King of Spades—10 points.
The Queen of Spades (Black Maria)—13 points.
The deal passes in rotation clockwise.

The game introduces two features: the discard and the play of the cards.

The inexperienced player, if he is dealt a high Spade, will assume that he cannot do better than pass it on to his right-hand opponent. It is, however, not always the best play. Provided a number of low Spades are held in support of the high ones, it is very often better to retain the high cards with a view to controlling the suit during the play of the hand. Indeed, a player who has been dealt any Spades or Hearts lower than the Queen would be well advised to keep them in order to protect himself against any top cards in the suits that may be passed on to him. The main principle of discarding should be to try and set up either a void suit—in order to get rid of penalty cards by discarding them during the play—or at obtaining long suits, provided low cards in them are held. A player who has been dealt:

cannot do better than pass on the three Diamonds. The Spades must be kept to protect against receiving a high card in the suit, the Hearts are adequately protected, and there is nothing to fear in Clubs.

An ability to count the cards is the first essential to success. Towards the end of a deal an experienced player will know pretty well which cards are still left to be played, and he will be able to make a shrewd guess who holds them. It is in the end-play, therefore, that opportunity comes for skilful play.

After fourteen tricks have been played the players should know who holds the remaining cards.

West is on lead and leads the **6 ♠**, North plays the **2 ♠** and East, perforce, wins with the **K ♠**. Now, if East returns the **5 ♦** West must win with the **7 ♦** and North saddles him with the **Q ♠** (Black Maria). If, however, East returns the **3 ♣**, North will have to win with the **6 ♣** on which West will have played the **A ♠**.

East's play will be directed by the score, and whether it is more advantageous to him to saddle West or North with all 20 points. The strategy is quite ethical so long as East puts his own interest first and is not moved by malice aforethought.

FOUR-HANDED BLACK MARIA is played in the same way as the parent game, except that no card is removed from the pack, and every player, therefore, receives thirteen cards. The players may play all against all, or two in partnership against the other two.

FIVE-HANDED BLACK MARIA is played in the same way as the parent game, but the 2 of Diamonds as well as the 2 of Clubs is removed from the pack. Each player, therefore, is dealt ten cards.

Cut-throat Bridge

Many suggestions have been made to make bridge (see page 125) suitable for three players. The most satisfactory is towie (see page 114) but what has become known as Cut-throat Bridge is the original and the simplest of the three-handed variations.

The players take seats at random and after drawing for deal, shuffling and cutting in the regular way, the dealer deals thirteen cards each to the three players and to a fourth hand that is temporarily set aside.

The auction, beginning with the dealer, is conducted as in the parent game, and when a player's bid, double or redouble has been passed by the other two players, the player on his left leads to the first trick. The player who has obtained the final contract then sorts the fourth hand, spreads it in front of him on the table, and plays it as his dummy, against the other two players in partnership with each other,

The play and scoring are the same as in the parent game, except that if a player loses his contract both his opponents score the penalty points. The winner of a rubber receives a bonus of 700 points if neither opponent has won a game, but 500 points if either has.

Very clearly the game is a gamble, because the players must bid in the hope of finding the cards they need in the dummy hand.

A variation designed to make the game less speculative is for every player to be dealt seventeen cards and the fifty-second card face downwards to the dummy. After looking at their cards, and before bidding them, every player contributes four of them, face downwards, to the dummy. This way, every player knows four out of the thirteen cards that he is bidding for.

In another variation, instead of bidding for the dummy, an agreed number of deals (that must be divisible by three) are played, and, in turn, every player plays the dummy against the other two playing in partnership.

In this variation rubbers are not played, but the player who bids and makes game scores a bonus of 300 points. There is no vulnerability.

Five Hundred

Five Hundred, a variation of euchre (see page 155), is one of the best of the very few card games for three players. It is played with a pack from which the 2s, 3s, 4s, 5s and 6s have been removed and a Joker added. In all thirty-three cards, which are dealt in bundles of three-two-three-two to the players, and three cards (the widow) face downwards to the table.

The rank of the cards in the trump suit is: **Joker**, **Right Bower** (Jack), **Left Bower** (Jack of the suit of the same colour), **A K Q 10 9 8 7**. In the three plain suits the cards rank in the usual order from Ace (high) to 7 (low).

The player on the left of the dealer bids first. The auction proceeds clockwise, and a player who has passed cannot make a further bid.

The denominations rank in the order: No-Trumps (highest), Hearts, Diamonds, Clubs, Spades (lowest), and the player nominates the number of tricks (not less than six) that he proposes to win in a specified suit or without a trump suit. In turn the other players must either pass or name a contract that scores higher. If all three players pass, the hand is played without a trump suit. No-one may take the widow, the player on the left of the dealer leads to the first trick, and the players score 10 points for each trick won.

In the trump suit there are ten cards, namely Joker, Right Bower, Left Bower, Ace, King, Queen, 10, 9, 8, 7. In the plain suit of the same colour as the trump suit there are only seven cards, because the Jack has been promoted as Left Bower to be third highest trump. In the other two plain suits there are eight cards in each. In No-Trumps there are eight cards in each suit, because there are no Bowers, but in practice one suit may consist of nine cards because if the holder of the Joker leads it he chooses the suit it represents (and the Joker wins) though he cannot nominate it to be a suit in which he has previously renounced. In the same way, the Joker wins if played to the lead of any suit, unless the player playing it has previously renounced the suit.

The values of the bids are:

	Six	Seven	Eight	Nine	Ten
Spades	40	140	240	340	440
Clubs	60	160	260	360	460
Diamonds	80	180	280	380	480
Hearts	100	200	300	400	500
No-Trumps	120	220	320	420	520

Other scoring tables are known, but this one, the Avondale Schedule, is the most satisfactory because the suit values mount by twenties, and for each trick over six (if one contracts to win it) an extra 100 points are added. It is the least complicated.

A player may score only for the number of tricks that he has contracted to win, but there is a bonus for winning all ten tricks (the slam) whether contracted for or not. The bonus varies. If the contract is worth less than 250 points, the bonus is 250 points; if the contract is worth more than 250 points, the bonus is the value of the contract. If, therefore, a player bids Eight Spades (240 points) and wins all ten tricks, he scores 490 points (240 + 250) but if he bids Eight Clubs (260 points) and wins all ten tricks, he scores 520 points (260 + 260). Since the game is won by the player who first reaches 500 points, it is possible for a player to win game in one deal.

The player who makes the final declaration takes the widow and discards three cards in its place. He need not show the cards to his opponents. He then leads to the first trick. A player must follow suit, if he can, and in a suit declaration, if the Joker or left Bower is led, the other players must play a trump on it, if they hold one. In No-Trumps, if the holder of the Joker leads it, the other players must follow to the suit nominated by the leader.

The winner of a trick leads to the next, and all ten tricks must be played, because the opponents of the declarer score 10 points for every trick that they win.

If a player fails to make his contract, both opponents score the value of the contract.

If more than one player scores game in the same deal, and one of them is the final declarer he wins if he makes his declaration. If neither is the final declarer, he who first takes enough tricks to score 500 points wins.

If a player fails to score 300 points he pays the winner double the face value of his loss; and if a player fails to score 100 points he pays the winner treble. Doubles and trebles, as they are called, are optional.

FIVE HUNDRED FOR TWO PLAYERS is played in much the same way as the parent game. The players sit facing each other, and, as well as the widow in the centre of the table, the dealer deals a hand, face downwards, to his immediate left. It is known as the dead hand.

The dead hand must not be looked at nor touched. The two players play against each other, as in the parent game, but their bids tend to be high, because bidding is largely a speculation on which cards are against the player and which are in the dead hand, and therefore, harmless.

FIVE HUNDRED FOR FOUR PLAYERS is played in the same way as the parent game, but with two playing in partnership against the other two. In order that every player may have ten cards and the widow three, the 33-card pack as used in the parent game, is increased to forty-three cards by including the 6s, 5s and two 4s.

Knaves

Knaves, a game for three players, is so called because the four Knaves are penalty cards and the object of the players is to avoid winning tricks that contain them.

Seventeen cards are dealt to each player and the last card is turned face upwards on the table to denote the trump suit. It takes no other part in the game.

The player on the left of the dealer leads to the first trick; thereafter the player who wins a trick leads to the next. A player must follow suit, if he can, to the card led. If he cannot he may either trump or discard a card of a plain suit.

The player who wins a trick scores 1 point for it, but 4 points are deducted from a player's score if he wins the Knave of Hearts, 3 points if he wins the Knave of Diamonds, 2 points if he wins the Knave of Clubs, and 1 point if he wins the Knave of Spades. The aggregate score for each deal, therefore, is 7 points (*i.e.* 17 points for tricks minus 10 points for Knaves) unless one of the Knaves is the card turned up to denote the trump suit. Game is won by the first player to score 20 points.

The players play all against all, but skilful play introduces temporary partnerships that add much to the interest of the game. If, for example, one player is in the lead and the other two are trailing behind, they will combine with the aim of preventing the leading player from winning still more, even if they cannot reduce his score by forcing him to win tricks that contain Knaves. In the same way, if two players have an advanced score, and the third is down the course, the two who are ahead will so play that such points as they cannot themselves win will go to the player with the low score rather than to the one with the high score.

The game, therefore, gives ample scope for clever play. Until the last Knave has been played, a player has to strike a balance between the incentive to take a trick, and so score a point, and the fear of being saddled with a Knave, resulting in a loss.

There is much more in the game than appears on the surface. Consider the hands on the right.

No score to anyone.

East deals and the **7 ♣** is turned up.

With his preponderance of trumps North appears to be in a position to score well. In reality his hand is far from being a good one, because, though the trumps give him the advantage of winning tricks, this advantage is more than offset by the fact that he is in the dangerous position of being forced to take Knaves. Indeed, North is very likely to come out with a poor score; against good play by West he will be hard put to avoid taking the Knaves of Hearts and Diamonds—for a loss of 7 points—and, in any case, he can hardly avoid taking one of them.

Oklahoma

Oklahoma may be played by any number of players from two to five, but is generally considered best when played by three.

Two packs of cards and one Joker are shuffled together, making in all a pack of 105 cards. The cards rank in the order from Ace to 2, but the Joker and all the 2s are wild and may represent any card that the holder chooses, and when making sequences the Ace may be high, as in **A K Q . . .** , or low, as in . . . **3 2 A**, but not round the corner, as in . . . **2 A K** . . .

Thirteen cards are dealt to each player. The rest of the pack (the stock) is placed face downwards on the table, and the top card of it is turned face upwards and placed alongside it.

The object of the game is to form sequences of three or more consecutive cards of the same suit, or sets of three or four cards of the same rank regardless of suits.

When the deal has been completed, the player on the left of the dealer has the right to take the exposed card into his hand or refuse it; if he refuses it, the player on his left has the same option; and so on. If a player takes the exposed card, he must immediately meld it with two or more cards in his hand, discard face upwards on the table a card from his hand, and expose his meld on the table in front of him.

If no player takes the exposed card, the play begins with the player on the left of the dealer, who takes the top card of the stock into his hand. He may or may not meld, and, whether he does or not, he discards a card from his hand face upwards on top of the exposed card.

The play continues round the table in this way, each player taking in his turn either the top card of the stock or the top card of the discard pile. When a player takes the top card of the discard pile he must immediately meld it, by adding it to one of his previous melds, by exchanging it for the Joker if he had already melded it, or by adding it to two or more cards in his hand and exposing them on the table as a meld. He then takes into his hand the rest of the cards in the discard pile, and may make further melds out of them before he discards from his hand.

A sequence may be melded up to fourteen cards (a complete suit with an Ace at each end) but not more than four cards of the same rank may be melded together as a set.

When melding with the Joker or one of the 2s, the player must announce the precise cards they represent. At a later turn a player may exchange the Joker for the card it represents, but he cannot exchange a 2, nor can he exchange the Joker if it is in the meld of another player.

A player may discard any card that he chooses, except a Queen of Spades which must be retained in the hand if the player holds any other card that he can discard.

The deal ends when a player has no cards left in his hand (goes out). The discard, however, must be made after melding so that if a player is left with **4 ♦ 4 ♠ 4 ♣** in his hand, he cannot go out, because if he melded them he would be left with no card to discard.

When play ends, the cards in a player's meld count in his favour, those left in his hand count against him.

	Melded	In hand
Joker	+100	−200
Q ♠	+ 50	−100
A	+ 20	− 20
2 (representing **K Q J 10 9 8** including **Q ♠**)	+ 10	− 20
K Q (excluding **Q ♠**) **J 10 9 8**	+ 10	− 10
7 6 5 4 3	+ 5	− 5
2 (representing **7 6 5 4 3** or **2**)	nil	− 20

The player who goes out receives a bonus of 100 points, but if a player draws the last card of the stock and discards without going out, the scores are totalled but no player receives the bonus.

A player who goes out on his first turn does not receive the bonus. A player who goes out on his second or later turn, and who has not made a meld on a previous turn is said to go out concealed and receives an additional bonus of 250 points, which, however, does not count towards reaching the game score.

The game score is 1,000 points, and the player who first reaches it receives a bonus of 200 points. If two or more players reach 1,000 points or more in the same deal, the highest score wins, and if there is a tie the bonus of 200 points is divided between them

Ombre

Ombre is a Spanish game of considerable antiquity. It was introduced into England by Katherine of Braganza, who married Charles II in 1662, and it immediately became very popular. Nowadays it is rarely played in Great Britain, but it is popular in Denmark (which saw the publication of a book about it in 1965) and it is played in Spain under the name of trefillo and in Latin America as rocamber. It deserves to be more popular.

The game is played with a pack of forty cards *i.e.* the regular pack from which the 10s, 9s and 8s have been removed. It is not a difficult game to play, but it is first necessary to master the rather involved and unusual order of the cards.

In plain suits the cards in the *red* suits rank in the order: **K Q J A 2 3 4 5 6 7**; those in the *black* suits rank in the normal order: **A K Q J 7 6 5 4 3 2**.

In trump suits if a *red* suit is trumps the order of the cards is: **A ♠** (Spadille), **7** (Manille), **A ♣** (Basto), **A** (Punto), **K Q J 2 3 4 5 6**; if a *black* suit is trumps the order of the cards is: **A ♠** (Spadille), **2** (Manille), **A ♣** (Basto), **K Q J 7 6 5 4 3**.

The three top trumps, Spadille, Manille and Basto, are collectively known as Matadores. The holder of one need not follow suit with it to a trump lead, but he must play one if a higher matadore is led and his hand contains no other trump card.

To determine the dealer, a card is dealt face upwards to each player in turn, and he who is first to receive a black Ace is dealer. It is here to be noted that, as in all games of Spanish origin, in dealing and play the game progresses anti-clockwise.

Nine cards are dealt to each player in bundles of three. The remaining thirteen cards are placed face downwards in the centre of the table.

Each deal is complete in itself. One player (ombre) plays against the other two playing in partnership. The player on the right of the dealer has first option of being ombre. It carries two privileges: he names the trump suit, he may discard from his hand as many cards as he chooses and draw fresh cards from the stock. If the player on the right of the dealer wishes to become ombre he says 'I play'. His right-hand neighbour may then announce that he wishes to become ombre, and, by so doing, he tacitly agrees that he will play without exchanging any of his cards. The first player may then reconsider the position, and is entitled to remain ombre if he is willing to play without exchanging any of his cards. If the second player passes, the third player (the dealer) may announce that he wishes to play without discarding. Again, the first player has a right to reconsider and may remain ombre without discarding.

If all three players pass, that is to say, if none wishes to play ombre the hand is abandoned.

If the first player is allowed to play ombre unopposed, he discards as many cards as he chooses from his hand, and draws cards from the stock to replace them. The second player does the same, and then the dealer. If any cards are left in the stock after the three players have made their exchanges, the dealer is entitled to look at them. If he does he must show them to the other two players: if he does not, the other two may not.

Ombre now names the trump suit and leads a card. The game proceeds, anti-clockwise, every player following suit, if he can, to the led card, or trumping or discarding if he cannot. The winner of a trick leads to the next, until all nine tricks have been played.

At the beginning of a deal each player puts an agreed sum in a pool. Now . . .

Sacardo. If ombre wins more tricks than either of his opponents individually, he takes all that is in the pool.

Codille. If one of the opponents wins more tricks than ombre, ombre pays him a sum equal to the amount in the pool, and the amount in the pool is carried forward to the next deal.

Puesta. If ombre and one, or both, of his opponents win the same number of tricks, ombre doubles the amount in the pool and it is carried forward to the next deal.

The deal does not pass in rotation. After every deal the dealer for the next is determined by dealing the cards round, face upwards, until one player receives a black Ace.

The deal that follows is a simple one to illustrate the mechanics of the game:

West	*North*	*East*
♥ K 7	♥ none	♥ 4 5 6
♦ 6	♦ 7	♦ 2 3 4 5
♠ 7 5	♠ J 6 4 3 2	♠ Q
♣ Ma Ba K 5	♣ Q J 6	♣ 7

North deals.

West says: 'I play'. East and North pass.

West discards 7 ♥ 6 ♦ 7 ♠ 5 ♠. He draws 3 ♥ Q ♦ A ♦ 4 ♣.

East discards 4 ♥ 5 ♥ 6 ♥. His hand is of no value and he hopes to end with a void suit. He draws Q ♥ A ♥ Spa.

North discards 7 ♦ J ♠ 6 ♠ 4 ♠ 3 ♠ 2 ♠. He draws J ♥ 2 ♥ K ♦ J ♦ K ♠ 3 ♣.

The hands are now:

West	*North*	*East*
♥ K 3	♥ J 2	♥ Q A
♦ Q A	♦ K J	♦ 2 3 4 5
♠ none	♠ K	♠ Q
♣ Ma Ba K 5 4	♣ Q J 6 3	♣ Spa 7

West names Clubs as the trump suit.

His hand is none too good, but the lead of a trump is called for. He, therefore, leads K ♣, and East wins with Spadille, because West would hardly have led the King of trumps if he did not hold Manille, and probably Basto as well. East has no better return than 7 ♣, on which North plays the **Jack**. West allows it to win, by playing **4 ♣**, because he is aware that North holds the more dangerous hand, and that sooner or later a trick in trumps must be lost to him. North must keep his top Diamonds and K ♠, and he cannot safely lead a Heart. He, therefore, leads a Club. West wins with Basto, draws North's last trump with Manille, and continues with **5 ♣**. It puts North on the spot. If he discards **J ♦**, West will lead the suit and later win K ♥ and a Diamond; if North discards **2 ♥** or **K ♠**, West will win K ♥, and continue with **3 ♥**, so that he will either win **Q ♦**, or North and East will divide their tricks three-two. Either way it is sacardo, and West scoops the pool.

Towie

Towie was originated by J. Leonard Replogle as a variation of bridge (see page 125). It may be played by any number of players, but is most acceptable as a game for three because only three take an active part in each deal.

Four hands of thirteen cards each are dealt in the usual way; the one to the quarter opposite the dealer is the dummy hand to be bid for. After dealing, the dealer chooses (without looking at them) six cards from the dummy hand, and faces them.

The players, beginning with the dealer, bid as in the parent game, but part scores are not reckoned and if the bidding ends without a game or higher contract being reached, there is a goulash deal, with further goulashes if necessary.*

When the bidding ends the player on the left of the declarer makes the opening lead. The dummy hand becomes the property of the declarer who sorts it, exposes it on the table, and plays it against the other two players in partnership, as in the parent game.

The scoring is the same as in bridge with the following differences:

1. In No-Trump contracts the trick score is 35 points a trick.
2. For winning a first game the declarer scores a bonus of 500 points and becomes vulnerable. For winning a second game—and with it the rubber—a player scores 1,000 points.
3. The declarer who makes a doubled or redoubled contract scores a bonus of 50 points if not vulnerable, and 100 points if vulnerable.
4. For undoubled overtricks the declarer scores 50 points each. If doubled or redoubled he scores for them as in the parent game.
5. The penalties for undertricks are:

   Not Vulnerable
   Undoubled: 50 points per trick
   Doubled: 100 points for the first and second tricks
               200 points for the third and fourth tricks
               400 points for the fifth and subsequent tricks

   Vulnerable
   Undoubled: 100 points for the first trick
              200 points for the second and subsequent tricks
   Doubled: 200 points for the first trick
              400 points for the second and subsequent tricks

   If the contract is redoubled the scores for doubled contracts are multiplied by two.

---

*For a goulash deal the players sort their cards into suits (the dealer sorts the dummy hand) and the hands are placed face downwards in a pile, one on top of the other, in front of the dealer. The cards are cut without being shuffled, and the same dealer deals the cards in bundles of five-five-three.

If there are more than three players participating in the game the inactive players are opponents of the declarer. They take no part in the bidding or play, but participate in the scoring, losing when the declarer makes his contract, and scoring the undertrick penalties when the declarer's contract is defeated.

At the end of a deal the declarer, whether he has won or lost his contract, retires from the table and his place is taken by one of the waiting players. The inactive players come into the game each in his turn, replacing the declarer of the previous deal. No vulnerable player, however, may re-enter the game if a non-vulnerable player is waiting to play.

The game ends when one player has won two deals.

Large penalties are not uncommon in towie because a player has no partner during the auction period and cannot do more than bid on the strength of his own hand, the six cards that he sees in dummy, and the seven cards that he expects to find there. Over-bidding is frequent, but risks must be taken, and the game is not for the chicken-hearted or cautious bidder. The play of the defence offers scope for skill, but, on the whole, the main object of a player must be to play the dummy, particularly when five are in the game.

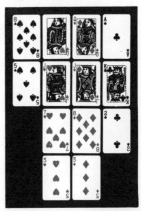

The dummy hand after the face-down cards have been exposed

South and East were vulnerable, and South dealt. He bid a cautious One Spade, and, after a pass by West, East bid Three No-Trumps. South lacked the courage to bid Four Spades, and East, with dummy's cards opposite him, had an easy ride for his contract.

Games for
Four players

Auction Pitch

Auction Pitch, commonly known as Pitch and sometimes as Set Back, is a variation of all fours (see page 48). It is at its best and most popular when played by four players, each playing for himself.

As in the parent game, the cards rank in the usual order from Ace (high) to 2 (low), and six are dealt to the players in two bundles of three each. No card, however, is turned up to determine the trump suit.

The player on the left of the dealer bids first, and each player, in his turn, may either make a bid or pass. A bid must be for at least two points, and for more than the preceding bid, except for the dealer, who is entitled to buy the hand for the same number of points as the preceding bid. The maximum number of points in a deal is 4, and a player who expects to win them bids Smudge. The dealer cannot take the declaration from him.

The successful bidder is known as the maker, and he pitches (leads) to the first trick. The card that he leads determines the trump suit.

At each trick a player must follow suit to the card led, if he can, otherwise he may discard or trump. The winner of a trick leads to the next.

As in the parent game, points are scored as follows:

High. The player who holds the highest trump scores 1 point.

Low. The player who holds the lowest trump scores 1 point.

Jack. The player who wins the trick that contains the Jack of the trump suit (if it is in play) scores 1 point.

Game. Counting the Ace as 4, the King as 3, the Queen as 2, the Jack as 1 and the Ten as 10, the player with the highest total in the tricks he has won scores 1 point. If there is a tie no-one scores the point.

Every player records what he scores, and if the maker fails to reach his bid he is set back by the full amount of it. He records the score and if it reduces him to a minus score he encircles it. A player with a minus score is said to be in the hole.

The game is won by the player who first reaches 7 points, and if the maker and one or more of the other players reach 7 points in the same deal, the maker wins. As between the other three players, the points are counted in the order High, Low, Jack, Game.

A player who smudges and wins all four points automatically wins the game regardless of his score, unless he was in the hole when he smudged. In this event he scores only 4 points.

Boston Whist

Boston Whist, or more simply Boston, is a variation of solo whist (see page 168) that, though an excellent game, is not as popular as the parent game because the scoring is rather complicated.

The game is for four players playing all against all, and the cards rank in the regular order from Ace (high) to 2 (low). Thirteen cards are dealt to each player in bundles of four-four-five. The player who faces the dealer cuts another pack of cards: the top card of the lower part of the pack determines what is known as the First Preference, and the other suit of the same colour is known as the Second Preference. The other two suits are known as the Plain Suits.

The player on the left of the dealer bids first. Each player bids in turn, and bidding continues until three players in their turn pass a bid. A player must make a higher bid than the previous one, and once a player has passed he cannot re-enter the bidding except to bid a Misère or Spread that is superior to the previous bid.

A player has the choice of fourteen bids, namely:

Pass.

Boston–A contract to win five tricks.

Six–A contract to win six tricks.

Seven–A contract to win seven tricks.

Little Misère–A contract to lose twelve tricks after discarding a card which is not shown.

Eight–A contract to win eight tricks.

Nine–A contract to win nine tricks.

Grand Misère–A contract to lose all thirteen tricks.

Ten–A contract to win ten tricks.

Eleven–A contract to win eleven tricks.

Little Spread–A contract to lose twelve tricks after discarding a card which is not shown, and the remaining cards exposed on the table.

Twelve–A contract to win twelve tricks.

Grand Spread–A contract to lose all thirteen tricks with the cards exposed on the table.

Grand Slam–A contract to win all thirteen tricks.

In this list any call is superior to any above it and, apart from the Misères (which are played without a trump suit) a bid in first preference takes precedence over one in second preference, and one in second preference takes precedence over one in a plain suit.

When a player makes a bid he does not name the denomination. He merely says 'Boston', 'Six', 'Seven', as the case may be. If a second player thinks that he can make the same number of tricks in the second preference he says 'I keep', and if a third player thinks he can make the same number of tricks in the first preference he says 'I keep over you'.

When the final bid has been made, the declarer names the trump suit and the player on the left of the dealer leads to the first trick. The object of the game is for the declarer to win his contract, and the other three players to try and prevent him from doing so. As is routine in games of the whist family, a player must follow suit to the card led, if he can, and if he cannot he may trump or discard.

The winner of a trick leads to the next.

Before the start of a hand the players put an agreed amount into a pool.

If a player makes his contract he receives from each of his opponents the number of units shown in the following table, and, if his contract was for Seven or higher, he takes the pool.

Number of Tricks contracted for	Number of Tricks actually won								
	5	6	7	8	9	10	11	12	13
Boston, 5	12	12	13	13	14	14	14	15	15
Six		15	16	16	17	18	19	20	20
Seven			18	20	21	22	23	24	26
Eight				23	24	26	28	29	31
Nine					32	34	36	39	41
Ten						42	45	48	52
Eleven							63	68	72
Twelve								106	114
Thirteen									166

In America the practice is to ignore overtricks. This is superior because it simplifies the scoring and leads to more skilful play as a player has to bid the full value of his hand to score the maximum.

The scoring is:

For Boston (5) = 10
    Six = 15
    Seven = 20
    Eight = 25
    Nine = 35
    Ten = 45
    Eleven = 65
    Twelve = 105
    Thirteen = 170

If a player fails to make his contract he doubles the amount in the pool, which is carried forward to the next deal, and to each of his opponents he pays the number of units shown in the following table.

PLATE 11 *(opposite)* A two-handed game of cribbage being played. Scores are 'pegged' on the standard cribbage or noddy board in the foreground

Number of Tricks contracted for	Number of Tricks by which a player Falls short of his contract												
	1	2	3	4	5	6	7	8	9	10	11	12	13
Boston, 5	10	20	30	40	50								
Six	15	25	35	45	55	65							
Seven	20	30	40	50	60	70	80						
Eight	25	35	45	55	65	75	85	95					
Nine	35	45	55	65	75	85	95	105	115				
Ten	45	55	65	75	85	95	105	115	125	135			
Eleven	70	80	90	100	110	120	130	140	150	160	170		
Twelve	120	130	140	150	160	170	180	190	200	210	220	230	
Thirteen	180	190	200	210	220	230	240	250	260	270	280	290	300

In Misères and Spreads the declarer wins or loses to or from each player as under:

Little Misère = 20
Grand Misère = 40
Little Spread = 80
Grand Spread = 100

The deal circulates clockwise, and by custom, between deals the pack is cut to the dealer, without shuffling, by his right-hand opponent.

BOSTON DE FONTAINEBLEAU is a variation of the parent game with general principles that are very similar, but with interesting modifications and simpler scoring.

There are no preferences: the suits rank in the order Diamonds, Hearts, Clubs, Spades,* and a player who bids Six Clubs overbids he who has bid Six Spades, and he who has bid Six Hearts overbids he who has bid Six Clubs, and so on. The introduction of a bid known as Piccolissimo, is a contract to make exactly one trick, without a trump suit, after discarding a card which is not shown; and an Open Slam is one to win all thirteen tricks with the cards exposed on the table.

The cards are dealt in bundles of four-four-five, as they are in the parent game, and the player on the left of the dealer bids first. There is, however, no pool.

PLATE 12 *(opposite)*
A game of piquet in progress

The bids rank in the order: Pass, Boston, Six, Little Misère, Seven, Piccolissimo, Eight, Grand Misère, Nine, Little Spread, Ten, Grand Spread, Eleven, Twelve, Grand Slam, Open Slam.

---

* So in England and America: in France the order is Hearts, Diamonds, Clubs, Spades.

As in the parent game, the bidding continues until three players pass a bid in turn, but once a player has passed he cannot re-enter the bidding.

Although the game is played all against all, a hand may sometimes be played under partnership conditions, because if a player has contracted for Boston, Six, Seven, Eight, Nine or Ten, he may call for a whister (partner). If accepted, the two partners play from where they are seated, and the whister has to make three extra tricks.

The player on the left of the dealer leads to the first trick, and the play continues as in the parent game.

If the hand is played with a trump suit, the Ace, King, Queen and Jack are honours. If the contract is made the declarer (or the declarer and the whister) scores for an extra four tricks if all four honours are held, and for an extra two tricks if three honours are held, but only if the contract is made, and only for contracts from Boston to Ten, excluding Misères, Piccolissimo and Little Spread.

The scoring table is set out below, the figures are the units that a player receives from, or pays to, each player if he is successful, or unsuccessful, in his contract. If the declarer plays with a whister the stakes, win or lose, are shared between them.

| | When the Trump Suit is: | | | For each Overtrick |
	♠/♣	♥	♦	
Boston, 5	10	20	30	5
Six	30	40	50	5
Little Misère 75				
Seven	50	60	70	5
Piccolissimo 100				
Eight	70	80	90	5
Grand Misère 150				
Nine	90	100	110	5
Little Spread 200				
Ten	110	120	130	5
Grand Spread 250				
Eleven	130	140	150	5
Twelve	150	160	170	5
Grand Slam	400	450	500	
Open Slam	600	700	800	

Bridge

Modern Bridge, more precisely Contract Bridge, but the 'Contract' has for long been dropped, was developed out of Auction Bridge and introduced to card players in the early 1920s. It took firm root quickly, and made rapid progress, to become the most popular game in the whole history of card-playing. To-day, half a century after its *début*, it is played by millions, rich and poor, from peers to peasants, and it has attracted to itself a vast literature in most European languages.

Bridge is played by four players, two playing in partnership against the other two, and with a standard pack of fifty-two cards. The cards rank in the order Ace (high) to 2 (low), and the Ace, King, Queen, Jack and Ten of a suit are known as the honour cards. The suits rank in the order Spades, Hearts, Diamonds, Clubs; the Spade and Heart suits are known as the major suits: the Diamond and Club suits as the minor suits. Although only one pack of cards is necessary, it is customary to use two, of different design or colour, and while one is being dealt the other is shuffled by the partner of the dealer, in readiness for the next dealer.

To determine partners, a pack is spread-eagled on the table. The four players draw cards from it, and the two who draw the two highest cards play in partnership against the other two. If two players draw cards of equal rank, precedence is determined by the rank of the suits. The player who draws the highest card has choice of seats and cards, and deals first. Thereafter the deal passes round the table clockwise. His partner sits opposite to him; the other two partners sit one on each side of him.

It is convenient to divide the game into two periods. The bidding, during which the two partnerships compete against each other to establish which suit shall be made trumps or whether the hand shall be played without a trump suit. The playing, during which the player who has won the contract strives to make it, playing his own hand and that of his partner exposed on the table, against the other partnership striving to prevent him.

The dealer bids first, and the bidding continues round the table clockwise. When a player bids he states the number of tricks in excess of six that he undertakes to win, and in the denomination that he undertakes to play. The lowest bid, therefore, is a bid of One (a contract to win seven tricks) and the highest is a bid of Seven (a contract to win all thirteen tricks). As No-Trumps takes precedence over the suits, and the suits rank in the descending order Spades, Hearts, Diamonds, Clubs, the lowest possible bid is One Club, and the ascending scale is: One Club, One Diamond, One Heart, One Spade, One No-Trump, Two Clubs, Two Diamonds . . . . Seven Hearts, Seven Spades, Seven No-Trumps. A contract of Six (to win twelve tricks) is called a small slam; a contract of Seven (to win all thirteen tricks) is called a grand slam.

In turn each bid must either name a greater number of tricks than the previous one, or an equal number of tricks in a higher denomination. If a player has no wish to contract to win tricks he says 'No Bid', and if all four players do so, the hand is thrown in and the deal passes.

In his turn any player may double a bid made by an opponent. The effect of a double is to increase the score whether the contract succeeds or fails: and the partnership whose contract has been doubled may redouble thereby increasing the score, win or lose, still further. Doubling and redoubling, however, do not increase the size of a contract: *e.g.* a bid of Four Hearts is superior to a bid of Four Diamonds and remains superior to it even though it may have been doubled and redoubled.

The bidding period continues until the last and highest bid has been followed by three passes. The player who first mentioned the denomination in the final contract then becomes the declarer.

It is usual to denote the four players by the cardinal points of the compass, and if we assume that South deals, a sequence of bidding to illustrate some of the points mentioned might be:

South	West	North	East
1 ♦	No bid	1 ♥	1 ♠
1 No-Trump	2 ♠	3 ♦	No bid
3 No-Trumps	Double	No bid	No bid
4 ♦	No Bid	5 ♦	Double
Redouble	No Bid	No Bid	No Bid

The final contract, therefore, is Five Diamonds, and the hand will be played by South, because he was the first on his side to mention Diamonds as the trump suit.

The playing period begins by the player on the left of the declarer leading to the first trick. As soon as he has done so, the partner of the declarer places his cards face downwards on the table as dummy. He takes no further part in the play except that he has a right to draw his partner's attention to certain irregularities, such as asking him if he has none of a suit when he fails to follow suit, and warning him against leading out of the wrong hand. The declarer plays the dummy hand as well as his own.

The play follows the normal routine of trick-taking games: if a player is able to do so he must follow suit to the card led; otherwise he may either discard or trump. The trick is won by the player who plays the highest card of the suit led, or the highest trump. The player who wins a trick leads to the next. Plate 13 shows the playing period of the game in progress.

When all thirteen tricks have been played, the players record their scores, and those of their opponents, on a marker, or sheet of paper, as shown in the accompanying diagram.

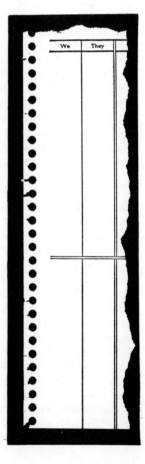

When a player makes his contract, the score for tricks won is entered below the horizontal line. All other scores are entered above this line.

A game is won when a partnership scores 100 points below the horizontal line, either in one or more deals. If a partnership scores less than game in one deal, it is said to have a part-score and if the opponents then score game the part-score cannot be carried forward towards the next game. When a partnership wins a game a line is drawn across the score sheet below it, and both partnerships begin the next game from a love score.

A partnership that wins a game becomes vulnerable and is subject to higher bonuses if it makes its contract, and increased penalties if it fails. Vulnerability, however, does not affect the points for winning the tricks contracted for.

The main object of the game is to win a rubber, which is the best out of three games.

If a partnership has bid and made its contract, it scores;
In No-Trumps: 40 points for the first trick and 30 points for each subsequent trick.
In Spades and Hearts: 30 points for each trick.
In Diamonds and Clubs: 20 points for each trick.
The scores for winning tricks are doubled if the contract has been doubled, and quadrupled if the contract has been redoubled.

If a partnership has made tricks in excess of its contract, it scores:
If undoubled: trick value for each trick.
If doubled: 100 points for each trick if not vulnerable.
200 points for each trick if vulnerable.
If redoubled: 200 points for each trick if not vulnerable.
400 points for each trick if vulnerable.

If a partnership has failed to make its contract, it loses:
If undoubled: 50 points for each trick if not vulnerable.
100 points for each trick if vulnerable.
If doubled: 100 points for the first trick; 200 points for each subsequent trick if not vulnerable.
200 points for the first trick; 300 points for each subsequent trick if vulnerable.
If redoubled: 200 points for the first trick; 400 points for each subsequent trick if not vulnerable.
400 points for the first trick; 600 points for each subsequent trick if vulnerable.

If a partnership wins a rubber, it scores:
In three games 500 points.
In two games 700 points.

A partnership scores bonuses of:
1,500 points, if vulnerable, for bidding and making a grand slam, 1,000 points if not vulnerable.
750 points, if vulnerable, for bidding and making a small slam, 500 points if not vulnerable.
150 points if either partner holds all four Aces in a No-Trump contract, or all five honours in a suit contract.
100 points if either partner holds any four honours in a suit contract.
50 points if a partnership makes a doubled or redoubled contract.

Bridge is not a difficult game unless a player makes it so by ill-advised bidding. Its most important feature is that a player scores below the line, towards game, only for the tricks that he has contracted to win, and, by a logical extension, he scores the big bonuses for slams only if the necessary number of tricks has been contracted for. It follows that it is of paramount importance for the partners to estimate the trick-taking power of their combined hands, and not only must a player estimate as accurately as possible the position of the adverse high cards and distribution (as revealed by the bids of the other players) but convey by his bidding as much information as possible to his partner. In short, bidding may be defined as a conversation between the partners, and both must speak the same language.

Most modern players value their hands by means of the well-known Milton Work count of 4 for an Ace, 3 for a King, 2 for a Queen, and 1 for a Jack.

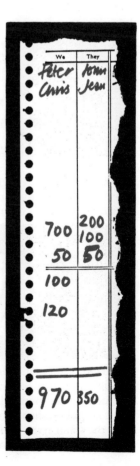

The player who opens the bidding with a bid of One of a suit, promises to make a further bid if his partner responds with One in a higher-ranking suit, or Two in a lower-ranking suit. For this reason a player should not open unless he can see a sound rebid in his hand over partner's most likely response.

The strength to justify an opening bid varies, but in general it may be said that a hand totalling at least 13 points should be opened. It is clear, however, that the more points a player holds the less length does he need in the trump suit, and the fewer points in the hand the greater must be the length in the trump suit. With less than 13 points in the hand the practice is to open an 11- or 12-point hand with a reasonable 5-card suit, and with only 10 points in the hand, sometimes less, a player needs a reasonable 6-card suit, or two 5-card suits.

Open One Heart. The hand totals only 11 points, but the Heart suit is worth showing and if it is not shown at once it may be too late.

Open One Spade. The hand totals only 11 points, but is strong by reason of its distribution. With two suits of equal length it is proper to bid the higher-ranking before the lower-ranking one.

Open One Spade. The hand totals a mere 10 points, but the 6-card Spade suit is too good to be held back.

There are 40 points in the pack and experience has taught that if the combined hands have a total of 25 points game will be made, if 33 the small slam, and if 37 the grand slam. There are, of course, exceptions, but in the long run the rule is to be relied on.

A bid of One No-Trump is advised with a total of 16 to 18 points. The bid should never step outside the stipulated range, because partner needs to rely on it for his response. With 9 points he will jump to Three No-Trumps; with 7 or 8 he will bid Two No-Trumps and leave it to the opener to pass with a minimum, but bid Three with a maximum. A NoTrump range of 16 to 18 points is known as a strong No-Trump. Some experienced players favour, particularly when not vulnerable, a range of 12 to 14 points. It is known as a weak No-Trump. Whether a strong or a weak No-Trump is played is a matter of personal choice, but it must be agreed between the partners before play begins, because if a weak No-Trump is played partner must increase his responses by 4 points.

In the same way, an opening bid of Two No-Trumps is advised on 20 to 22 points, leaving it to partner to raise to Three if he holds 5 points, and to pass with less.

Opening bids of One No-Trump and Two No-Trumps postulate a balanced distribution of 4-3-3-3 or 4-4-3-2. A bid of Three No-Trumps is tactical. It shows a hand containing a solid minor suit, and altogether a hand that has a reasonable prospect of winning nine tricks if partner has one or two top cards in the right places.

The hand qualifies for an opening bid of Three No-Trumps. There is every prospect of making the contract; if not it will not cost a lot and there is the consolation that it has probably stopped the opponents from bidding a game that would have been a greater loss.

The partner of the player who opens the bidding with No-Trumps raises on a very precise number of points. The number of points, however, may be reduced slightly if the responder holds a 5-card suit. Over a bid of One No-Trump, partner holds:

The hand totals 8 points and 9 points are normally necessary to jump to Three No-Trumps. Here, however, the jump to Three No-Trumps is justified on the length of the Spade suit, and the good intermediate cards. It is unwise to bid Spades because if it is assumed that partner holds a balanced 16-point hand he is just as likely to win nine tricks in No-Trumps as the responder is to win ten in Spades. If Three No-Trumps cannot be made there is no reason to suppose that Four Spades can.

A jump take out into a suit is a game force. It does not, however, promise a very strong hand: rather it means that the responder, who knows the precise strength of his partner's bid, can foresee game for the partnership but cannot tell whether the combined hands will play better in No-Trumps or in a suit.

West	East
♠ Q J 4 3	♠ K 10 9 7 2
♥ A Q 2	♥ J 6 4
♦ K 9 3	♦ A J 8 2
♣ A 7 6	♣ 8

Bidding	Bidding
1 No-Trump	3 ♠
4 ♠	No Bid

Over West's opening bid of One No-Trump (16 to 18 points) East who has 9 points has enough to jump to Three No-Trumps. He prefers Three-Spades, however, which West raises to game, because game in Spades can hardly fail, but in No-Trumps will be defeated if a Club is led.

Another important feature of responding to a No-Trump bid is the Stayman convention. It is a bid of Two Clubs over partner's One No-Trump, or Three Clubs over his Two No-Trumps, made, irrespective of the holding in the suit, to ask partner to bid his better 4-card major suit, or, if he lacks one, to bid Diamonds.

West	East
♠ K Q 2	♠ A J 4 3
♥ A J 6 2	♥ K Q 8 4
♦ Q 6 4	♦ 3 2
♣ A Q 4	♣ J 8 5

Bidding	Bidding
1 No-Trump	2 ♣
2 ♥	4 ♥
No Bid.	

Without the convention East, with 11 points, would have no alternative except to jump his partner's opening bid of One No-Trump (16 to 18 points) to Three. The combined total of 29 points is more than adequate for the bid, but Three No-Trumps may be defeated if a Diamond is led and Four Hearts can hardly fail.

There is a large range of bids which show weakness and that may be recognized as such by the logic of the situation.

West	East
1 ♠	2 No-Trumps
3 ♠	?

East's bid of Two No-Trumps shows a count of from 11 to 13 points, and over it West cannot do more than repeat his suit. His hand, therefore, cannot be strong, and his bid of Three Spades no more than the cheapest way of keeping his promise to rebid, which he made when he opened with One Spade.

In the same way, if the bidding is:

West	East
1 No-Trump	2 ♠
?	

West should pass. East's bid must be showing a weak hand that he considers will play better in a suit than in No-Trumps, otherwise, over an opening bid of One No-Trump, it would be impossible for partner ever to play in Two of a suit.

Or we may consider the following sequences:

West	East	West	East	West	East
1 ♥	2 ♥	1 ♥	2 ♣	1 ♣	1 ♥
3 ♣	3 ♥	2 ♥	3 ♦	1 ♠	2 ♥
		3 ♥		2 ♠	3 ♥

In all these sequences the bid of Three Hearts shows weakness. A player cannot be holding much of a hand when he cannot do better than rebid his suit at the lowest level, and it is particularly pronounced when he rebids it twice.

An opening bid of Three of a suit is also a weakness bid. It is made with a hand that has little, if any, defensive strength, offers small chance of success of game, and with one long suit that, if trumps, is unlikely to be defeated by more than two tricks if vulnerable and three if not vulnerable.

This type of hand qualifies for an opening bid of Three Spades if only because, even if doubled and partner has no support, it cannot cost more than 500 points (two down). It is a reasonable loss if the opponents have a game in one of the other suits.

There is also a range of strong bids. The strongest of all is an opening bid of Two Clubs. It is strictly conventional and may be made even if the player is void in the suit. The bid guarantees either five or more high cards and distributional strength, or 23 or more points and a balanced distribution. With one exception the bid is forcing to game. Partner must respond no matter how weak his hand is, and with a weak hand he bids Two Diamonds. Any other response by him shows an Ace and a King or two King-Queen combinations or the equivalent in high cards. The exception to the bid not being forcing to game occurs when the opener has bid Two Clubs with a balanced hand and, after the negative response of Two Diamonds, has rebid Two No-Trumps.

West	East
♠ K J 3	♠ Q 6 2
♥ A Q 6	♥ 9 7 4
♦ A K 4	♦ 8 5 3 2
♣ A Q J 2	♣ 7 4 3

Bidding	Bidding
2 ♣	2 ♦
2 No-Trumps	No Bid

West, with 24 points, is too strong to open with any other bid than Two Clubs, and over East's negative response he cannot do better than rebid Two No-Trumps. East with only 2 points in his hand does well to pass, but another point in his hand would make a big difference and with 3 points or more he would bid Three No-Trumps.

The opening bid of Two in any other suit is forcing for one round, and shows a hand containing not fewer than eight playing tricks and at least one powerful suit.

This hand is best opened with Two Spades. If it is opened with One Spade there is no satisfactory way of coping with a response of Two Hearts.

A strong 2-suited hand also qualifies for an opening bid of Two. The higher-ranking suit is bid first.

A 1-suited hand may also be opened with a Two bid. This hand should be opened with a bid of Two Spades, and Three Spades should be bid over any response made by partner.

The responses to opening Two bids (of suits other than Clubs) are not so well-defined and clear-cut as the responses to an opening bid of Two Clubs. In general, if partner holds a biddable suit he should bid it at the lowest level. If he lacks a biddable suit, but has a total of from 10 to 12 points, he should bid Three No-Trumps. If he lacks a biddable suit and insufficient points to bid Three No-Trumps, but has adequate support (*i.e.* **x x x** or **Q x**) for partner's suit and a count of 5, he should give a simple raise in partner's suit. If he lacks a biddable suit, insufficient points for Three No-Trumps, and insufficient support for partner's suit, he should make the negative response of Two No-Trumps.

As well as an opening bid of Two Clubs there are several other bids that are forcing to game. The most frequent is a jump bid in a new suit.

West	*East*
♠ Q 8 4	♠ A K 6
♥ 9 2	♥ A Q J 10 6 4
♦ A J 3	♦ 8 2
♣ A K 9 3 2	♣ J 4
Bidding	Bidding
1 ♣	2 ♥

The situation is typical. East's bid of Two Hearts sets up a forcing situation. It is true that a bid of One Heart by East cannot be passed by West, but it is better for East to get the hand off his chest, and by bidding Two Hearts he makes certain that the bidding will not be dropped until a game level is reached.

It is much the same if the opener makes a jump in a new suit over his partner's response:

West	*East*
♠ K J 6	♠ A Q 9 2
♥ A K J 7 4	♥ 10 8 3
♦ 6	♦ K Q 9
♣ K Q J 7	♣ 10 6 3
Bidding	Bidding
1 ♥	1 ♠
3 ♣	

In this situation (or a similar one) West's bid of Three Clubs is a game force and East cannot pass it.

In many cases a forcing situation is set up by reason of the logic behind the bidding.

West	*East*
♠ A K 9 6 3	♠ Q 7 4 2
♥ K J 9 2	♥ Q 10 8 3
♦ A 8 4	♦ K 6 2
♣ 9	♣ 5 4
Bidding	Bidding
1 ♠	1 ♠
3 ♥	?

As West rebid at the level of Three, over East's weak response of Two Spades, and when there was no need for him to rebid, he must have a very strong hand, and East must make a further bid. He bids Four Hearts and West passes.

An inferential force is even more pronounced in a sequence such as:

West	East
1 ♥	1 ♠
2 No-Trumps	3 ♥
?	

West must not pass because East is very clearly inviting him to choose between playing the hand in Three No-Trumps or Four Hearts, whichever contract best suits him.

When the bidding of the partners shows that they hold between them the balance of strength, they should consider bidding a slam. As a guide it may be said that prospects of a slam are good when a player holds enough to make a positive response to a forcing bid; or when the point count of the combined hands totals at least 33; or when a player has enough for an opening bid opposite a partner who has opened with a bid of Two, or who has opened the bidding and made a jump rebid.

Before a slam can be bid with a measure of safety, it is essential for the partners to find out if they hold between them control of the vital suits. The Blackwood convention has been designed to enable the partners to learn how many Aces and Kings are held by the partnership.

When the trump suit has been agreed either directly by support or by implication, or if a forcing situation has been set up, a bid of Four No-Trumps by either partner asks the other to bid Five Clubs if he lacks an Ace or holds all four, Five Diamonds if he holds one Ace, Five Hearts if he holds two and Five Spades if he holds three. If the player who has bid Four No-Trumps, after his partner's response continues with a bid of Five No-Trumps, he is showing that he holds all four Aces and is asking his partner to bid Six Clubs if he lacks a King, Six Diamonds if he holds one King, Six Hearts if he holds two, Six Spades if he holds three and Six No-Trumps if he holds all four.

Bidding	Bidding
1 ♠	2 ♥
3 No-Trumps	4 ♠
4 No-Trumps	5 ♥
6 ♠	No Bid

Once East has shown that he has support for Spades, West, with support for Hearts, visualises a slam. His bid of Four No-Trumps asks East how many Aces he holds, and East's response of Five Hearts tells West that he holds two. It is important for West to bid the slam in Spades, because if East plays in Hearts and his two Aces are in Hearts and Clubs (as they are) the opening lead of a Diamond from South may break Six Hearts out of hand. When West plays in Six Spades, the King of Diamonds is protected against the opening lead and twelve tricks are assured.

As West knows that there is an Ace against the hand the grand slam is out of the question and West, therefore, has no need to bid Five No-Trumps to ask East how many Kings he holds.

The convention is a very useful one, but it must be used with discretion, because if partner lacks the necessary Aces the partnership may find itself carried out of its depth. As a rule, it may be said that if the final contract is to be in Clubs the bid of Four No-Trumps should not be made unless the bidder holds at least two Aces, and if the contract is to be in Diamonds he should hold at least one Ace.

A limit bid is a bid that informs partner of the precise strength of the hand, and so permits him to estimate the combined strength of the partnership, and drop the bidding if he can see no future for it.

No-Trump bids are limit bids because they are made on an agreed number of points in the hand. A single raise of partner's suit is a limit bid that shows moderate strength and support for the suit; a double raise of partner's suit shows that the hand is too good for a mere simple raise and invites him to bid game if his hand is above average; a triple raise is distributional, it promises good support for the suit and a few scattered points, but no more because with good support for the suit coupled with high-card strength it would be more in order to make a gradual advance to a possible slam.

When an opponent has bid a suit at the level of One, a player should enter the auction only if he can be reasonably sure that his bid, if passed out, will not be defeated by more than two tricks if vulnerable and three if not vulnerable. This general rule, however, must be accepted with some reservation. It would, for example, not be wrong for a player who holds

to bid One Heart over an opponent's One Diamond. The bid might prove costly, but not very often, and it is cowardly not to contest the part-score for fear of the worst happening. A player has a right to assume that even if his partner has a blank hand and only two or three low Hearts, the hand will win three tricks in Hearts and one in each of the black suits.

A jump overcall shows strength, and, though it is not forcing, partner is expected to take action if he holds the values that would justify a response to a bid of One.

An overcall should be based on a 5-card or longer suit, though it is reasonable to overcall with **A K Q x** or **K Q J x** at the level of One. It is nearly always very unwise to overcall with a broken suit.

In general, when an opponent has opened the bidding with a bid of One of a suit, it is better to counter it with a take-out double than with a weak overcall. A double in this situation shows weakness in the suit doubled and a total of about 13 or 14 points with a balanced hand and 11 or 12 with an unbalanced one. Postulating that the doubler's partner has not bid (if he has the double is for a penalty) the doubler invites partner to bid his best suit.

West	*East*
♠ K J 9 6 2	♠ 5 3
♥ K J 9 2	♥ A Q 8 3
♦ 6	♦ K 7 2
♣ A Q 7	♣ 10 8 6 2

If South has bid One Diamond, West should double. East bids Hearts and the good fit has been found. If West bids One Spade over South's One Diamond the Heart fit will never be found and a good result will be exchanged for a bad one.

If partner's best suit is the one that has been doubled, either he bids No-Trumps or passes for a penalty if he holds length in the suit.

A double of One No-Trump is made with a balanced hand and a count of about 2 points more than the No-Trump bidder's average. With a weak hand partner will take out into his best suit, but if the combined count totals 23 or more he will pass for a penalty.

A pre-emptive bid is defined as an opening bid at the level of Three or higher. It is a bid of great value because either it prevents the opponents from entering the auction or compels one of them to bid at a level that is dangerously high when he has no notion of what cards his partner may be holding. Postulating that the bid of Three is weak and that an opponent holds strength in the other three suits, the most practical way of countering the pre-empt is to bid Three Diamonds over Three Clubs and Three No-Trumps over Three Spades, Hearts or Diamonds. Either bid invites partner to bid his best suit.

When the bidding period ends, and the playing period begins, the player on the left of the declarer leads to the first trick. It is only after he has led that the partner of the declarer exposes his hand on the table as dummy. It follows, therefore, that the opening lead has to be made in the dark, since the player can see only his own hand and is left to judge the best lead from it, coupled with the information that he has obtained from the bidding. The opening lead must be chosen with care. It is of great importance, because quite often the choice of a good or bad lead will decide whether or not the declarer's contract will be made.

Against a No-Trump contract, if partner has bid a suit, leading it usually offers the best chance of defeating the contract, unless the player on lead holds only a singleton in the suit or he has a good suit of his own.

With two cards of partner's suit the higher should be led; with three cards the highest should be led, unless the suit is headed by the Ace, King, Queen or Jack, when the lowest should be preferred. With two honours in partner's suit the higher should be led; with a sequence (a combination of three or more cards of adjacent rank) the highest should be led. In all other cases the fourth highest should be led.

When a player leads his own suit, he should lead the fourth highest of his longest suit, unless he holds a sequence (when he should lead the highest), a long suit headed by the Ace and King and an entry in another suit (when he should lead the King), or an intermediate honour sequence *e.g.* **A Q J x** or **K J 10 x** (when the higher of the two touching honours should be led).

The reason for leading the fourth highest card of a suit is that if partner subtracts the number of the card from eleven, the remainder will be the number of higher cards held by the other three players. The Rule of Eleven.

Q 9 7

	Dummy		
5 led	W	E	**K 10 8**
	Declarer		

West leads the 5. As $11 - 5 = 6$, and East can see six cards higher than the 5 in dummy and in his own hand, he will know that the declarer cannot hold a card higher than the 4, so that whichever card is played from dummy he can win the trick by playing the card just higher.

Against a suit contract it is usually best to lead partner's suit, if he has bid one. If he has not, and the player on lead has to lead from his own suit, he should give preference to leading the top card of an honour sequence. He should avoid leading a card that may cost a trick *e.g.* leading the King from **K Q x**, or a card that may enable the declarer to win a trick with a card that might have been captured *e.g.* leading the Ace from **A Q x**. The lead of a trump is a good lead if the bidding has suggested that the dummy will be able to trump side suits.

After the opening lead has been made, and the dummy hand exposed, it is of first importance for the declarer, before he plays a card from dummy, to take stock of the position and decide upon the best way to play the cards.

Against West's contract of Three No-Trumps, North leads the Queen of Spades. At first sight it may seem immaterial whether West wins the trick with the Ace in dummy or with the King in his own hand. In the event, it matters a lot in which hand he wins the trick. If West gives consideration to the position he will appreciate that he must win the first trick with the King of

Spades in his hand, win the King, Queen and Jack of Clubs, reach dummy, by leading the 4 of Spades to the Ace, to win dummy's Ace and 7 of Clubs, and finally the two red Aces in his own hand. If West wins the first trick with dummy's Ace of Spades, he will lose the contract if the adverse Clubs fail to divide 3-2, because he has left himself with no side entry to the Clubs.

When the declarer is playing a No-Trump contract, usually his first aim should be to establish his longest suit. In many cases, however, it is better to develop a short and strong suit rather than a long and weak one.

PLATE 13 *(opposite)* **A game of bridge. Declarer is in Four Hearts, and having won the first trick with the Ace of Diamonds is about to ruff in dummy a second Diamond. His contract seems safe**

North leads a Club against West's contract of Three No-Trumps. Consideration shows that West's best play is to win with the King of Clubs and play on Spades to knock out the Ace. This way, West makes sure of his contract with three tricks in Spades, three in Hearts, one in Diamonds and two in Clubs. The Diamond suit is longer than the Spade suit, but West cannot develop East's Diamonds without first losing the lead twice. By then the opponents will have set up the Clubs and broken the contract; in any case, only three tricks in Diamonds will be developed for eight in all, which is not enough.

In a suit contract, it is usually the right play for the declarer to draw the adverse trumps at the first opportunity. Trumps, however, should not be drawn if the declarer can find a better use for them.

West plays in Four Hearts, and North leads a Club. West wins the first trick with the Ace of Clubs, and if he draws the trumps at once his contract will depend on the finesse of the Queen of Spades being successful. It is no more than an even chance. The

contract is a certainty if West, after winning the first trick with the Ace of Clubs, leads either the 7 or 3 of the suit. It does not matter whether North or South wins the trick, or what card is returned. Declarer wins the next trick and trumps a Club in dummy. Now the adverse trumps may be drawn, and West comes to ten tricks with one Spade, five Hearts, two Diamonds and one Club by straight leads, and the ruff of a Club on the table.

A valuable weapon in the armoury of the declarer is the ability to manage a suit to make the most tricks out of it.

West	*East*
A 9 3 2	**K Q 10 5 4**

In this position it is vital to play the King first. Then, if either North or South is void of the suit, there is a marked finessing position over the Jack, and five tricks in the suit will be made.

The unthinking player who first plays the Ace, on the assumption that it does not matter which high card he plays first because the outstanding cards will normally divide 3-1 or 2-2, will lose a trick in the suit whenever North is void and South holds **J 8 7 6**. It will occur about five times in every hundred.

West	*East*
A K 10 5 3	**9 7 6**

If West cannot afford to lose more than one trick in the suit, his play is to win either the Ace or King; if both opponents follow suit, he enters East's hand in a side suit, leads the 7 from the table and if South plays the 8, plays the 10 from his own hand. This protects him against losing two tricks in the suit if South started with **Q J 8 x**.

There is a percentage play or a safety play for almost every combination of a suit, and it may be found by analysing the division of the remaining cards in the suit.

West	*East*
♠ **A K 4 2**	♠ **5 3**
♥ **A 9 7**	♥ **10 6 2**
♦ **A 9 4**	♦ **K 8 7**
♣ **K 7 6**	♣ **A 10 5 4 3**

Against West's contract of Three No-Trumps, North leads a Spade. West can make his contract only if he wins four tricks in Clubs. After winning the first trick with the King of Spades, the right play is for West to win the King of Clubs. If North and South both follow suit, West continues with the 7 of Clubs and plays the 4 from dummy if North plays an honour, but the 10 if North plays a low card. If South follows suit, there is only one more outstanding Club and it will fall under East's Ace. If North shows out on the second round of Clubs, then South started with **Q J x x** of the suit and West cannot do anything about it. The directed play, however, guarantees that he will win four tricks in the suit if North originally held **Q J x x** of the suit.

Most important of all, however, is an ability to count the cards. It is not all that difficult, and, in the main, is largely a matter of drawing deductions from the bidding and previous play of the cards, coupled with training oneself to think along the right lines.

PLATE 14 *(opposite)* Canasta in progress. Both sides have melded. One side also has two red 3s on the table and is freezing the discard pile with a black 3

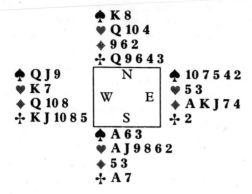

♠ K 8
♥ Q 10 4
♦ 9 6 2
♣ Q 9 6 4 3

♠ Q J 9   ♠ 10 7 5 4 2
♥ K 7   ♥ 5 3
♦ Q 10 8   ♦ A K J 7 4
♣ K J 10 8 5   ♣ 2

♠ A 6 3
♥ A J 9 8 6 2
♦ 5 3
♣ A 7

West deals at love all, and the auction is:

West	North	East	South
1 ♣	No Bid	1 ♦	1 ♥
2 ♦	2 ♥	2 ♠	4 ♥
No Bid	No Bid	No Bid	

West leads Diamonds and East wins the first two tricks with the Ace and King of the suit. A third round of Diamonds is ruffed by South with the 8 of Hearts.

As South has lost two tricks, it would seem that his contract is doomed, because West, by reason of his opening bid and lacking either the Ace or King of Diamonds, must surely be holding the Kings of Hearts and Clubs.

South, however, has a partial count of the hand that will enable him to make his contract if he knows how to take advantage of it. On the assumption that West almost certainly started with three Diamonds and probably five Clubs, he cannot have more than five cards in Spades and Hearts. South, therefore, wins the Ace of Hearts (in case the King is singleton) and when the King of Hearts does not come down, he leads a Spade to dummy's King, a Spade from dummy to the Ace in the closed hand, and then trumps his last Spade with dummy's 10 of Hearts. As West played the 7 of Hearts under South's Ace and followed to the three rounds of Spades, South may reconstruct the position as:

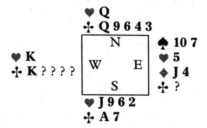

♥ Q
♣ Q 9 6 4 3

♥ K   ♠ 10 7
♣ K ? ? ? ?   ♥ 5
                 ♦ J 4
                 ♣ ?

♥ J 9 6 2
♣ A 7

Now, by leading the Queen of Hearts from dummy, West is put on lead with the King, and as he must return a Club, South wins two tricks in the suit.

The play of the defenders is more difficult than that of the declarer, because a defender has to combine his hand with that of the unseen one held by his partner. They have the slight advantage of a partnership language that enables them to exchange information and advice, but, for the most part, success in defence comes mainly from drawing the right deductions from the bidding, and the cards that have been played to previous tricks.

To lead the highest card of a sequence, to win with the lowest, and to follow suit as the situation dictates, is a general rule that does not need to be enlarged on. Most of the general rules for defence play, however, have been handed down from the days when whist was the fashionable game. At bridge reservations have to be made, because the bidding and the exposed dummy hand allow for modifications of what were only broad generalities in the first place.

To return the suit that partner has led is not always the best play. Sometimes it is more important to take time by the forelock.

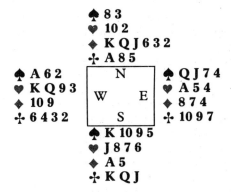

South deals and opens the auction with One No-Trump (12 to 14 points) and North jumps him to Three.

West leads the 3 of Hearts and East wins with the Ace. If East returns a Heart, South has no difficulty in making nine tricks, because dummy's 10 of Hearts protects the Jack in the closed hand and the defenders cannot win more than one trick in Spades and three in Hearts. With the 2 of Hearts on the table, East should appreciate that his partner cannot hold more than four Hearts and that they cannot be better than **K Q 9 3**, because if they were **K Q J 3** he would have led the King and not the 3. As once East gives up the lead he can never regain it, he must take advantage of the time factor, the tempo, and lead the Queen of Spades. The only chance of defeating the contract is to find West holding the Ace of Spades, and as South's bid of One No-Trump postulates a maximum of 14 points, East, who holds 7 points and can count 10 on the table, can count West with just enough room in his hand for the Ace of Spades as well as for the King and Queen of Hearts.

To cover an honour with an honour may be good play in many cases, but it is not when the honour has been led from a sequence.

The Queen is led from dummy. If East covers with the King, the declarer will win four tricks in the suit by winning with the Ace and returning the suit to finesse against West's 10. East, therefore, should not cover. The Queen will win, but now the defenders will always win a trick in the suit because if the declarer continues with dummy's Jack, the lead is no longer from a sequence and East covers it with the King. With **K x** only, East should cover the Queen, otherwise the declarer, after winning dummy's Queen may continue with a low Spade (not the Jack) from the table and East's King will be wasted.

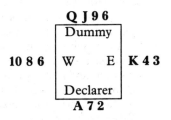

Second hand plays low; third hand plays high, is another general rule that has been handed down from the past. It is, perhaps, a rule worth remembering, because exceptions when second hand should play high are few and far between, and when third hand sees only low cards on his right, there are virtually no exceptions to his playing high.

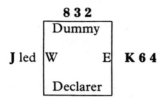

8 3 2

Dummy

J led | W   E | **K 6 4**

Declarer

West leads the Jack. East should play the King like a man. He knows that the declarer holds the Queen (otherwise West would have led it in preference to the Jack) and if declarer holds the Ace as well the King is doomed. East, therefore, must play on the chance that West has led from **A J 10 x** and that declarer holds **Q x x**.

A very important weapon in the armoury of the defenders is the echo or peter, sometimes called the come-on or high-low signal. Reduced to its simplest terms, when a defender plays a higher card followed by a lower one of the same suit, it is a request to partner to play the suit. In many cases a defender can afford to play the suit only once. In such a case to play a 7 or a higher card is an encouragement to partner, and, by contrary, to play a lower card is a discouragement to him. Against a trump contract, the high-low play in a side suit shows that a doubleton is held and that the third round can be trumped. If the play is made in the trump suit itself, it shows that three trumps are held. Against a No-Trump contract, the echo shows length in the suit, usually four cards.

The defenders are frequently compelled to discard, and nearly always discarding presents them with a problem. The general rules to follow are not to retain the same suit as partner; not to discard from a suit in which you have the same length as dummy or suspect the declarer has in his hand; and never to discard so that the declarer is given information.

Counting the cards is, of course, as important to the defenders as it is to the declarer. In some ways, however, the defenders have it a bit easier. If the declarer is in a No-Trump contract he will have limited his hand to an agreed number of points. It follows, therefore, that if the declarer's limit is 16 to 18 points and he has shown up with 15 points, the defenders know that he has left in his hand no more than a King or its equivalent. In much the same way, in a suit contract the declarer and his dummy will rarely hold less than eight trump cards between them. It follows, therefore, that if a defender holds three trumps, he knows that his partner is probably holding not more than two.

In conclusion, it may be said that good defence consists in playing those cards that give as much information as possible to partner, and making things as easy as possible for him; by contrary, in playing those cards that give as little information as possible to the declarer and making things as difficult as possible for him. Whenever it is possible to do so, a defender should play the cards that the declarer knows are in his hand, and retain those of which he knows nothing. If all this comes as a counsel of perfection – the best bridge players are perfectionists.

Brint

Brint was originated by J. B. Chambers in 1929. It is a hybrid of bridge (see page 125) and vint, the national card game of Russia. It has been described as bridge with vint scoring, because the score that counts towards game, and recorded below the line, depends entirely upon the level to which the bidding has been carried. No-Trumps and the suits retain their rank, but each trick (over six) at the level of One is worth 10 points, at the level of Two 20 points, and so on up to Seven when each trick is worth 70 points.

The full scoring table is:

When the Contract is at the level of:	Each Odd-trick (whether Doubled or not) is worth:	When the Declarer is Not Vulnerable		
		Undoubled	Doubled	
		Penalty for each Undertrick	Bonus for Contract and each Overtrick	Penalty for each Undertrick
One	10	50	50	100
Two	20	50	50	100
Three	30	50	50	100
Four	40	100	100	200
Five	50	150	150	300
Six	60	200	200	400
Seven	70	250	250	500

The score for tricks made is unaffected by a double, but if a doubled contract is redoubled the trick score, as well as the bonus and penalty for a doubled contract, is doubled. The bonuses and penalties are increased by 100 points each if the player is vulnerable.

A game is won by the pair that first reaches a trick score of 160 points.

The bonuses for bidding and making slams and games, and for holding honours, recorded above the line as at bridge, are:

For a successful bid of Seven – 1000 points
For a successful bid of Six – 500 points
For a successful bid of Five – 250 points
For a successful bid of Four – 500 points if vulnerable
　　　　　　　　　　　　　　　250 points if not vulnerable
In a No-Trump contract for four Aces in one hand – 150 points
In a Suit contract for *five* honours in one hand – 200 points
In a Suit contract for *four* honours in one hand – 100 points
They are unaffected by vulnerability, doubling and redoubling.

Calypso

Calypso was invented by R. W. Willis of Trinidad: it dates from the mid-1950s, and though designed on entirely new lines, inevitably borrows some of the best features of bridge (see page 125) and canasta (see page 149).

The game is played with four packs of cards (with identical backs) shuffled together, but the cards are shuffled only at the start of a game, and a player holds only thirteen of them at a time.

Four players take part, and it is a novel feature of the game that each player has his own trump suit. Spades and Hearts play in partnership against Diamonds and Clubs. The players cut for seats and trump suits. The highest has choice of both, and his partner takes the corresponding suit and sits facing him. The choice of a trump suit conveys no advantage; it is purely a matter of personal preference.

Thirteen cards are dealt to each player, and the dealer places the rest of the pack to his left, ready for the next dealer after the hand has been played.

The player on the left of the dealer leads to the first trick. Thereafter the lead is made by the player who wins a trick. When playing to a trick a player must follow suit if he can; otherwise he may either discard or trump by playing a card of his own trump suit.

A trick is won by he who has played the highest card of the suit led, or by he who has trumped it, or over-trumped it by playing a higher trump of his own trump suit. If two or more players play identical cards, the first played takes priority for the purpose of winning tricks, and perhaps the most important feature of the game is that if a player leads a card of his own trump suit, he wins the trick automatically unless it is trumped by another player or over-trumped by still another player. To illustrate:

North ♣	East ♠	South ♦	West ♥
8 ♥	J ♥	10 ♥	3 ♥

North has led the 8 of Hearts, and East wins the trick because he has played the highest Heart.

4 ♦	6 ♠	7 ♦	3 ♦

North has led the 4 of Diamonds, and East wins the trick because he has trumped. South has merely followed suit to North's lead.

3 ♥	4 ♠	6 ♦	J ♥

North has led the 3 of Hearts, and South wins the trick, because although East has trumped, he has over-trumped. West has merely followed suit to North's lead.

9 ♣	J ♣	6 ♣	5 ♣

North has led the 9 of Clubs and wins the trick because Clubs is his own trump suit. That East has played a higher Club does not score.

North ♣	East ♠	South ♦	West ♥
6 ♣	7 ♠	9 ♦	5 ♣

North has led the 6 of Clubs, East has trumped, but South wins the trick because he has over-trumped.

6 ♥	Q ♥	Q ♥	10 ♥

North has led the 6 of Hearts, and the trick is won by East as his Queen of Hearts was played before South's.

The object of the game is to build calypsoes. A calypso is a complete suit (from Ace to 2) in a player's trump suit.

When a player wins a trick, he leaves exposed on the table, in front of him, any cards that will help him to build a calypso, passes to his partner any cards that will help him to build a calypso, and discards the others, face downwards, on his right.

North (whose trump suit is Clubs) leads the 4 of Clubs and wins the trick:

4 ♣	6 ♣	J ♣	6 ♣

North places the **4 ♣**, **6 ♣** and **J ♣** face upwards on the table in front of him, and discards the second **6 ♣**. He then leads the **8 ♣** and the trick is:

8 ♣	J ♣	7 ♣	8 ♦

Again North wins the trick. He keeps the **7 ♣** and **8 ♣** for his calypso, passes the 8 ♦ to his partner for his calypso, and discards the **J ♣** because he already has one.

The play continues until all thirteen tricks have been played; the next player then deals another hand of thirteen cards each.

A player may build only one calypso at a time, but once a calypso has been built the player may begin another. He may use any cards in the trick with which a calypso has been completed, but he cannot use any cards from his discard pile. These cards are dead.

The game ends when each player has dealt once. The score is then made up as follows:

For the first calypso—500 points.
For the second calypso—750 points   ⎱When obtained by
For any subsequent calypso—1,000 points ⎰ the individual players.
For each card in an incomplete calypso—20 points.
For each card in the discard pile—10 points.

The two partners add their totals together, and stakes are paid on the difference between the totals of the two sides.

A serious view is taken of revoking. A revoke does not become established until a player of the offending side has played to the next trick, and a revoke made in the twelfth never becomes established, but if established a revoke suffers a penalty of 260 points.

SOLO CALYPSO is played by four players but each plays for himself. The play is more or less identical with the parent game, the main difference between the two is that, in solo calypso, the players draw cards for choice of seats and trump suits; the highest has first choice, the lowest takes what is left.

CALYPSO FOR THREE PLAYERS is played with three packs of cards and one complete suit (it does not matter which) removed from all three packs. The game consists of three deals. Each player plays for himself.

Canasta

Canasta is a variation of rummy (see page 149) that was developed in South America as an independent game. It may be played by any number of players from two to six, but is at its most skilful when played by four. If two or three play each plays for himself; if four they play as two partners against the other two, the partners sitting facing each other; if five they play two against three, but of the three only two play at a time and rotate so that at each deal a different player sits out; if six play they play as three partners against the other three, the partners sitting alternately around the table.

The game is played with two 52-card packs and two Jokers to each pack. The four Jokers and the eight 2s are wild cards: they may be named as any other card.

The dealer deals eleven cards to each player* and the rest of the pack (the stock) is placed face downwards in the centre of the table. The top card is turned face upwards and placed alongside it. It is known as the up-card, and is the start of the discard pile. If it is a wild card or a red 3 it is covered with the next card of the stock, and if this also is a wild card or a red 3 it is covered with the next card of the stock, and so on.

The red 3s are bonus cards that count for or against the side to which they fall. They do not form part of a player's hand, and at his turn to play he who holds a red 3 must place it face upwards on the table in front of him and refill his hand by drawing the top card of the stock. If a red 3 is taken in the discard pile, it is similarly faced, but the player does not refill his hand from the stock.

The object of the game is to form melds of three or more cards of the same rank, with or without the help of wild cards. Sequences are not recognized as melds.

The player on the left of the dealer plays first. Thereafter play continues clockwise round the table. A play consists of a player drawing a card, melding (optional), discarding. A game in progress is shown in Plate 14.

The Draw The player takes either the top card of the stock or the up-card of the discard pile provided he can meld with it. In the latter case, however, he must take with it the whole of the discard pile subject to its not being frozen. At the beginning of the game the discard pile is frozen until a side has made its first meld; it is then unfrozen for that side only. Even for a side that has melded the discard pile is frozen at any time that a red 3 or a wild card is the up-card. It remains frozen until it is taken by a player, because the fresh discard pile is not frozen unless the player starts the fresh pile with a wild card. If a player plays a black 3 to the discard pile it is frozen for the next player only.

---

* If two play each is dealt fifteen cards; if three play each is dealt thirteen cards.

The Meld A meld is valid if it contains at least two 'natural' (*i.e.* not wild) cards of the same rank, and not more than three wild cards. Black 3s, however, may not be melded unless the player melds out in the same turn. Wild cards may not be melded separately from natural cards. A meld must be placed face upwards on the table, and the melds of the two partners are placed in front of only one of them. A player may add one or more cards of the same rank, or wild cards, to a meld previously faced by his side. A player may make as many melds as he chooses, including the addition of cards to melds made by his side; also he may not add cards to the melds of his opponents. Wild cards, once melded, cannot be replaced with natural cards.

A canasta is a meld of seven or more cards, and may be built up from an initial meld of three or more cards. If a canasta contains no wild cards it is a natural canasta; if it is formed with one, two or three wild cards it is a mixed canasta. Wild cards may be added in any number to a canasta, but other melds are limited to three (see illustration).

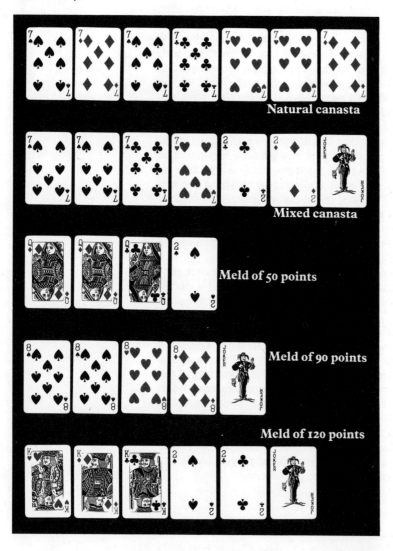

Natural canasta

Mixed canasta

Meld of 50 points

Meld of 90 points

Meld of 120 points

Every card melded has the following point value:

Jokers – 50 points each.

Aces and 2s – 20 points each.

Kings, Queens, Jacks, 10s, 9s and 8s – 10 points each.

7s, 6s, 5s, 4s, and black 3s – 5 points each.

These points count to the credit of a side if the cards are melded when a deal ends, and to its debit if they are not melded.

The red 3s have a value of 100 points each, unless a side holds all four of them, when each has a value of 200 points. At the end of the deal a side that has made any meld scores all its red 3s as a plus bonus: a side that has made no meld deducts the value of its red 3s from its score.

The first meld is governed by a strict rule. If the score of a side is under 1500 points the first meld must total at least 50 points; if the score is between 1500 and 2995 points it must total at least 90 points; and if the score is 3000 points or more it must total at least 120 points. There is no minimum total for a side that has a minus score.

The Discard. After a player has made a draw and melded if he has chosen to, he must play a card to the discard pile. The card must be played from hand and not from a meld on the table. The discard, however, is optional when the player melds every card in his hand (called melding out). It sometimes happens that a player is able to meld all his cards in one turn, he not having melded previously. It is known as melding out blind, and the bonus is doubled. Either way, however, a player must have, or be able to complete, a canasta, and as melding out may not suit partner he should first always ask him: 'May I go out?' Partner's reply to the question must be a simple 'Yes' or 'No', and, whichever it is, is binding on the partnership. Indeed, if the partner says 'Yes' and the player cannot, after all, meld out he suffers a penalty of 100 points.

The side that goes out totals the point values of the cards in its melds; adds a bonus of 100 points for melding out (200 points if it has melded out blind); 100 for each red 3 (800 points if the partnership holds all four red 3s); 500 points for each natural canasta and 300 points for each mixed canasta. From this is subtracted the total point value of the cards left in the hand of the partner.

The score of the side that did not meld out is determined in the same way, and it is deducted from that of the side that melded out. If it has not made a meld the value of its red 3s are deducted from, instead of added to, its total.

The game is won by the side that first reaches a total of 5,000 points, or the higher total if both sides pass 5,000 in the same deal.

The chief aim of a player must be to make canastas. If there is a choice, it is best to begin as many melds as possible, because each is a start towards a canasta. One should take advantage of the fact that, to fulfil the minimum count, a player may take two or more different melds at the same turn. At the same time, it is unwise to meld every meldable card as soon as you can. It depletes the hand and leaves you at the mercy of the opponents until you are able to go out. A good general rule is that it is unwise to make a first meld if it reduces the hand to less than six cards. A first meld should always be made if it can with the minimum number of cards.

A player should always try to retain at least one wild card in his hand, and, except to help complete a canasta, he should not add unnecessarily to a meld when there is the risk that the opponents will go out.

Nearly always it is unwise to discard Aces; they pull more weight when melded.

Since black 3s have no constructive value there is a tendency to discard them at the first opportunity. It is not bad play to do so, and it has the advantage of freezing the pack for one's left-hand opponent. In general, however, it is better to retain a black 3 until one is faced with the problem of finding a safe discard.

As the two partners hold between them only eleven cards, it stands out that at best they are unlikely to make more than one canasta out of them. There are, however, sixty-four cards that have not been dealt to the four players. Clearly, therefore, taking the pack must be to a player's advantage, because he can make so many more canastas out of it.

If your side wins the first pack, do not reduce your hand unnecessarily. Do not be frightened to discard from your longest holdings. By contrast, if your side loses the first pack your only defence is to play to go out. There is a very important difference between attacking and defending play.

When the pack is frozen, try to build up a hand in pairs. Pairs are very valuable, because every meld must contain at least two cards of the same suit—a pair that is.

THREE-PACK CANASTA, or Samba, may be played by any number of players from two to six, but is a satisfactory game only for six playing in three partnerships of two each. One player sits between two opponents, one of each of the other partnerships.

Three 52-card packs with two Jokers each are used. Thirteen cards are dealt to each player. Game is 10,000 points, and when a side reaches 7,000 its minimum count for its first meld is 150 points. Five red 3s have a value of 1,000 points; six 1,200 points. A side must have two canastas to meld out.

Cinch

Cinch, Double Pedro or High Five, is a variation of all fours (see page 48) that, though it may be played by any number from two to six, is nearly always played by four, two playing in partnership against the other two.

It is played with the regular 52-card pack. The 5 of the trump suit is known as Right Pedro and the 5 of the suit of the same colour as Left Pedro. The cards rank in the order from Ace (high) to 2 (low) with the exception that Left Pedro ranks between Right Pedro and the 4 of the trump suit.

Each player is dealt nine cards in bundles of three, and each in turn, beginning with the player on the left of the dealer, may either pass or bid. A bid is made by naming a number from one to fourteen that must be higher than any previous one. After all have either passed or bid, the player who made the highest bid names the trump suit. If, however, all the other players pass, the dealer (who bids last) may name the trump suit without specifying any contract: each side scores for whatever points it makes.

When the final bid has been made and the trump suit named, all the players, except the dealer, discard from their hands all the cards that are not trumps. These discards are placed face upwards on the table where they may be inspected.

The dealer then deals to each player, in turn, sufficient cards to fill his hand to six cards. He then robs the pack. That is to say he discards face upwards on the table all non-trump cards in his hand, looks through the balance of the pack, and picks out any cards he wishes to fill his hand to six cards.

As the players start the game with six cards each, it follows that any player who has been dealt more than six trump cards must discard sufficient to reduce his hand to six cards.

The object of the game is to win tricks containing cards that score as follows:

Ace of the trump suit (High) = 1 point.	10 of the trump suit (Game) = 1 point.
2 of the trump suit (Low) = 1 point.	Right Pedro = 5 points.
Jack of the trump suit (Jack) = 1 point.	Left Pedro = 5 points.

The player who made the highest bid (the maker) leads to the first trick. Thereafter the player who wins a trick leads to the next. If a trump is led a player must follow suit to it if he can: if a plain suit is led a player must not discard if he can follow suit to it, but he may trump even though he is able to follow suit.

The total number of points in each deal is 14, and when all six tricks have been played each side counts the points it has won. If the maker's side has fulfilled at least its contract, the difference between the two counts is credited to the side with the higher count. It is not necessarily the maker's side. If the maker's side has failed to make its contract, his side scores nothing and the opposing side scores the points it has won plus the count of the contract.

The game is won by the side that is first to reach a total of 51 points.

As a player is allowed to play a trump to the lead of a plain suit, it follows that very few tricks are won with a plain-suit card. For all practical purposes, cinch is a 1-suit game with the plain-suit cards serving only to enable a player to get off lead.

On average nine trump cards will be dealt originally, so that a player has no justification to expect more than one in the draw. In the long run the number of points that a player may expect to win is the same as the number of trumps held by the partners.

Experienced players, however, have developed a number of conventional bids in order that the first bidder of a partnership may give information about his trump holding. These bids are an essential feature of the game because each player has only one bid.

With any Pedro a bid of Five is made.

With **A x x** or **A x x x** a bid of Six is made.

With Ace and King of a suit, even doubleton, a bid of Seven is made.

With **A K J x x** a bid of Eleven is made.

With **A K Q x** a bid of Eleven or Twelve is made.

South deals:

West	North	East	South
♠ A K	♠ 6 4	♠ Q 10 8 2	♠ 7 3
♥ 6 3	♥ A J 8	♥ K 9	♥ 4 2
♦ 10 8 5	♦ 9 2	♦ K 4	♦ A Q 6
♣ 8 4	♣ 7 6	♣ K	♣ 3 2

West, with Spades as trumps in mind, bids Seven. North passes, and as East can see from his cards that West's Ace-King combination is in Spades, bids Eleven. As a player has only one bid, it is good practice to bid as high as possible, to stop an opponent over-bidding, rather than try to buy the contract at a low level. South passes.

East, the maker, names Spades as trumps.

West discards: ♥ 6 3 ♦ 10 8 5 ♣ 8 4 and receives in exchange: ♠ 5 (Right Pedro) ♥ 7 ♦ 3 ♣ 10

North discards: ♥ A J 8 ♦ 9 2 ♣ 7 6 and receives in exchange: ♥ Q 10 ♣ 9 5 (Left Pedro).

East discards: ♥ K 9 ♦ K 4 ♣ K and receives in exchange: ♥ 5 ♣ J.

South discards: ♥ 4 2 ♦ A Q 6 ♣ 3 2 and robs the pack of: ♠ J 9 ♣ A Q.

The hands are now:

West	North	East	South
♠ A K 5	♠ 6 4	♠ Q 10 8 2	♠ J 9 7 3
♥ 7	♥ Q 10	♥ 5	♥ none
♦ 3	♦ none	♦ none	♦ none
♣ 10	♣ 9 5	♣ J	♣ A Q

East leads the 2♠ which West wins with the A♠. This gives the partnership 2 points for high (A♠) and low (2♠). The play always centres about capturing the two Pedros, and as West holds Right Pedro (5♠) and will win it, East and West will make their contract if they can locate and capture Left Pedro (5♣).

Euchre

Euchre, a game always more popular in the New World than in the Old, and made famous by Bret Harte's witty *Plain Language from Truthful James*, has several variations. The standard game is suitable for from two to six players, but is best for four, two playing in partnership against the other two.

The game is played with the 32-card or short pack, that is the regular pack from which the 6s and lower cards have been removed. The cards rank in the order from Ace (high) to 7 (low) with the exception that the Jack of the trump suit (Right Bower) takes precedence over all other trump cards, and the Jack of the suit of the same colour (Left Bower) ranks as the second highest trump.

There is some advantage in dealing. The players, therefore, must draw cards to decide who shall deal. The highest takes first deal, which, thereafter, passes round the table clockwise.

The dealer gives five cards to each player either in bundles of two then three, or three then two. It does not matter which, but he must be consistent throughout the game. The rest of the pack is placed face downwards in the centre of the table, and the top card is turned face upwards. It is the potential trump suit, and, beginning with the player on the left of the dealer, each player in turn has the option of either refusing or accepting it.

To accept it as the trump suit the opponents of the dealer say: 'I order it up'; the dealer's partner says: 'I assist'; and the dealer himself says nothing, but accepts by making his discard. To refuse the card as the trump suit, the opponents and partner of the dealer say: 'I pass'; the dealer signifies refusal by taking the card from the top of the pack and placing it, face upwards, partly underneath the pack.

If all four players pass on the first round, there is a second round. Beginning with the player on the left of the dealer, each player in turn may now either pass, or name any suit he likes (other than that of the turned up card) as trumps. If all four players pass on the second round, the hand is abandoned and the deal passes.

When the trump suit has been settled, the player who has named it (the maker) has the right to go it alone, but he must announce his intention to do so before a card has been led. His partner places his cards face downwards on the table, and takes no active part in the hand. The maker (he is the only one of the four who can go alone) plays his hand against the two opponents in partnership. If he wins the march (all five tricks) he scores 4 points; if he wins three or four tricks he scores 1 point; if he is euchred (*i.e.* fails to win at least three tricks) the opponents score 2 points each.

Euchre is a trick-taking game. The player on the left of the dealer (or the player on the left of the maker if he is going it alone) leads to the first trick. Thereafter the player who wins a trick leads to the next. A player must follow suit to the card led if he can, if not he may either discard or trump.

If the partnership that made the trump suit wins the march it scores 2 points; if it wins three or four tricks it scores 1 point; if it is euchred the opposing side scores 2 points. It is customary for each side to keep the score by using a 3 and a 4 (cards not needed in the game) as shown in the illustration. The side that is first to score five points wins.

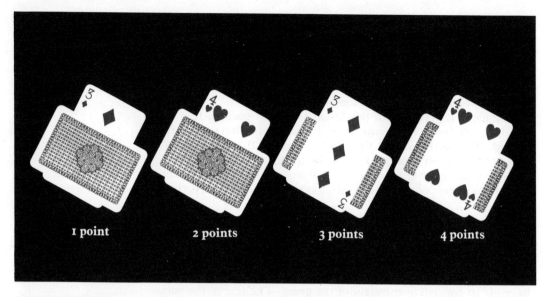

| 1 point | 2 points | 3 points | 4 points |

TWO-HANDED EUCHRE is played in exactly the same way as the parent game except that the pack is reduced to twenty-four cards by removing the 8s and all lower cards, and, obviously, there is no declaration of going it alone.

THREE-HANDED EUCHRE is played in the same way as the parent game except that the maker of the trump suit plays against the other two in partnership. If the maker wins the march he scores 3 points; if he wins three or four tricks he scores 1 point; and if he is euchred each of his opponents scores 2 points.

CALL-ACE EUCHRE is a variation that may be played by four, five or six players, each playing for himself. It is played in the same way as the parent game with the exception that the maker has the option of either playing for himself or of calling for a partner by saying: 'I call on the Ace of . . .' and he names a suit. The player who holds the Ace of this suit then plays in partnership with the maker against the other players, but he does not reveal himself. It follows, therefore, that until the Ace is played, and it may not be in the deal, everyone except the holder of the Ace (if it is in play) is left to guess where his interest lies.

The scoring is rather different to that of the other variations as fundamentally the game is all against all. For winning the march a lone player scores 1 point for every player in the game; in a partnership hand the score is 2 points each if three or four players are in the game, and 3 points each if five or six players are in the game. For winning three or four tricks a lone player scores 1 point; in a partnership hand both players score 1 point. If a lone player or a partnership is euchred the other players score 2 points each.

Hearts

Hearts and its several variations is very similar in principle to black maria (see page 104) because the object of the game is to avoid taking tricks that contain certain specified cards. The play itself follows the general principles of trick-taking games: the player on the left of the dealer leads to the first trick, and thereafter the winner of a trick leads to the next; a player must follow suit to the card led if he can, and if he cannot he may discard any card that suits him.

The game may be played by any reasonable number of players, but it is at its most interesting and skilful as a game for four, each playing for himself.*

The Queen of Spades and all cards of the Heart suit are penalty cards. Every deal is a separate event, and the usual method of settling is to debit he who wins the Queen of Spades with 13 points, and those who win Hearts with 1 point for each card.

A revoke is heavily penalized. A player may correct a revoke if he does so before a card is led to the next trick; otherwise the revoke is established, the hand is abandoned, and the revoking player is debited with all 26 points.

The game is not a difficult one, but it calls for an ability to count the cards, read the distribution and visualize possibilities. It is instructive to consider the play in the deal below if West has to make the opening lead and assumes that the best lead is the 2 of Hearts because one of the other players will certainly have to win the trick.

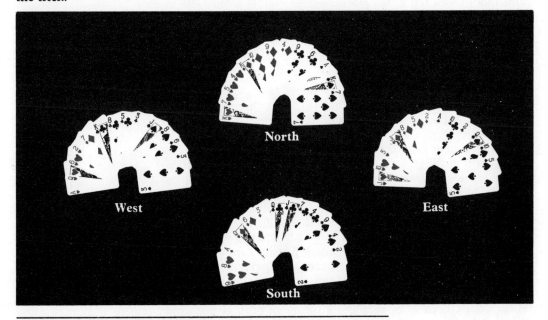

North

West

East

South

---

*When the game is played by three players or by more than four, low cards are removed from the pack to reduce it to a number that allows every player to be dealt the same number of cards.

Against West's opening lead of the 2 of Hearts the play will be short and sharp, and West will come off worst of all because good play by his opponents will saddle him with the Queen of Spades.

West	North	East	South
2 ♥	4 ♥	3 ♥	8 ♥
6 ♥	7 ♥	10 ♥	9 ♥
Q ♥	K ♥	J ♥	A ♦
A ♥	5 ♥	Q ♠	Q ♦

A more experienced West would have kept off leading a Heart. It is probable that his best lead is the singleton Diamond, because he has nothing to fear in the Spade suit, and, once he has got rid of his Diamond, he gives himself the best chance to get rid of the dangerous Ace and Queen of Hearts.

In **DOMINO HEARTS** the players are dealt only six cards each, and the rest of the pack is placed face downwards in the centre of the table. The player on the left of the dealer leads to the first trick, and the game is played in the same way as the parent game except that if a player cannot follow suit to a card that has been led he must draw a card from the stock, and continue to do so until he draws a card of the suit led. Only after the stock has been exhausted may a player discard from his hand if he cannot follow suit to a lead.

Play continues until all the cards have been taken in tricks, each player dropping out as his hand is exhausted. If a player wins a trick with the last card in his hand, the next active player on his left leads to the next trick. The last player to be left in the game retains all the cards left in his hand, and takes into it any cards that may be left in the stock.

The Queen of Spades is not a penalty card; only cards of the Heart suit are, and 1 point is lost for each one taken in a trick or left in the hand of the surviving player.

In **GREEK HEARTS**, as in black maria (see page 104) each player, before the opening lead is made, passes three cards to his right-hand opponent and receives three from his left-hand opponent.

As in the parent game the penalty cards are the Queen of Spades and all cards of the Heart suit, and the penalties for winning them are the same; if, however, a player wins all the Hearts and the Queen of Spades, instead of losing 26 points, he receives 26 points from each of the other players.

The game calls for some considerable skill, because, before passing on his cards, a player has to decide whether he will take the easy road and play to avoid winning penalty cards, or try for the big prize by winning all. The decision is never an easy one, because by discarding a high Heart one may be helping an opponent to a better score, and oneself lose a good score if one receives the Queen of Spades and a couple of high Hearts from one's left-hand opponent.

HEARTSETTE is played in the same way as the parent game, but with a widow hand. If three or four take part in the game the 2 of Spades is removed from the pack, and if five or six take part the full pack is used.

When there are three players, each is dealt sixteen cards, when four, twelve cards, when five, ten cards and when six, eight cards. The remaining cards are placed face downwards in the centre of the table.

The player on the left of the dealer leads to the first trick and whoever wins it takes the widow and discards from his hand to reduce it to the proper number of cards. No-one else sees the widow nor the cards that have been discarded.

The play continues in the same way as in the parent game with the same penalty cards and penalties for winning them.

OMNIBUS HEARTS or Hit the Moon, combines most of the features that have been added to the parent game. Like it it is at its best when played by four, each playing for himself.

Thirteen cards are dealt to each player, and before the opening lead is made each player passes three cards to his right-hand opponent and receives three from his left-hand opponent.

The play is the same as in the parent game. All the Hearts and the Queen of Spades are penalty cards, but a novel feature is that the 10 of Diamonds is a bonus card. A player loses 1 point for every Heart that he wins and 13 points if he wins the Queen of Spades. By contrary, he wins 10 points if he takes the 10 of Diamonds, and if he wins all the Hearts, the Queen of Spades and the 10 of Diamonds (known as hitting the moon—no longer such a feat as it once was) he wins 26 points instead of losing 16.

The game is won by the player who has the highest plus score, or lowest minus score, when one player reaches a score of −100.

The game calls for skill both in discarding to the right-hand opponent and in the play. Good discarding is dictated by the fact that only the Club suit is neutral and harmless. Every Heart is a liability and top Spades are dangerous (unless adequately supported by low cards) though top Diamonds are advantageous the low ones may be liabilities.

In play it is necessary to aim at forcing the lead into the hand of the least dangerous opponent. All the time temporary partnerships must be formed. If the score stands at: North −83, East −41, South +32, West +47, it is obvious that West will be doing his best to win the game by driving North to −100 as quickly as possible. A skilful South, therefore, will enter into a tacit partnership with North to try and save him by prolonging the game and so give himself more time to pull ahead of West. The strategy is perfectly proper because both players are acting in their own interests.

PIP HEARTS is played in the same way as the parent game, but the Queen of Spades is not a penalty card and the penalty for winning a Heart is increased to the pip value of the card, the court cards counting Jack 11, Queen 12, King 13 and Ace 14.

Pinocle

(see footnote page 91)

Pinocle has much in common with bezique (see page 50) and originated in Europe. It has, however, long since crossed the Atlantic, and, if we exclude the ubiquitous bridge (see page 125) it shares with poker (see page 189) the honour of being the national card game of the U.S.A.

In its original form, pinocle is a game for two players and is described on page 91. American card-players, however, have developed a number of variations suitable for more than two. The most popular is Auction Pinocle, a rather remarkable game because though fundamentally a game for three it makes a better game when played by four.

In every deal only three players take an active part. If four play the dealer deals no cards to himself; and if five wish to take part the dealer deals no cards to the second player on his left as well as none to himself. The inactive players, as they are called, take no part in the bidding and play, but participate in the settlement.

The pinocle pack consists of forty-eight cards, namely the **A 10 K Q J 9** (in that order) of each suit, duplicated. The dealer deals fifteen cards face downwards to the active players, either in five bundles of three each, or in three bundles of four each and one of three, and after the first round, three cards face downwards to the table as a widow-hand.

A bid is a contract to score either by melds, by cards won in tricks, or by both, the number of points named, and the player on the left of the dealer makes the first bid which must be at least 300. After this, each player in turn may either pass or make a higher bid. Bids must be in multiples of ten, and once a player has passed he cannot re-enter the auction. When two players pass a bid the player who made it becomes the bidder, his bid the contract, and the other two players his opponents.

If the opening bid of 300 is passed by the other two players the bidder may concede defeat by throwing in his cards without looking at the widow. He pays 3 units to the kitty (but nothing to his opponents) and the deal passes to the next player.

If the bid is for more than 300, or if the bidder does not wish to concede defeat, he shows the widow to his opponents and takes the cards into his hand. He then names the trump suit, and places on the table in front of him his melds. They are scored for as follows:

Class A
A 10 K Q J of the trump suit = 150 points
K Q of the trump suit (royal marriage) = 40 points
K Q of a plain suit (common marriage) = 20 points

Class B
Pinocle (**Q ♠** and **J ♦**) = 40 points
Dis (**9** of the trump suit) = 10 points

Class C
Four Aces—one of each suit = 100 points
Four Kings—one of each suit = 80 points
Four Queens—one of each suit = 60 points
Four Jacks—one of each suit = 40 points

No card may be used twice in melds of the same class, but the same card may be used in two or more melds of different classes. Only the bidder melds. He then discards face downwards (buries) three cards from his hand in order to reduce it to fifteen cards: later the cards that he discards will be counted for him as won in a trick. The discards must be made from the cards in his hand, not from those in his melds, but before he leads to the first trick he may change the cards that he has discarded, change the melds and the trump suit.

When the bidder and his opponents have agreed on the value of the melds and how many more points (if any) he needs to fulfil his contract, the bidder leads to the first trick. If, however, he thinks he will not be able to make his contract he may concede defeat (called *single béte*) and pay to the players, active and inactive, the value of his bid.

When playing to a trick a player must follow suit if he can, and if he cannot he must play to win the trick by trumping or over-trumping it. Only if he has no card of the suit led and no trump card may he discard. If a trump is led, the subsequent players must try to win it. A trick is won by the highest card of the suit led or the highest trump if the led card has been trumped. If two identical cards are played the one first to be played wins the trick, if the trick is to be won by the card.

When all the tricks have been played, the players score for each Ace 11 points, each Ten 10 points, each King 4 points, each Queen 3 points, each Jack 2 points, and for winning the last trick 10 points. It gives a total of 250 points to be won in tricks.

Every deal is a separate event and settlement is made before the next deal begins. It is usual to reduce the contract to units on which payment is made.

Contract	Unit Value	
300–340	3	
350–390	5	If Spades
400–440	10	are trumps
450–490	15	the unit
500–540	20	values are
550–590	25	doubled.
600 and more	30	

The bidder pays double (called *double béte*) if his score for melds and cards taken in tricks fails to equal his contract; he receives if his score equals or exceeds his contract, but he does not receive more than the unit value of his contract.

Payment is made to and from all players, active and inactive, and to and from a kitty if the contract is for 350 or more.

The kitty is a separate account and is the common property of the players. They make good any deficiency if it owes, and divide any surplus when the game breaks up.

As the name implies **PARTNERSHIP PINOCLE** is played by four players two playing in partnership against the other two. The partners face each other.

The 48-card pinocle pack is used. The dealer gives each player twelve cards in bundles of three each, and turns up the last card dealt to himself to determine the trump suit. In turn, beginning with the player on the left of the dealer, any player who holds the dis (9 of the trump suit) may exchange it for the turned-up card, and if the dealer turns up the dis as the trump card he scores 10 points. Each original holder of a dis, whether or not he exchanges it with the turned-up card, scores 10 points for it.

The players expose their melds on the table in front of them, and in addition to the melds for auction pinocle (page 160) melds and the scores for them are as follows:

Double Trump Sequence **A 10 K Q J**	1,500 points
Double Pinocle	300 points
All Eight Aces	1,000 points
All Eight Kings	800 points
All Eight Queens	600 points
All Eight Jacks	400 points

When the players have shown their melds and scored for them, they return them to their hands. No meld, however, finally counts unless the partnership wins a trick, and when a trick is won both partners score for their melds.

The player on the left of the dealer leads to the first trick, and the play continues as in auction pinocle.

When all twelve tricks have been played, the players count 10 points for every Ace and 10 won, 5 points for every King and Queen, and 10 points for winning the last trick. As in auction pinocle the total is 250 points.

The game is won by the partnership that first wins 1,000 points in melds and cards won in tricks, but if both partnerships reach 1,000 or more points in the same deal the game continues to 1,250 points, and, if it happens again, to 1,500 points, and so on.

At any time during the game a player may claim that he has scored 1,000 points or more and won the game. Play is brought to an end and the claim is verified. If the claim is found to be correct his partnership wins the game; if the claim is found to be wrong his partnership loses the game. In either case, what the opposing side has scored makes no difference to the result.

PARTNERSHIP PINOCLE FOR MORE THAN FOUR PLAYERS is played with two 48-card pinocle packs shuffled together. Six players form two partnerships of three players each sitting alternately at the table: eight players form two partnerships of four players each sitting alternately.

The dealer gives 16 cards to each player in bundles of four each and turns up the last card dealt to himself to denote the trump suit.

The game is played in the same way as partnership pinocle, but in addition to the melds opposite, melds and the scores for them are as follows:

Triple Trump Sequence **A 10 K Q J**	3,000 points
Double Trump Sequence **A 10 K Q J**	1,500 points
Four Kings and Four Queens of the same suit	1,200 points
Three Kings and Three Queens of the same suit	600 points
Two Kings and Two Queens of the same suit	300 points
Quadruple Pinocle	1,200 points
Triple Pinocle	600 points
Double Pinocle	300 points
Fifteen Aces, Kings, Queens and Jacks	3,000 points
Twelve Aces	2,000 points
Twelve Kings	1,600 points
Twelve Queens	1,200 points
Twelve Jacks	800 points
Eight Aces	1,000 points
Eight Kings	800 points
Eight Queens	600 points
Eight Jacks	400 points

FIREHOUSE PINOCLE is played as a partnership game for four, two playing in partnership against the other two. Twelve cards are dealt to each player. As in auction pinocle the trump suit is bid for; the player on the left of the dealer bids first; each player has only one bid or pass, and the minimum bid is 200. The bidder makes the trump suit and leads to the first trick. Game is won by the partnership that first reaches 1,000 points. The score of the bidder's side is counted first, and the game is played to the end. A partnership cannot concede defeat.

CHECK PINOCLE was developed some say in Texas, out of firehouse pinocle, and is considered one of the best and most skilful of all partnership games, not excluding bridge.

The game is played by four players, two playing in partnership against the other two, with the regular 48-card pinocle pack.

Twelve cards are dealt to each player in bundles of three at a time, and each player in turn, beginning with the player on the left of the dealer, must either bid or pass. The lowest bid is 200, subsequent bids must be made in multiples of ten, and once a player has passed he may not re-enter the bidding. None of the first three players may make a bid unless he holds a marriage (King and Queen of one suit) but if all three pass the dealer must bid at least 200 and he does not need a marriage to do so; if, however, he wishes to make a higher bid than 200 he must hold one. The bidding ends when a bid has been passed by the three other players, and the bidder then names the trump suit.

The players then expose their melds on the table. The melds and the scores for them are the same as in auction pinocle (page 160) and the partners add the values of their melds together and record the total as a single score.

Some melds have what is known as a check (chip) value; a Trump Sequence (**A 10 K Q J**) and Four Aces each of a different suit are each worth 2 checks, Four Kings, Four Queens, Four Jacks each of a different suit, and Double Pinocle are all worth 1 check. Check values are paid across the table as the game procedes.

The players return the melds to their hands, and the play is the same as in partnership pinocle. When all twelve tricks have been played a partnership scores 10 points for every Ace and 10 that it has won, 5 points for every King and Queen, and 10 points if it has won the last trick.

The bidding side adds these points to those that it has already scored for its melds, and if the total is at least equal to the bid the contract has been made and the partnership scores for everything that it makes; if its total is less than its bid the amount of its bid is deducted from its score. In all cases the opposing side scores for everything that it makes.

The game is won by the partnership that first scores 1,000 points. The score of the bidding partnership is counted first, and as the game is over when it reaches 1,000 points, the opposing partnership scores nothing in the final deal.

At the end of each deal a partnership is entitled to checks on the following scale:

Contract	*If Made*	
200–240	2 checks	If the contract is
250–290	4 checks	defeated the
300–340	7 checks	bidding partnership
350–390	10 checks	pays double checks
400–440	13 checks	to the opposing
and 3 added checks for		partnership.
each series of 50 points.		

A partnership that wins all twelve tricks in a deal receives 4 checks; for winning the game it receives 7 checks and 1 check for each 100 points (or part thereof) by which the score of the winning partnership exceeds that of the losing partnership; and if the losing partnership has a net minus score, the winning partnership receives an additional 4 checks.

Polignac

Polignac is sometimes played as a party game with the 52-card pack. It is, however, better as a serious game for four, playing all against all, with the 32-card pack – the 6s and lower cards removed.

Eight cards are dealt face downwards to each player. The player on the left of the dealer leads to the first trick. Thereafter the player who wins a trick leads to the next. A player must follow suit to the card led, if he can, otherwise he may discard.

The object of the game is to avoid taking tricks that contain a Jack, and 1 point is lost for every Jack taken, with the exception of the Jack of Spades (Polignac) which costs the winner 2 points.

The usual method of scoring is to play a pre-arranged number of deals (that should be a multiple of four) and he who loses the least number of points is the winner.

It is a very simple game, but some skill is called for particularly in choosing the best card to lead after a trick has been won, correct discarding when unable to follow suit, and deciding whether or not to win a trick when the choice is available.

Slobberhannes

If we may judge by its name, Slobberhannes is either of Dutch or German origin. It is a very simple game that is played in exactly the same way as polignac (see above). The only difference is that a player loses 1 point if he wins the first trick, 1 point if he wins the last, 1 point if he wins the trick containing the Queen of Clubs, and a further 1 point (making 4 points in all) if he wins all three tricks.

Quinto

Quinto was invented by Angelo Lewis ('Professor Hoffman') as a partnership game for four players, two playing against the other two, that calls for a high degree of skill. It is played with the regular 52-card pack to which the Joker has been added.

The dealer places the five top cards of the pack face downwards on the table in front of him. It is known as the cachette. The remaining forty-eight cards are dealt twelve each, to the players. After looking at their cards, each player in turn, beginning with the player on the left of the dealer, has the opportunity of doubling the value of each trick, and of quadrupling it by redoubling a double made by an opponent of his side.

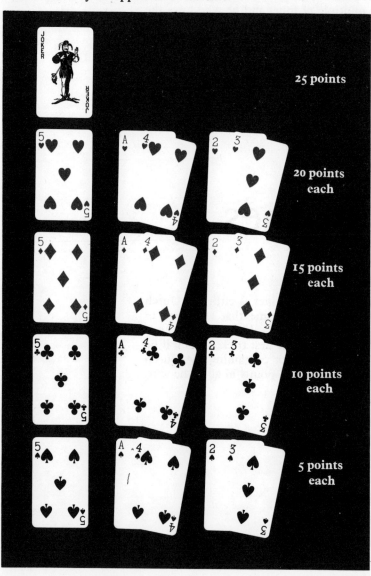

25 points

20 points each

15 points each

10 points each

5 points each

The player on the left of the dealer leads to the first trick. Thereafter the winner of a trick leads to the next. A player must follow suit if he can, if not he may either discard or trump.

Unlike at most games trumps are pre-arranged, and not dictated by a player or by facing a card. In descending order the suits rank: Hearts, Diamonds, Clubs, Spades, and a higher suit is trumps over a lower one. That is to say, every Spade may be trumped by any Club, Diamond and Heart, every Club by any Diamond and Heart, and so on. The highest trump, therefore, is the Ace of Hearts, the lowest the 2 of Clubs.

The Joker has no trick-taking value. It may be played by its holder when he chooses to do so, and irrespective of his obligation to follow suit. It is won by the player who takes the trick to which it has been played.

A side scores 5 points for every trick that it wins, and this is increased to 10 points if doubled and 20 points if redoubled. When all twelve tricks have been played, the player who has won the last trick takes the cachette and counts it as a trick won by his side in play.

The Joker is known as Quint Royal, and the 5 of every suit, and every pair of cards in a suit that total five are known as quints. The partnership that wins a quint in a trick scores for them as in the illustration.

Game is 250 points, and whereas the score for tricks is not recorded until the deal is played, the score for quints is recorded as the trick is won.

A rubber (best of three games) is played and the winner of it scores a bonus of 100 points.

In **THREE-HANDED QUINTO** two play in partnership against the other playing with a dummy hand. As this gives him a considerable advantage he begins with a handicap of 25 points that is credited to the opponents before a game begins.

The player who plays the dummy-hand deals first in every game. Thereafter the deal passes clockwise. When either opponent of the dummy-player deals, the dummy-player must look first at the hand from which he will have to make the opening lead, and must double or redouble before he looks at the other hand.

Rubbers are not played. Each game is a separate event; the three players taking the dummy-hand in turn.

Solo Whist

Solo Whist, more commonly called Solo, is one of the classical games for four players. It is played with the full pack of fifty-two cards. Thirteen cards are dealt to each player in three bundles of three cards each, and the last four cards singly. The dealer turns up the last card to indicate the trump suit.

Each player in turn, beginning with the player on the left of the dealer, must either pass or make a bid. The bids (declarations) are:

Proposal. The player who makes a Proposal asks for a partner with the object of making eight tricks in partnership with him against the other two players. In turn, any other player may Accept, and the two play as partners from the seats in which they are sitting. The declaration of Proposal and Acceptance is usually called Prop and Cop.

Solo is a declaration to win five tricks against the other three players.

Misère is a declaration to lose all thirteen tricks. The hand is played without a trump suit.

Abundance is a declaration to win nine tricks against the other three players; the declarer chooses his own trump suit. A player who wishes to play abundance with the turned-up suit as trumps may overcall with Royal Abundance, but the stake value of the bid remains unchanged.

Open Misère is a declaration to lose every trick, and after the first trick has been played with his cards exposed on the table in front of him. There is no trump suit.

Declared Abundance is a declaration to win all thirteen tricks with a trump suit of his own choice.

Every bid must be higher than the previous one, and with the exception of the player on the left of the dealer, who may accept a proposal after passing, no player may re-enter the bidding once he has passed. The bidding ends when a bid has been passed by the other three players.

If the final bid is Declared Abundance, the declarer leads to the first trick. Against any other declaration the opening lead is made by the player on the left of the dealer. The play follows the general principles of trick-taking games: a player must follow suit if he is able to, otherwise he may either discard or trump, and the winner of a trick leads to the next.

Stakes are scaled to the value of the bids:

Proposal and Acceptance = 2 units*	Abundance = 4 units
Solo = 2 units	Open Misère = 6 units
Misère = 3 units	Declared Abundance = 8 units

*Proposal and Acceptance does not carry equivalent stakes to Solo because they are paid by and received from two players, whereas in Solo (and higher declarations) they are paid to and received from three players.

Solo is a combination of whist and nap(oleon). It is a fairly simple game, and by far the simplest of the declarations is Proposal and Acceptance. As no player will propose without some strength in trumps, the partnership hardly ever fails to make eight tricks. It is a notoriously dull contract, therefore, and most modern players reject it.

The declaration of Solo is another that is fairly easy to win, though it must never be forgotten that the player has to compete against three. It is unwise to bid Solo without a good trump suit, and the dealer is in the ideal position to bid it with success because he plays last to the first trick: it gives him the best chance to win it and make an immediate attack on the trump suit.

Misère is not such an easy declaration as it may seem. A 5-card suit, unless it contains the 2, is likely to spell defeat. If a player holds **7 6 5 4 3** of a suit he will usually be defeated if another holds four of the suit including the 2.

Abundance should not be attempted without a very good trump suit, and Declared Abundance is best avoided by any except an experienced player.

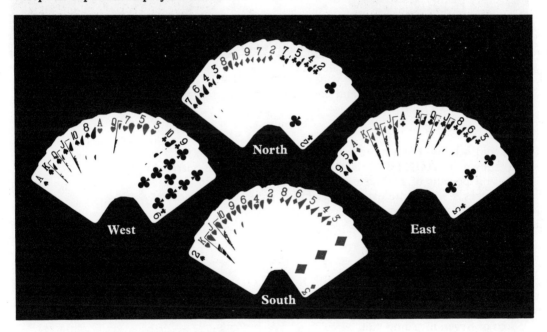

South deals and turns up the 2 of Spades.

West	North	East	South
Solo	Misère	Abundance	Open Misère
Pass	Pass	Pass	

West's Solo is the obviously correct bid. He cannot fail to win less than five tricks and it is too much to expect the Hearts to develop three tricks to make Abundance a good call.

North's Misère is optimistic. Had he been left to play it, the opening lead of a Heart would have broken him out of hand.

East's Abundance is a certainty with eleven tricks (and him needing only nine) for the taking of them.

South's Open Misère is not to be advised. As already pointed out a 5-card suit missing the 2 is a danger spot. As it happens it is the Heart suit that proves his downfall.

West leads the 10 of Clubs, and the play is:

West	North	East	South
10 ♣	7 ♣	J ♣	K ♥
9 ♣	5 ♣	A ♣	J ♥
A ♠	4 ♣	3 ♣	10 ♥
A ♥	8 ♥	A ♦	6 ♥

The position is down to:

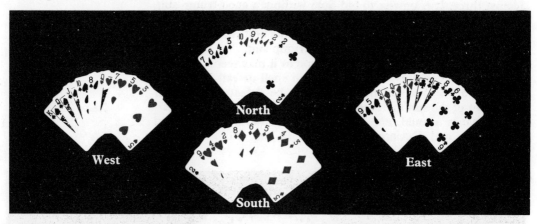

South is doomed because West wins the 7 ♥ and 5 ♥ (on which South plays the 4 ♥ and 2 ♥) and continues with the 3 ♥ which South must win with the 9 ♥.

As solo is limited to a mere handful of declarations, the variation known as **AUCTION SOLO** is much to be preferred, because it permits of a larger number of declarations and, therefore, makes a more interesting and skilful game. In ascending order the declarations are:

Proposal and Acceptance.
Solo of Five in own suit.
Solo of Five in trump suit.
Solo of Six in own suit.
Solo of Six in trump suit.
Solo of Seven in own suit.
Solo of Seven in trump suit.
Solo of Eight in own suit.
Solo of Eight in trump suit.
Misère.
Abundance of Nine in own suit.
Abundance of Nine in trump suit.
Abundance of Ten in own suit.
Abundance of Ten in trump suit.
Abundance of Eleven in own suit.
Abundance of Eleven in trump suit.
Abundance of Twelve in own suit.
Abundance of Twelve in trump suit.
Open Misère.
Declared Abundance with no trump suit (bidder has the lead).
Declared Abundance in the original trump suit (bidder does
    not have the lead).

Such, at least, are the declarations in the original version of the game, but modern players do not recognize all of them. Proposal and Acceptance are nearly always omitted, so also are Solo of Five in own suit, and Declared Abundance in the original trump suit.

Once the players have agreed on which declarations are admissible and which not, the game is played in the same way as the parent game.

Settlement is made in the following way:

Proposal and Acceptance
  For success: receive 6 units each plus 1 unit for each overtrick.
  For failure: pay 6 units each plus 1 unit for each undertrick.
Solo
  For success: receive 6 units from each player plus 3 units for each overtrick.
  For failure: pay 6 units to each player plus 3 units for each undertrick.
Misère
  For success: receive 12 units from each player.
  For failure: pay 12 units to each player.
Abundance
  For success: receive 18 units from each player plus 3 units for each overtrick.
  For failure: pay 18 units to each player plus 3 units for each undertrick.
Open Misère
  For success: receive 24 units from each player.
  For failure: pay 24 units to each player.
Declared Abundance
  For success: receive 36 units from each player.
  For failure: pay 36 units to each player.

The stake-values of Solo and Abundance are unchanged whether the contract is for five, six, seven or eight, or nine, ten, eleven or twelve tricks, overtricks and undertricks count from the number of tricks that are contracted for.

The method of scoring appears to encourage underbidding. In practice, however, it is not so and as first bidder a player would be well advised to declare his full strength at once, especially if his hand is worth no more than six tricks. With six tricks in a plain suit a player should bid it at once, no matter what his position at the table, but if the tricks are in the original trump suit it is reasonable to bid only a Solo of Five: he may get away with it, and, if not, a Solo of Six in the trump suit will overcall an opponent's Six in a plain suit. The penultimate player should make it a rule always to bid his hand to the limit; if he does not the last player will and then there may be no second chance.

Whist

Whist developed out of the sixteenth-century game of triumph. At first its practice was confined to the lower classes, but in 1718 it was taken up by a party of gentlemen, Lord Folkestone among them, who met at the famous Crown Coffee House, and they, with the help of Edmond Hoyle, introduced the game to fashionable society. At this time the game was known as whisk: soon after it was changed to whist in order to underline the silence in which it was proper to play the game.

During the eighteenth and nineteenth centuries it was by far the most popular card game of the English-speaking nations, but at the close of the nineteenth-century it lost much of its popularity due to the introduction of bridge (see page 125). It is, however, still extensively played.

In principle whist is a very simple game, played by four players, two playing in partnership against the other two. The partners sit facing each other. Thirteen cards are dealt singly to each person, and the dealer exposes the last card to denote the trump suit. He takes it into his hand after he has played to the first trick.

The player on the left of the dealer leads to the first trick. Thereafter the player who wins a trick leads to the next. A player must follow suit to the card led if he can, if not he may either discard or trump.

The object of the game is to win a rubber (best out of three games), and a game is won when one side has won 5 points. The first six tricks (the book) do not count for scoring: a side scores 1 point for each trick that it wins over six. The Ace, King, Queen and Jack of the trump suit are known as honours, and any side that is dealt all four of them scores 4 points, and any three 2 points. If, however, at the beginning of a deal a side has a score of 4 points it cannot score for honours.

The deal passes in a clockwise rotation.

Skill at whist is largely a matter of playing in close collaboration with one's partner, and estimating from the cards held and those that have been played, the most likely position of those that remain to be played.

To this end, there are a number of recognized plays which should be departed from only under special circumstances, to be learnt by experience. It is, for example, good tactics for second player to play low and third high; a player should not finesse against his partner; and if an opponent plays an honour it is usually profitable to play a higher honour on it.

A player who holds five or more trumps in his hand should make it a rule to lead one; and if a player fails to lead a trump and wishes his partner to do so, he calls for the lead of one by first playing an unnecessarily high card in a suit and following it with a low card in the same suit.

The lead is a good opportunity for a player to give his partner information about his hand, and the leads listed in the table on page 175 are standard practice and should be known to all players.

PLATE 15 *(opposite)* Children playing a game of old maid. The choice of card to take is a solemn affair

In plain suits:

Holding	1st Lead	2nd Lead
A K Q J	K	J
A K Q	K	Q
A K x and more	K	A
A K	A	K
K Q J x	K	J
K Q J x x	J	K
K Q J x x x and more	J	Q
A x x x and more	A	4th best of remainder
K Q x and more	K	4th best of remainder
A Q J	A	Q
A Q J x	A	Q
A Q J x x and more	A	J
K J 10 9	9	K (if A or Q falls)
Q J x	Q	
Q J x x and more	4th best	

In the trump suit:

Holding	1st Lead	2nd Lead
A K Q J	J	Q
A K Q	Q	K
A K x x x x x and more	K	A
A K x x x x	4th best	

PLATE 16 *(opposite, above)* A Pope Joan board at present in the Cheltenham Art Gallery and Museum
PLATE 17 *(opposite, below)* A game of fan tan in progress

Lacking any of these combinations the fourth highest of the longest suit should be led.

In the deal below the mechanics of the game are illustrated.

South deals and turns up the 4 of Spades to denote trumps.
West leads the 5 of Diamonds, and the play is:

West	North	East	South
5 ♦	J ♦	A ♦	3 ♦

West leads the fourth highest of his longest suit, commonly
called fourth-best. East wins with the **A ♦**. It would be finessing
against his partner if he played the **Q ♦**. In the event it makes no
difference, because East has no better play than to return his
partner's suit, and it is proper to lead the highest from an original
holding of three.

2 ♦	7 ♦	Q ♦	K ♦

South, therefore, wins the second trick, instead of the first,
with the **K ♦**.

West	North	East	South
5 ♣	3 ♣	A ♣	K ♣
8 ♣	6 ♣	7 ♣	Q ♣

East has no better lead than the **7 ♣**. He knows that South holds the **Q ♣**, because without it South would not have led the **K ♣** at the previous trick, but it offers a chance of trumping if West can take the lead early in the play.

10 ♦	5 ♠	4 ♦	9 ♦
6 ♠	A ♠	3 ♠	2 ♠
10 ♠	K ♠	8 ♠	4 ♠
J ♣	9 ♣	2 ♥	2 ♣

North has no better lead than the **9 ♣**.

8 ♦	3 ♥	J ♠	4 ♣
6 ♦	7 ♠	Q ♠	9 ♠

East pulls the remaining trumps.

K ♥	A ♥	J ♥	Q ♥

The end position has come down to:

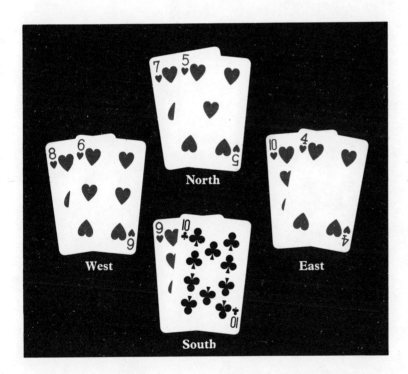

It is North's lead. North and South have won six tricks, East and West five tricks. North, therefore, leads the **5 ♥**. If East wins with the **10 ♥** his side will win the odd trick as West will win the last trick with the **8 ♥**. North's only hope is that East will make the mistake of playing the **4 ♥**, because then South will win with the **9 ♥** and the last trick with the **10 ♣**.

6 ♥	5 ♥	10 ♥	9 ♥

East makes no mistake.

8 ♥	7 ♥	4 ♥	10 ♣

East and West, therefore, have won the odd trick and score 1 point. There is no score for honours as both sides held two.

Games for Five or more players

Blackout

Blackout, or Oh Well!, may be played by any number from three to seven, but is considered best as a game for five.

The full 52-card pack is used, but in order that every player starts with the same number of cards, if three players take part in the game a card is removed from the pack, if five two cards, if six four cards, and if seven three cards. These cards should not be seen by the players, and, after playing a deal, the cards are returned to the pack, which is then shuffled and fresh cards removed before the next deal.

The cards are dealt face downwards to the players, and the last card is turned face upwards to denote the trump suit.

The player on the left of the dealer announces how many tricks he thinks he will win; if he thinks that he will not be able to take a trick he announces 'None'. The player on his left then announces how many tricks he thinks he will be able to win, and so on, round the table in a clockwise direction. These declarations should be recorded by a scorer (appointed before the game begins) who will also be held responsible for recording the scores of the players at the end of each deal.

The player on the left of the dealer leads to the first trick. A player must follow suit to the card led if he can, otherwise he may either discard or trump. The winner of a trick leads to the next.

When the cards have been played out, the tricks won by the players are counted, and any player who has made the exact number of tricks that he has contracted to win scores a bonus of 10 points, and 1 point for every trick won. A player who has declared 'None' scores a bonus of 10 points if he has not won a trick. Any player who scores more or less tricks than he contracted for does not score the bonus of 10 points but only 1 point for every trick that he has won.

The deal passes round the table clockwise, and the game ends when one of the players reaches a total of 100 points.

At any time during the play a player has a right to ask how many tricks a player has announced he will win and how many he has already won; and it is a rule of honour that if at any time a player realises that he cannot possibly fulfil his declaration he must not communicate the fact to the other players.

Skill is shown largely by judging from their bids and plays what cards the other players hold. Nothing is to be gained by announcing 'None' with the intention of scoring the bonus of 10 points by not winning a trick: the opponents will combine to force you to win one. In the same way, if a player has made the number of tricks he has declared, the opponents will do their best to force him to win another and so deprive him of the 10-points bonus.

Brag

Brag is almost certainly the ancestor of poker (see page 189) and itself probably derived from the Spanish game of primero, the popular card game of Tudor England and, so far as we can trace, the first card game to be played scientifically in this country.

The game is played with the full 52-card pack, and by any number of players from five to eight. The general principle of the game is quite simple. The players stake on the respective merits of their cards, and the best hand is determined by certain arbitrary rules. Bluffing is an important feature of the game. The Ace of Diamonds, Jack of Clubs and 9 of Diamonds are known as braggers, and rank as Jokers or wild cards.

In **SINGLE-STAKE BRAG** the dealer puts up a stake to the agreed limit, and deals three cards face downwards to each player. In turn, beginning with the player on the left of the dealer, each player must either drop out of the game for the round in progress, or put up a stake at least equal to that of the dealer's. If he chooses he may raise the stake, in which event, any player coming into the

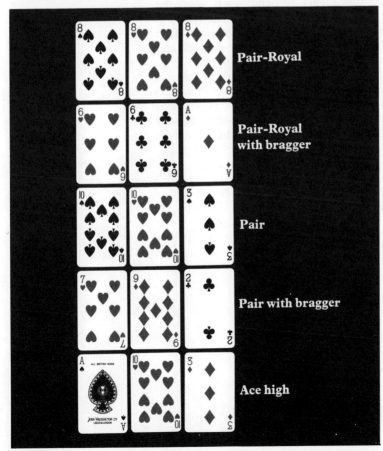

Pair-Royal

Pair-Royal with bragger

Pair

Pair with bragger

Ace high

The classes of brag hands, the highest at the top

game, or already in the game, must raise his bet to as much as the highest individual stake, or drop out of the game and lose what he has already staked. If no-one meets the dealer's stake he withdraws it, and receives an agreed amount from the other players. The deal then passes to the next player.

Unlike at poker, there is no discarding and drawing more cards. When all those who wish to play have raised their bets to an equal amount, the cards are shown and the player with the best hand collects all the stakes.

Flushes and sequences are of no value. The best hand is a Pair-Royal; it consists of three cards of equal rank (the Aces high the 2s low) and a hand of three natural cards takes precedence over one with braggers. The next best hand is a Pair, with a preference for a natural pair over one with a bragger, and if two players have equal pairs the one with the higher third card wins. If no player holds either a Pair-Royal or a Pair, the player with the highest single card wins and if two players hold exactly equal hands the winner is he who was first to stake.

In **THREE-STAKE BRAG** the game begins by each player putting up three separate stakes; the dealer then deals two cards face downwards and one card face upwards to each player.

The first stake is won by the player who is dealt the highest face-upwards card. For this round of the game the braggers take their normal position in the pack, and if two or more players are dealt cards of equal rank, precedence is determined as in the single-stake game.

The hand is next played as in single-stake, and the winner takes the second stake. If no-one bets, the hands are exposed and the highest hand wins.

Finally, the players expose their cards and the third stake is won by the player whose cards most nearly total 31 (over or under) the Aces counting 11, the court cards 10 each and the other cards at their pip values. A player whose hand totals less than 31 may draw a card from the remainder of the pack, but if his total then exceeds 31 he automatically loses the game.

Coon Can

In the U.S.A. Coon Can is known as Double Rum. It is no bad name for it because it is a variation of rummy (see page 197) played with two packs of cards shuffled together with two Jokers.

The game may be played by any number of players up to eight; each plays for himself.

Ten cards are dealt face downwards to each player. The rest of the pack (the stock) is placed face downwards in the centre of the table, and the top card of it is turned face upwards and placed alongside it to start the discard pile.

The object of the game is to get rid of all the cards held, by melding them face upwards on the table, either in sets of three or more of the same rank, or in sequences of three or more of the same suit, the Ace either high or low but not round-the-corner. A Joker may be used to represent any card that the holder chooses.

Each player, beginning with the one on the left of the dealer, plays in turn. He is under no obligation to meld, but he must take into his hand either the top card of the stock or the top card of the discard pile, and discard a card to reduce his hand to ten cards. If he chooses to meld he must do so between drawing a card and discarding one, and as well as melding, at the same time, he may add cards to melds that he has already made, and to those of his opponents.

A Joker may be moved from one end of a meld to the other, provided the player has the natural card to replace it. If, for example, a sequence is: **6 ♠ 7 ♠ 8 ♠ Joker**, a player who holds a **9 ♠** may play it in room of the Joker and transfer the Joker to represent the **5 ♠**. Once moved, however, a Joker cannot be moved a second time and a player who holds a **5 ♠** cannot play it in room of the Joker and place the Joker elsewhere. Nor can a Joker be moved if it is in the interior of a sequence, as in **4 ♠ 5 ♠ 6 ♠ Joker 8 ♠**. The Joker cannot be replaced by a **7 ♠**. When a Joker cannot be moved it is customary to place it crosswise, as a reminder to the other players.

The game is won by the player who is first to meld all his cards. The remaining players pay him the same number of units as the pip value of the unmelded cards left in their hands – a Joker counting 15, an Ace 11, the court cards 10 each, and all other cards their pip values.

Rarely it happens that the stock will be exhausted before the game has been won. In this event the game continues and the players draw cards from the discard pile, discarding a different card to that drawn. If this proves insufficient to finish the game, the pip values of the hands are counted and placed into a pool to be scored by the winner of the next hand.

Loo

The modern player may be forgiven if he mistakes the meaning of the name which has been attached to this game. In fact it is a truncation of the now obsolete lanterloo, from the French *lanturlu* a word best translated by our succint, if vulgar, fiddle-sticks.

There are several variations of the game, but all are played with the full 52-card pack and are suitable for any reasonable number of players, though six or seven, each playing for himself, is best.

In **THREE-CARD LOO** the first player to deal puts into a pool an agreed number of units. It may be any number, but it must be one that is divisible by three. Three cards are then dealt, one card at a time, to each player, and to an extra hand that is known as Miss. The top card of the remainder of the pack is turned up to denote the trump suit.

The dealer offers the player on his immediate left the choice of refusing to play, playing with the cards dealt to him, or exchanging his cards for Miss and playing with those. In turn, each player is offered the same choice, though, of course, once a player has chosen to exchange his hand for Miss, a subsequent player is reduced to choosing between playing with the cards dealt to him or not playing the hand. Once a player has made a decision he must stand by it, and if he has chosen not to play he throws his cards face downwards towards the centre of the table.

The player who first chose to play leads to the first trick. Thereafter the player who wins a trick leads to the next. The play is governed by the following rules:

1. A player must follow suit if he can, and must head the trick if he can.
2. If a player cannot follow suit he must trump if he can, and if the trick has already been trumped he must overtrump if he can.
3. If the player on lead holds the Ace of trumps (or the King if the Ace has been turned up) he must lead it.
4. If the player on lead holds two or more trumps he must lead one of them, and if there are only two players in the game he must lead the highest.

A player who fails to comply with any of these rules, when able to do so, is deemed to have revoked; the pool is divided among the non-offenders, and the offender pays the full amount back to the pool.

When the hand has been played those who have won tricks divide the pool between them: one-third of the amount in it to the winner of each trick.

Those who have not won a trick are looed, and must put into the pool as many units as there were in it at the beginning of the deal. Unlimited loo, however, can come very expensive, and in practice it is essential for the players to agree upon limiting the losses of looed players.

If no player is looed, the next dealer replenishes the pool as at the beginning of the game.

If every player refuses to play, the dealer takes the entire pool and the next dealer replenishes it.

If only one player chooses to play the dealer must come into the game against him, but if he holds a weak hand, he may protect himself against loss by announcing that he will play for the pool. In this event he is not looed if he fails to win a trick, and, in return for the concession, he leaves in the pool any amount to which he may be entitled by reason of his having won tricks.

FIVE-CARD LOO is a variation of the parent game that differs from it in the following five particulars:

1. Every player is dealt five cards, and as there are five tricks to be won the number of units paid into the pool must be divisible by five.
2. There is no Miss.
3. A player may exchange cards by drawing them from the stock. He may exchange any number of cards that he chooses, and once he has exchanged a card he must enter the game.
4. The highest card in the pack is the Jack of Clubs. It is known as Pam ('Even mighty Pam that kings and queens o'erthrew, And mowed down armies in the fights of Lu.*) It ranks as a trump and takes precedence even over the Ace; if, however, a player leads the Ace of trumps and announces 'Pam be civil' the holder of Pam is debarred from playing it to the trick.
5. If a player holds five cards of a suit, or four cards of a suit and Pam, he is said to hold a flush and must expose his hand at once. He wins the pool and all the other players, except those who may hold flushes or Pam, are looed. If two or more players hold flushes, one in the trump suit wins over one in a plain suit, and as between two or more in a plain suit, the one with the highest card wins. If two or more in plain suits are exactly equal the pool is divided.

IRISH LOO is a combination of the three-card and five-card games, and is considered by competent players to be the best of the several variations.

Every player is dealt three cards, there is no Pam and no Miss, but a player is allowed to exchange cards by drawing from the stock. The game is played in the same way as the parent game, with the added novelty that if Clubs are trumps everyone must enter the game. It is known as Club Law and makes it imperative that the penalty for being looed must be limited to a reasonable amount.

Loo, in all its variations, is so bound up by hard and fast rules of play, already mentioned, that there is very little to be said about the play of the cards. At best one can only say that the most successful player is not he who knows how to play, but he who knows when to elect and when to refuse to play.

The most important point to note is that, apart from Pam at 5-card loo, there are only three certain tricks, namely the Ace, the King-Queen combination and the Queen-Jack-10 combination of

---

*Alexander Pope, *The Rape of the Lock*, Canto iii, Lines 61 and 62.

the trump suit. Usually the player who holds the **Q J 9** of trumps will win a trick, but it is by no means certain that he will, and he may be looed if he is in an unfavourable position at the table. It is the same if a player holds **K 3** of the trump suit. He will certainly win a trick if the suit is led and he is the last to play, but if he is not, he may not win a trick, because if the **4** is played he is compelled to play the King and a later player may win with the Ace. It leaves him only with the remote possibility of winning a trick with the lone **3** of trumps.

Perhaps in practice the picture is not so depressing as it appears in theory, because, even if there are seven players in the game, a large number of cards remain in the stock. Some of the high cards, therefore, may not be active and a combination such as **J 10 9** of trumps, or even **J 10** and a card in a plain suit, may win a trick.

In general a player is advised not to be too cautious about electing to play if he holds a weak hand, but he is advised to be careful. In practice he should keep a close watch on the number of units in the pool and weigh up the possible loss against the possible gain. If, for example, there are 15 units in the pool at 5-card loo and the cost of being looed is 10 units it is not worth while entering the play with a weak hand because, look at it which way you like, the cost of being looed is three times more than the possible gain that will accrue by winning one trick. It is not a good bet.

Napoleon

Napoleon, usually called Nap, is one of the simplest of all card games. It is played with the full pack of fifty-two cards, by any number of players up to six, each playing for himself.

Each player is dealt five cards, and, beginning with the player on the left of the dealer, every player in turn must either pass or declare to win a specified number of tricks in the ascending order: Two, Three, Four and Nap (a declaration to win all five tricks).

The player who has contracted to win most tricks leads to the first trick and the card that he leads determines the trump suit. Play follows the usual routine of trick-taking games: a player must follow suit if he can, otherwise he may discard or trump, and the player who wins a trick leads to the next.

Stakes are paid only on the number of tricks contracted for. Those won above, or lost below, the number contracted for are ignored. The usual method of settlement is by means of a level-money transaction:

Declaration	Declarer wins	Declarer loses
Two	2 units	2 units
Three	3 units	3 units
Four	4 units	4 units
Nap	10 units	5 units

Payment is made to, and received from, all players at the table.

Nap(oleon) is such an elementary game that in some circles interest is added to it by introducing a number of extraordinary declarations:

Misery is a declaration to lose every trick. It ranks between the declarations on Three and Four, and though normally it is played without a trump suit, some play it with a trump suit, determined as in the parent game by the opening lead. It pays and wins 3 units.

Wellington is a declaration to win all five tricks at double stakes. It cannot be declared, however, except over a declaration of Nap.

Blücher is a declaration to win all five tricks at triple stakes. It cannot be declared, however, except over a declaration of Wellington.

Peep Nap sanctions the player who has declared Nap (or Wellington or Blücher if these declarations are permitted) to exchange the top card of the pack for a card in his own hand.

Purchase Nap sanctions each player before declaring to exchange any number of cards in his hand for fresh cards, by paying into a pool 1 unit for every card exchanged. The pool is carried forward from deal to deal and taken by the first player to win Nap (or Wellington or Blücher if these declarations are permitted).

SEVEN-CARD NAPOLEON is a variation of the parent game
in which seven cards are dealt to each player, and a player cannot
contract to win less than three tricks. There is no Wellington and
no Blücher. Misery is optional and, if permitted, ranks between
Nap and Six.

Apart from these amendments, the game is played in the same
way as the parent game.

Settlement is made as follows:

Declaration	Declarer wins	Declarer loses
Three	3 units	3 units
Four	4 units	4 units
Nap (five tricks)	10 units	5 units
Misery (if played)	10 units	5 units
Six	18 units	9 units
Seven	28 units	14 units

Payment is made to, and received from, all players at the table

Poker

Poker is not a difficult game to learn, but by no means an easy one to play well because skill at the game is born only of experience coupled with some knowledge of arithmetic. Fundamentally, poker is a game of calculating chances.

The parent game, commonly called straight poker, but more correctly straight draw poker, is played with the 52-card pack by any reasonable number of players: five, six or seven is considered the ideal number.

Each player is dealt five cards face downwards, and the object of the game is to make the best hand by an exchange of cards, and then bet on it against the other players.

The cards rank in the order from Ace high to 2 low, suits are equal and in ascending order the nine classes of poker hands, together with the approximate odds against their being dealt to a player, are:

Highest Card: any five odd cards. Evens.
One Pair: two cards of the same rank and three odd cards. 15 to 11.
Two pairs: two cards of the same rank, two other cards of the same rank and an odd card. 20 to 1.
Threes: three cards of the same rank and two odd cards. 46 to 1.
Straight: any five cards in sequence, not of the same suit; An Ace may be either high or low. 254 to 1.
Flush: any five cards of the same suit. 508 to 1.
Full House: three cards of the same rank and two other cards of the same rank. 693 to 1.
Fours: four cards of the same rank and an odd card. 4,164 to 1.
Straight Flush: a sequence of five cards all of the same suit: an Ace may be either high or low. 64,973 to 1.

Examples of each hand are illustrated. They are valued on the highest combination, and if the combination of two or more players is equal, by the highest odd card. In the event of two or more players holding exactly equal hands the stakes are divided.

The player on the left of the dealer begins the game by putting up an agreed amount, known as the ante. For convenience we will assume that it is 1 chip. The player on his left then puts up a straddle of 2 chips.*

The dealer now deals, face downwards, to each player five cards. After looking at his cards, the player on the left of the straddle has the option of playing or not. If he decides not to play he throws his cards face downwards towards the centre of the table, and takes no further interest in the deal in progress. If he decides to play he puts up 4 chips. The player on his left now has the choice of

---

* Throughout the game every player puts his chips on the table in front of him.

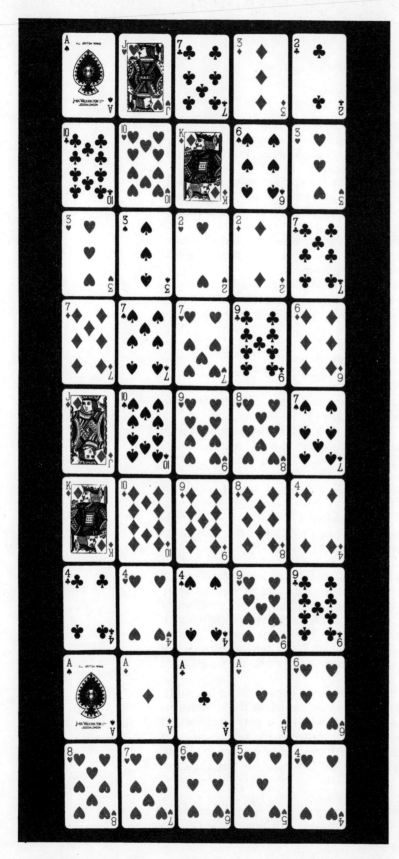

The classes of poker hand, the highest at the bottom. The numbers of possible ways in which each hand can be made up are as follows:

highest card: 1,302,540
one pair: 1,098,240
two pairs: 123,552
three: 54,912
straight: 10,200
flush: 5,108
full house: 3,744
four: 624
straight flush: 40

PLATE 18 (opposite) A baccarat layout in a casino, with a dealing shoe in the foreground. The enticing atmosphere is well conveyed

throwing in his hand, coming into the game for 4 chips, or doubling (*i.e.* coming into the game for 8 chips). In the same way, in turn, every player has the choice of throwing in his hand, coming into the game, for the same stake as the previous player, or raising the stakes until the agreed maximum is reached.

When staking reaches the ante and straddle, they can either throw in their hands and sacrifice what they have already put up, or come into the game by raising their stakes to the appropriate amount.

If no player comes into the game, the straddle recovers his 2 chips and takes the 1 chip put up by the ante.

Staking continues for some little time, because if a player has come into the game and a subsequent player has doubled, it is open to those who have already staked to increase their stakes, and this progressive staking continues until no-one increases the stakes or the agreed limit is reached.

When all have staked, those left in the game have the chance to improve their hands by exchanging cards. The dealer ignores those who have already thrown in their hands, but gives all the other players in turn as many cards as they wish after they have discarded those cards that they do not wish to retain. A player may discard any number of his cards, but no experienced player would remain in the game to exchange four cards, and only one who has taken leave of his senses will do so to exchange all five cards. Most players will exchange one, two, or three cards.

When cards have been exchanged, the player who was first to come in begins the betting. Either he throws in his hand (sacrificing the stake he has already made to come in) checks (signifies his intention to remain in the game without increasing his stake) or raises (increases his stake to any amount up to the agreed limit).

If he checks, all the players who follow him have, in their turn, the same choice. If no-one raises those left in the game show their cards and the player with the best hand takes all that has been staked. If a player raises, the subsequent players, in turn, have the option of throwing in their hands, putting up sufficient chips to meet the raise, or raise still further.

In this way the betting continues until the final bet is either called or not. If the final bet is called, the players left in the game show their cards and the player with the best hand wins all that has been staked: if the final bet is not called, the player whose bet has not been called wins all that has been staked with no need to show his hand.

Poker falls naturally into two parts: the staking and the betting. The staking is the easier part of the game because it is open to a precise arithmetical analysis. We may suppose that a player is dealt:

10 ♠ 6 ♠ 5 ♠ 2 ♠ 9 ♥

Since a pair of 10s is of small value, the player's aim must be to discard the 9 of Hearts hoping to draw a Spade to fill the flush.

There are 47 cards from which to draw, and of them only 9 are Spades, the other 38 are non-Spades. It follows, therefore, that the odds against drawing a Spade are 38 to 9, or approximately $4\frac{1}{4}$ to 1. If three players have come into the game with 4 chips each, making 15 chips on the table with the ante and straddle, it is not worth while playing because it costs 4 chips to come in so that the table is offering odds of 15 to 4 ($3\frac{3}{4}$ to 1) and the chance of improving is $4\frac{1}{4}$ to 1. If, however, four players have come in it will be just worth while coming into the game, because now there will be 19 chips on the table so that the table is offering odds of $4\frac{3}{4}$ to 1, which is better than the odds against improving.

Poker players should study very carefully the mathematical chances, because the whole theory of staking may be summed up by asking oneself two questions: What are the chances of improving my hand? What odds are the table laying me? Then, if the answer to the first question is greater than to the second the player should come in, if it is not he should throw in his hand.

The betting is the more difficult part of the game because it is largely psychology. At the same time, a player has to be gifted with the quality that we call judgement because his betting must be dictated by the manner in which the other players are betting, and how they, on their part, will interpret his betting. Particular note should be taken of the number of cards drawn by each of the other players and deductions drawn from the information gained. The subsequent betting should go a long way towards confirming whether the deductions are correct or not, and whether the player has improved on the draw.

A good poker player is inscrutable and unpredictable, because he varies his game to make the most with his good hands and lose the least with his bad ones. He profits by the advice of Saint Matthew—'let not thy left hand know what thy right hand doeth'—and he is always imperturbable, because there is no future in gloating over a win and wailing over a loss. If he thinks that he holds the best hand he bets on it boldly: if he thinks that he is beaten he throws in his cards and cuts his losses.

Pot-Deals, commonly called Pots, are widely played, and are an important feature of all variations of the game. When a pot is played there is no ante and no straddle; instead every player contributes an agreed amount to a pot, or pool, that is independent of the staking and betting. The player on the immediate left of the dealer has first decision whether to open the game by staking or not. If he does not open, the option passes to the player on his left, and so on.

The essence of a pot is that a player is debarred from opening the game, by putting up a stake, unless his hand qualifies him to do so by a pre-arranged standard. If no player opens, the deal passes, and the players sweeten the pot, by adding to it, for the next deal. If the pot is opened, other players may come in even if their hands are below standard, and he who wins the deal also wins the amount in the pot as well as all the stakes put up by the other players. The player who opened the game must show that his hand qualified for opening.

In a *Jackpot* a player must have a pair of Jacks, or better, to qualify for opening.

In a *Progressive Jackpot*, if no-one opens the first deal, the second deal is a Queenpot, and if no-one opens it the next is a King-pot, and so on. Some stop at Acepots, others continue to two pairs before beginning again at a Jackpot if no-one has opened the game.

In a *Freak Pot*, sometimes called Deuces Wild, all the 2s are wild cards and may be used to represent any cards that the holder chooses. Fives (five cards of the same rank) is now a possible hand, and it is classed above a straight flush, but is beaten if the straight flush is headed by an Ace.

In a *Double Pot*, or Legs, any type of pot is chosen, but a player must win it twice before he may take his winnings.

WILD WIDOW is a variation of the parent game, but, after four cards have been dealt to each player, a card is turned face upwards in the centre of the table and is left there for the duration of the deal. The dealer then gives each player one more card, and the game is played with the three other cards of the same rank as the exposed card wild.

In **SPIT IN THE OCEAN** only four cards are dealt to each player. A card is then dealt face upwards in the centre of the table. Each player considers this card as the fifth card of his hand. It is a wild card, as also are the other three cards of the same rank.

STUD POKER is a variation of the parent game the main feature of which is that some of the cards are dealt face upwards and some face downwards. There are several ways of playing the game.

In *Five-card Stud* there is no ante unless agreed on. The dealer gives each player a card face downwards (it is known as the hole card) and then a card face upwards. The deal is then interrupted for a betting interval. After the betting interval the dealer gives each active player another three cards face upwards, and after each there is a betting interval. If two or more players remain in the game after the last betting interval, they turn up their hole cards and the player with the best hand wins.

Each betting interval begins with the player who holds the best combination of cards exposed, and if two or more players have equal combination the one nearest to the dealer's left bets first. At the first betting interval the player who opens must make a bet; at subsequent intervals he may check. Any player who drops out of the game must turn his exposed cards face downwards.

Seven-card Stud, sometimes called Down the River, or Peek Poker, is played in the same way as five-card stud, except that the dealer first deals to each player two cards face downwards and one card face upwards. There is a betting interval, and, after this, the active players are dealt three cards face upwards and one face downwards, with the deal interrupted for a betting interval after each round of dealing. At the showdown, a player exposes his hole cards and selects five of his seven cards to form his hand.

WHISKEY POKER is so called because it was originally played in the American lumber camps to decide who should pay for the drinks.

Every player contributes an agreed amount to a pool. The dealer deals an extra hand (widow) to the centre of the table, immediately before dealing cards to himself. The player on the left of the dealer, after looking at his cards, may either exchange his hand for the widow, pass (in which case the option of taking the widow passes to his left-hand neighbour) or indicates, by knocking the table, that he will play with the cards dealt to him.

If the player on the left of the dealer (or any subsequent player) takes the widow, he puts his own cards face upwards on the table as a new widow. The player on his left may now either take the whole of the exposed widow in exchange for his own hand, take one or more cards from it in exchange for cards in his hand, or knock. A player, however, cannot draw cards from the widow and knock at the same turn, and the option to exchange the widow or cards with it, continues until a player knocks. As soon as a player does so, the remaining players have one turn each to exchange their hands or cards for it. After the player on the right of the knocker has had his turn, the players expose their cards and the best hand wins the pot.

If no-one takes the widow before it is the turn of the dealer, he must either take the widow or turn it face upwards on the table. Even if he decides to knock, without making an exchange, he must still turn up the widow.

In **KNOCK POKER** every player puts up an ante. The dealer gives every player five cards, as in the parent game, and the rest of the pack (the stock) is placed face downwards in the centre of the table. The player on the left of the dealer draws the top card of the stock and discards a card from his hand. Thereafter each player in turn draws either the top card of the stock or the top card of the discard pile, and discards a card from his hand.

At any time after drawing a card and before discarding one, a player may knock the table. He then discards a card from his hand. The other players have one more turn each to draw and discard a card, or drop out of the game by paying the knocker the amount of the ante. After the player on the right of the knocker has drawn and discarded, or dropped out of the game, all players remaining in the game show their cards and settlement is made as follows:

1. If the knocker has the best hand, all who are in the game pay him twice the ante.
2. If the knocker and one or more other players have equal hands they divide the winnings except for the amount paid to the knocker by those who dropped out of the game.
3. If the knocker does not have the best hand he pays twice the ante to every player remaining in the game, and the player with the best hand wins the antes.

HIGH-LOW POKER. Any variation of poker may be played high-low. As a rule the hand is played as a pot. The player plays his hand for either high or low, but does not have to announce which until the last card is dealt. The highest and the lowest hands divide the pot between them. An Ace is always high and cannot be counted as a low card except as part of a sequence in the high hand.

In **STRIP POKER** the dealer deals five cards, face downwards, to each player. There is no ante and no straddle. After an exchange of cards (as in the parent game) the players expose their cards and the one with the worst poker hand pays the table by removing an article of clothing.

The game, with all its voluptuous prospects, is said to be at its best in mixed company during a heat wave!

Rummy

Rummy, the name is frequently truncated to Rum, is one of the most popular of all card games. It is played with the full 52-card pack, and is suitable for any number of players up to five or six, each playing for himself. More than six players should prefer coon can (see page 183) or the variation known as continental rummy.

Ten cards are dealt to each player if only two play; seven cards if three or four play; and six cards if five or six play. The rest of the pack (the stock) is placed face downwards in the centre of the table, and the top card of it is turned face upwards and laid alongside it to start the discard pile.

Each player in turn, beginning with the one on the left of the dealer, must take into his hand either the top card of the stock or the top card of the discard pile, and discard a card from his hand, but if he has drawn the top card of the discard pile he must not discard it in the same turn.

The object of the game is to make sets of three or more cards of the same rank, or sequences of three or more cards of the same suit (the Ace being low) and declare them by exposing them on the table, after drawing a card from the stock or discard pile and before discarding a card from the hand. At the same time a player may add one or more proper cards to sequences and sets already declared either by himself or the other players.

If the stock is exhausted before any player declares all his hand, the discard pile is turned face downwards and becomes the stock.

The player who is first to declare all his cards wins the hand, and the other players pay him for every court card left in their hands 10 points each, for every Ace 1 point, and for every other card its pip value. If a player declares all his cards in one turn he scores rummy and is paid double.

Rummy is a very simple game that has lent itself to a number of improvements.

In **BOATHOUSE RUMMY** a player may draw the top card of the stock; or he may draw the top card of the discard pile and then either the top card of the stock or the next card of the discard pile. He may, however, discard only one card from his hand.

In a sequence the Ace may be either high, low, or round the corner.

The play does not come to an end until a player can declare his entire hand in one turn.

A losing player pays only for the unmatched cards in his hand, but Aces are paid for at 11 points each.

CONTINENTAL RUMMY is a variation of the parent game that is suitable for any number of players up to twelve. If two to five play two packs with two Jokers are used; if six to eight play three packs with three Jokers are used; and if nine to twelve play four packs with four Jokers are used.

Each player receives fifteen cards. A player may not declare until all fifteen of his cards are melded either in five 3-card sequences, or in three 4-card sequences and one 3-card sequence, or in one 5-card, one 4-card and two 3-card sequences. Sets of three or more cards of the same rank are of no value. A Joker may be used to represent any card. The Ace may be high or low, but not round the corner.

There are many ways of scoring, but generally the winner collects from all the other players 1 unit from each for winning, and 2 units from each for every Joker in his hand.

GAMBLER'S RUMMY is so called because it is the variation of the parent game that is most frequently played for high stakes.

Only four players take part and each is dealt seven cards. The Ace is low and, as in the parent game, counts only 1 point in the settlement. A player is not allowed to declare all his hand in one turn. He must declare it in at least two turns, but he is not debarred from going out second turn even if on his previous turn he played off only one card on another player's declaration.

The stock is gone through only once. When it is exhausted the players must draw the top card of the discard pile, and the game ends when a player refuses it.

KNOCK RUMMY, or Poker Rum, is played in the same way as the parent game, but a player does not declare his sequences and sets by exposing them on the table. Instead, after drawing a card, he knocks on the table, and then discards. Play comes to an end. The players separate their matched cards from their un-matched ones, and each announces the count of his unmatched cards, as reckoned in the parent game. The player with the lowest count wins the difference in counts from all the other players. If a player ties with the knocker for the lowest count he wins over the knocker. If the knocker does not have the lowest count he pays a penalty of an extra 10 points to the player with the lowest count. If the knocker goes rummy (has all his cards matched when he knocks) and wins, he receives an extra 25 points from all the other players.

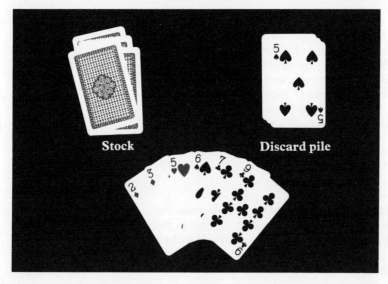

Stock   Discard pile

The player should take the 5 ♠ and discard 9 ♣, as 5 ♠ offers alternative chances of melding: with either 5 ♥ or 6 ♠

Scotch Whist

Scotch Whist, sometimes called Catch the Ten because one of the objects of the game is to win the trick that contains the 10 of the trump suit, is played with a pack of thirty-six cards. The 2s, 3s, 4s, and 5s are removed from the standard pack. The cards rank from Ace (high) to 6 (low) with the exception that the Jack of the trump suit is promoted above the Ace.

The game is suitable for any number of players from two to eight, but, as every player must begin with the same number of cards, if five or seven players take part the 6 of Spades is removed from the pack, and if eight take part all four 6s are. If two, three, five or seven play, each plays for himself. If four, six or eight play they may either play each for himself, or form into partnerships.

Dealing varies with the number of players taking part in the game. If two play each receives eighteen cards that are dealt in three separate hands of six cards each, to be played independently; if three play each receives twelve cards that are dealt in two separate hands of six cards each, to be played independently; if four or more play the cards are dealt in the normal clockwise rotation. In every case the dealer turns up the last card to indicate the trump suit.

The player on the left of the dealer leads to the first trick. Thereafter the player who wins a trick leads to the next. Play follows the usual routine of trick-taking games: a player must follow suit, if he can, to the suit led, if he cannot he may either trump the trick or discard on it.

The object of the game is to win tricks containing the five top trump cards, and the player, or partnership, that does so scores 11 points for the Jack, 4 points for the Ace, 3 points for the King, 2 points for the Queen, and 10 points for the Ten. Over and above this, each player, or partnership, counts the number of cards taken in tricks, and scores 1 point for every card more than the number originally dealt to him, or it.

The game ends when a player, or partnership, has reached an agreed total, usually 41 points.

It stands out that a player must direct his play towards winning tricks that contain the top cards of the trump suit, particularly the trick that contains the 10, since the Jack can only go to the player to whom it has been dealt, and usually the luck of the deal determines who will win the tricks that contain the Ace, King and Queen.

In a partnership game the player who has been dealt the 10, either singleton or doubleton, would be well advised to lead it. It gives a good score if his partner is able to win with the Jack; if an opponent wins the trick the partnership must hope to recover by aiming to win as many tricks as possible. If the game is being played all against all, the player who has been dealt the 10 should try and get rid of all the cards in his shortest suit, so that he can win the 10 by trumping with it.

Spoil Five

Spoil Five, sometimes called Forty-five, is an excellent game for any reasonable number of players, but is best for five or six, as it calls for some show of skill.

It is played with the full pack of fifty-two cards, but that it is rarely, if ever, played outside its native Ireland may be ascribed to the eccentric order of the cards. The 5 of the trump suit is always the highest trump, the Jack of the trump suit is the second highest, and the Ace of Hearts the third highest. Thereafter, if a black suit is trumps the cards rank in the order **A K Q 2 3 4 6 7 8 9 10** and if a red suit is trumps in the order **A** (if Diamonds are trumps) **K Q 10 9 8 7 6 4 3 2**. In plain suits, the black suits rank in the order **K Q J A 2 3 4 5 6 7 8 9 10**; the red suits in the order **K Q J 10 9 8 7 6 5 4 3 2 A** (except in Hearts). It is concisely expressed as 'highest in red; lowest in black', but even with this help it is all rather involved.

Five cards are dealt to each player either in bundles of two then three, or three then two. The next card is exposed to determine the trump suit. A pool is formed to which every player contributes an agreed amount, and it is usual to fix a maximum and, after the first deal, only the player whose turn it is to deal contributes to the pool.

The object of the game is to win three tricks, and, at the same time, prevent another player from winning them.

The player who wins three tricks takes the pool; and if no-one wins three tricks (a spoil) the deal passes to the next player. When a player has won three tricks the hand ends and the deal passes, unless the player who has won them declares 'Jinx'. It is an undertaking to win the remaining two tricks. Play then continues and if he fails to win the two tricks he loses the pool; on the other hand, if he wins the two tricks not only does he take the pool but the other players each pay him the amount that they originally contributed to the pool.

The player on the left of the dealer leads to the first trick. Thereafter the winner of a trick leads to the next. The rules of play are precise and peculiar to the game:

1. If the card turned up to denote the trump suit is an Ace, the dealer may rob. He may, that is, exchange the Ace for a card in his hand, but he must do so before the player on his left leads to the first trick.
2. Any player who has been dealt the Ace of the trump suit may exchange any card in his hand for the turn-up card, but he need not do so until it is his turn to play.
3. If a trump is led a player must follow suit if he can, but the 5 and Jack of the trump suit and the Ace of Hearts are exempt from following suit to the lead of a lower trump. It is called reneging. It means that the 5 of the trump suit need not be played if the Jack of the trump suit is led, and the Jack of the trump suit need not be played if the Ace of Hearts is led; if, however, the 5 of the trump suit is led no trump can renege.
4. If a plain suit is led a player may follow suit or trump as he

chooses, but he must not discard from another plain suit if he is able to follow suit or trump.

5. If a player misdeals the deal passes to the next player.

North

West

East

South

In a 4-handed game, South deals and turns up the **9 ♦**.

West leads the **J ♦**. North may renege the **5 ♦**, but it would hardly be good play not to use it to win the second highest trump, so he plays it. East, who holds the **A ♦**, robs by exchanging the **8 ♣** for the **9 ♦** and, of course, plays it. West who started with the hope of a jinx is now not so sure that he will win even three tricks. His prospects, however, improve when South, perforce, plays the **A ♥**. At least South cannot hold another trump.

North leads the **J ♣**, East plays the **5 ♣**, South the **7 ♣**, and West wins with the **2 ♦**.

West leads the **K ♠**, North plays the **6 ♠**, and East sees the possibility of himself winning three tricks. He trumps with the **A ♦**, and South plays the **9 ♠**. With any luck East should be able to win the last two tricks with the **J ♠** and **5 ♠**.

As it happens, however, East's play has enabled West to win three tricks, because when East leads the **J ♠**, West wins with the **3 ♦** and the last trick with the **2 ♠**.

East is dealt the 8 ♣, but exchanges it for the 9 ♦

Party Games

Authors

Authors is a simple game played with the full pack.

The cards are dealt one at a time to each player until the pack is exhausted.

The object of the game is to complete a trick of four cards of the same rank. The winner of the game is he who wins most tricks.

The game begins by the player on the left of the dealer asking another player for a specified card. He may ask for any card he chooses so long as he himself holds a card of the same rank. If the player asked holds the card, he surrenders it to the asker who continues by asking any player for another card. If a player has not got the card asked for, the privilege of asking passes to him. When a player has collected four cards of the same rank, he shows them and places them face downwards on the table in front of him as a trick.

A good memory is essential to success, and some guile is advantageous. There is, for example, nothing unethical in asking a player for a card already in one's hand, in an attempt to deter another player from spoiling one's hand by asking for the card.

Go Fish

Go Fish is a similar, but simpler, game to the above. If two or three players are in the game each is dealt seven cards; if four or five each is dealt five cards. The remainder of the pack (the stock) is placed face downwards in the centre of the table.

The game begins by the player on the left of the dealer asking one of the others for all the cards of a specified rank that he may hold. The asker may specify any rank he chooses so long as he himself holds at least one card of the same rank.

The player who has been asked must hand over all the cards of the specified rank that he holds; but if he holds none he says: 'Go fish'. The asker must then draw the top card of the stock.

A player's turn to ask continues for as long as he is successful in obtaining the cards he asked for. If he has to fish, and he draws a card of the specified rank from the stock, he must show it before continuing to ask. If a player fails to obtain a card of the rank asked for, either from the player asked or from the stock after being told to fish, the privilege of asking passes to the player on his left.

When a player obtains all four cards of one rank, he shows them and places them face downwards as a trick on the table in front of him.

The game ends when all thirteen tricks have been won, the winner of the game being he who has won most tricks.

Cheating

Cheating is an amusing game suitable for any number of players. It is played with two, three or even four packs of cards, shuffled together, according to the number of players, and sufficient cards are removed in order that every player may begin with the same number.

The cards are dealt one at a time, face downwards, to the players, and the dealer begins the game by playing a card, face downwards, to the centre of the table, and saying 'Six' or whatever he chooses. The next player plays a card face downwards on top of it and says 'Seven', the next 'Eight', and so on up to 'King', when the next player says 'Ace', the next 'Two', and so on.

The feature of the game is that a player need not necessarily play the card he announces – indeed he may not always be able to – and after a player has announced a card anyone may challenge him by calling 'Cheating'. The card is then exposed. If it is found that the player has not played the card he announced he must take into his hand all the cards on the table; on the other hand, if he has played the card that he announced the challenger must take all the cards on the table into his hand.

After a challenge the player on the left of the one challenged restarts the game by playing a card to the centre of the table and announcing it.

The game is won by the player who is first to get rid of all his cards.

The game is an hilarious one and a general shout of 'Cheating' is likely to lead to an argument as to who was first. It is best, therefore, for each player to stand out of the game in turn and act as an umpire.

Fan Tan

Fan Tan is also known as Card Dominoes, Parliament and Sevens, and must not be confused with the gambling game that is played in China under the same name. In fact, the well-known Chinese game is not a card game.

The game is played with the standard 52-card pack the cards ranking in the order from King (high) to Ace (low).

Before each deal an agreed amount is placed by each player into a pool. The cards are dealt one by one, face downwards, until the pack is exhausted, and play begins by the player on the left of the dealer placing a 7 face upwards in the centre of the table. If he has no 7 he contributes 1 unit to the pool, and the player on his left now has to play a 7 to the centre of the table or contribute 1 unit to the pool, and so on.

As soon as a 7 has been played to the centre of the table, the next player must play either the 6 of the same suit on its left, or the 8 of the same suit on its right, or the 7 of another suit below it. The game continues clockwise round the table, the players building up to the Kings on the right of the 7s and down to the Aces on the left of them.

Any player who is unable to play in his turn contributes 1 unit to the pool, and if he revokes, by failing to play when he could do so, he forfeits 3 units to the pool, and 5 units each to the holders of the 6 and 8 if he fails to play a 7 when he could and should have played it.

The game is won by the player who is first to get rid of all his cards. He receives all that is in the pool and from each of the other players 1 unit for every card that the player holds.

Skill comes into the game by holding up the opponents. As a general rule a 7, unless it is accompanied by several cards of the same suit, should be kept in hand for as long as possible; and, if a player has a choice of plays, he should prefer the card that will allow him later to play a lower or higher one of the same suit, rather than one that can only help the opponents.

With the situation of the game as in the illustration opposite, the player plays the **10 ♣** because when the **J ♣** is played he can follow with the **Q ♣**. It would be an error of judgement to play the **6 ♥**, because it doesn't help him, but might help the opponents.

On another level, the game can be played by children, without the need for a pool. Plate 17 shows children enjoying fan tan.

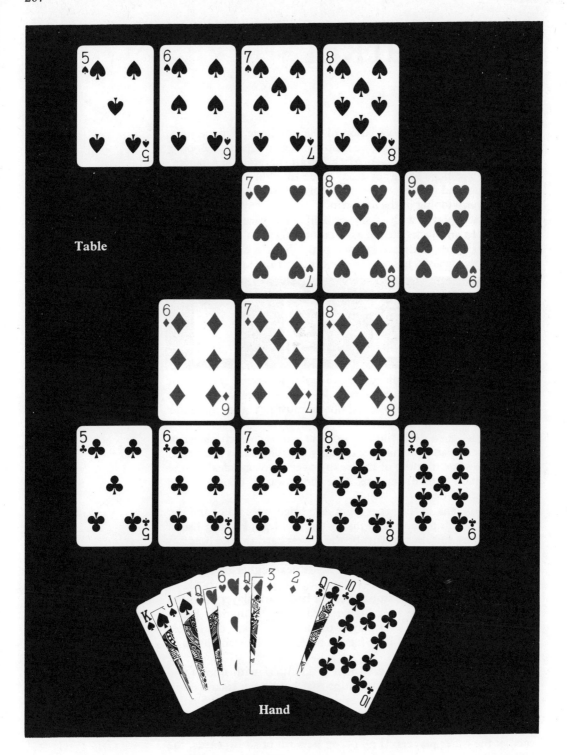

Table

Hand

Newmarket

Newmarket is a modern variation of the old game of pope joan (see page 211) and is known by a number of other names—Boodle and Stops in England; Chicago, Michigan and Saratoga in America.

It is an excellent game for from three to eight players that is easy to learn and contains an element of skill that guarantees the better player winning in the long run.

The game is played with a full pack of fifty-two cards, and an Ace, King, Queen and Jack (each of a different suit) from another pack. These four extra cards are known as the boodle cards, and are placed, face upwards, in a row in the centre of the table.

Before the deal each player has to stake an agreed number of chips (usually, but not necessarily, 10) on the boodle cards. He may stake his chips as he pleases, but he must not stake more nor less than the agreed number.

The dealer then deals the cards one at a time to each player in rotation, and to an extra hand or dummy. As the players must each receive the same number of cards, any over-cards are dealt to the dummy hand which remains face downwards on the table throughout the deal.

The cards rank in the order from Ace (high) to 2 (low) and the player on the left of the dealer makes the first lead. He may lead a card from any suit, but it must be the lowest card that he holds in the suit. The players do not play in rotation round the table. The next play is made by the player who holds next higher cards in the suit, then the next higher card is played by the player who holds it, and so on, until the run is stopped either because a player plays the Ace of the suit, or the next higher card is in the dummy hand. Either way, the player who played the last card leads the lowest card of another suit, and if he has no other suit the lead passes to the player on his left.

When a player plays a card that is identical with one of the boodle cards he collects all the chips that have been staked on it.

The object of the game, however, is not only to win the chips that have been staked on the boodle cards, but to get rid of all one's cards, because the player who is first to do so receives one chip from each of the other players. If no player gets rid of all his cards, the one who holds the fewest number of cards wins the hand, and if two players are left with an equal number of fewest cards they divide the winnings.

If when a deal comes to an end the chips on one or more of the boodle cards have not been claimed, because the corresponding cards to the boodle cards are in the dummy hand, they are carried forward to the next deal.

Old Maid

Old Maid may be played by any reasonable number of players. It is played with the standard 52-card pack from which one of the Queens is removed.

The dealer deals the cards one at a time, face downwards, to each player until the pack is exhausted. That some players may have a card more than the others does not matter.

The players then discard from their hands all pairs of cards (a player with three cards of the same rank discards two of them and retains the other). Then the dealer offers his hand to his left-hand neighbour who takes a card from it. If he has drawn a card that pairs with one of his he discards the pair; if not he mixes it with the cards in his hand. Either way he offers his hand to his left-hand neighbour who draws a card from it, and so on. Play continues round and round the table until all the cards have been paired and discarded, with the exception that one player will be left holding an odd Queen—the old maid.

A player is dealt:

He pairs off the 8 ♠ and 8 ♣, two of his 6s, and the 2 ♥ and 2 ♦. It leaves him with:

He shuffles the cards and presents them, face downwards, to his left-hand opponent, at the same time offering up a silent prayer that he will draw the Q ♦ or, if not that, when the time comes for him to draw a card from his right-hand opponent, the will draw a Queen to pair off with it. Children enjoy this game, as Plate 15 shows.

Pip-Pip

Pip-Pip may be played by any reasonable number of players. It is played with two packs of cards shuffled together and, with the exception that the 2s are promoted to rank above the Aces, the order of the cards is the same as in most trick-taking games.

The players draw cards. He who shows the highest deals first, and the card drawn determines the trump suit.

Seven cards are dealt face downwards to each player, and the remainder of the pack is placed face downwards in the centre of the table (the stock).

The object of the game is to win tricks containing 2s, Aces, Kings, Queens and Jacks, and for winning them a player scores 11 points for each 2, 10 points for each Ace, 5 points for each King, 4 points for each Queen and 3 points for each Jack.

The player on the left of the dealer leads to the first trick. Thereafter the player who wins a trick leads to the next. A player must follow suit if he can; if not he may either discard or trump. If two players play identical cards, the player of the second is deemed to have played the higher card.

Immediately after a player has played to a trick he draws a card from the stock; if he now holds in his hand the King and Queen of the same suit, other than of the trump suit, he may call 'Pip-Pip', and place the two cards face upwards on the table in front of him. For calling 'Pip-Pip' a player scores 50 points and, at the end of the current trick, the trump suit changes to that of the exposed King and Queen.

'Pip-Pip' may be called and 50 points scored if a player is dealt the King and Queen of a suit—other than of the trump suit. The trump suit is then changed before the first trick is played. If two or more players are dealt the King and Queen of a suit—other than of the trump suit—each scores 50 points if he calls 'Pip-Pip'. The trump suit is changed to that of the player who was first to call. 'Pip-Pip' may be called twice in the same suit provided the player has both Kings and both Queens of it. A King or a Queen once paired cannot be paired a second time. It is not compulsory to call 'Pip-Pip' if a player holds the King and Queen of a suit, but if he does not call he cannot score the bonus of 50 points.

Drawing cards from the stock continues until it contains insufficient cards to enable every player to draw one. The remaining cards in the stock are then turned face upwards and the players play the last seven tricks with the cards left in their hands.

The game ends when every player has dealt an equal number of times.

Pope Joan

Pope Joan is a very old card game that at one time was exceptionally popular in Scotland. The 9 of Diamonds is given the name of Pope, and as the Pope was the Antichrist of Scottish reformers, there is reason to think that it was for this reason that the nickname of Curse of Scotland became attached to the card.

The game is played with a standard pack of fifty-two cards from which the 8 of Diamonds is removed. Originally a special board, consisting of a circular tray divided into eight compartments, and revolving about a central pillar, was used (see Plate 16). To-day these boards are museum pieces, and modern players must make do with eight saucers labelled: *Pope* (**9 ♦**), *Ace, King, Queen, Jack, Matrimony, Intrigue, Game*, placed in the centre of the table.

Each player begins with the same number of counters of an agreed value, and the dealer places six in the saucer labelled Pope (**9 ♦**), two each in Matrimony and Intrigue, and one each in Ace, King, Queen, Jack and Game. It is called dressing the board.

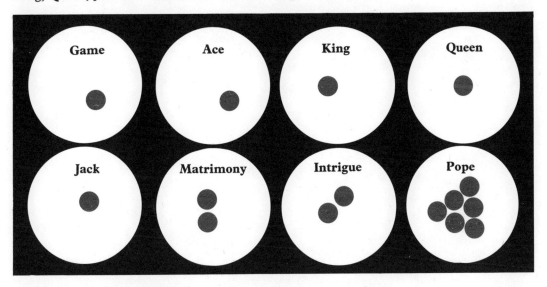

Cards are then dealt to the players and to an extra hand (widow) in the centre of the table. The number of cards dealt to each player and the widow depends on the number of players in the game. The players must each hold the same number of cards, so any over-cards go to the widow. The last card is turned face upwards to denote the trump suit, and if it is either the Pope (**9 ♦**) or an Ace, King, Queen or Jack, the dealer wins the counters in the corresponding saucer.

The player on the left of the dealer leads to the first trick. He may lead any card he chooses, and at the same time he announces it. Suppose it is the 6 of Clubs. Then the player who holds the 7 of Clubs plays it and announces it, the player who holds the 8 of Clubs plays it and announces it, and so on, until the run comes to an end.

The four Kings are stop cards, and in the Diamond suit the 7 is as well, because the 8 has been removed from the pack. In practice, of course, any card may be a stop card on account of the cards in the widow hand, and because the next higher card may already have been played.

When a run comes to an end, the player of the stop card starts a fresh run by leading any card he likes. In this way the game continues until one of the players has played all his cards. He is then entitled to the counters in the Game saucer, and, in addition, he receives from each player 1 counter for every card left in his hand. The player who is left with the Pope (9 ♦), however, is exempt from paying the winner so long as he holds the card in his hand. If he has played it in the course of the game he loses this advantage.

During the course of the game, any player who plays the Ace, King, Queen or Jack of the trump suit, or the Pope (9 ♦), wins the counters in the corresponding saucers; if the same player plays the King and Queen of the trump suit he wins the counters in matrimony, and if the same player plays the Queen and Jack of the trump suit he wins those in Intrigue.

The deal passes round the table clockwise, and any counters that have not been won in a deal are carried forward to the next.

Ranter Go Round

Ranter Go Round is an old Cornish game with the rather more appropriate alternative name of Cuckoo.

It may be played by any reasonable number, with a standard pack of fifty-two cards. The cards rank in order from King (high) to Ace (low); the suits have no rank. Each player begins with an agreed number of units, usually three. The dealer deals one card face downwards to each player. The object of the game is to avoid being left with the lowest card.

The player on the left of the dealer begins the game. He may either retain his card or offer it to his left-hand neighbour with the command 'Change'. There is no choice about it. The player so commanded must exchange cards with his right-hand neighbour unless he holds a King, when he says 'King', and the game is continued by the player on his left.

When an exchange has been made, the player who has been compelled to do so may pass on the card he has received in the same way, and so on, clockwise round the table, until the card is brought to a halt either by a King or by a player receiving a high card in exchange, so that he has nothing to gain by passing it on.

Any player giving an Ace, 2 or 3, in obedience to the command 'Change', must announce the rank of the card.

The dealer is last to play, and if he wishes to exchange his card, he does so by cutting the remainder of the pack and taking the top card of the cut.

If in doing this he draws a King he loses the hand and contributes one unit to the pool. If he does not draw a King, all the players expose their cards and the one with the lowest contributes one unit to the pool. If two or more tie for lowest card, all contribute to the pool.

When a player has contributed all his units to the pool, he retires from the game. The others continue, and the game is won by he who is left with at least one unit in hand.

Red Dog

Although in Red Dog, or High-card Pool, players stake on their cards, it is usually accepted as a party game, rather than a banking game, because the players stake against a pool and not against a banker.

The game may be played by any number up to ten, with the standard pack of fifty-two cards, ranking from Ace (high) to 2 (low). The suits have no rank.

The players contribute to the pool an agreed number of units, and each player is dealt five cards (only four cards if nine or ten players are in the game). Beginning with the player on the left of the dealer, each in turn stakes a minimum of one unit and a maximum that must not exceed the number of units in the pool, that he holds a card that is higher than, and in the same suit as, the top card of the stock when it is his turn to play.

The dealer faces the top card of the stock. If the player can beat it, he shows his card and is paid out of the pool. His remaining cards are not seen. If he cannot beat it, his stake is added to the pool and his cards are shown to the other players.

If at any time a player's winning bet takes all in the pool, a new pool is started as at the beginning of a game.

Rockaway

Rockaway or Go Boom is a game that may be played by any reasonable number of players.

Two packs of cards are shuffled together, and the dealer deals seven cards, face downwards, to each player. The next card (the widow) is placed face upwards in the centre of the table, and the rest of the pack (the stock) is placed face downwards on the table.

In turn, and beginning with the player on the left of the dealer, each player covers the widow either with a card of the same rank, of the same suit, or with an Ace, drawn from his hand. If he has no card in his hand to comply with the rule he draws a card from the stock and continues to draw one until he draws a card that permits him to cover the widow.

The card that covers the widow then becomes the widow for the next player, and so on, round the table in a clockwise direction.

When the stock is exhausted, the players play out the cards in their hands, and a player who cannot cover the widow misses his turn.

The hand comes to an end when a player has exhausted the cards in his hand. The remaining players expose their cards, which are scored against them: an Ace counting 15 points, a court card 10 points, and all other cards their pip value.

The deal passes round the table in a clockwise direction, and the game comes to an end when every player has dealt an equal number of times, by arrangement before the game begins.

E dealt. A, therefore, leads first, and the play is:

A	B	C	D	E
6 ♣	2 ♣	2 ♦	K ♦	A ♠

As an Ace counts 15 points against a player who is left with it, E plays A ♠ rather than one of his Diamonds.

| 10 ♠ | 9 ♠ | J ♠ | 8 ♠ | ? |

As E has no Spade, no 8 and no Ace in his hand, he must draw from the stock, and continue to do so until he draws a playable card.

It can be seen that E was foolish to play his Ace first round. As no opponent can go out in less than seven rounds, E would have been wise to keep his Ace for six rounds at least. He would not then have found himself in such a bad position on the second round. Usually, an Ace should not be played if another choice is available.

Spinado

Spinado is a less complicated version of pope joan (see page 211). No board is necessary (if you could find one) and there are only three pools: Matrimony, Intrigue and Game.

Before dealing, the dealer contributes 12 counters to the Matrimony pool, and 6 each to the Intrigue and Game pools. The other players contribute three counters each to the Game pool.

Matrimony is the King and Queen of Diamonds: Intrigue is the Queen and Jack of Diamonds.

The four 2s and the 8 of Diamonds are removed from a standard 52-card pack, and the dealer deals the cards to the players and to an extra hand (widow). As the players must each hold the same number of cards, over-cards go to the widow hand.

The player on the left of the dealer starts the game by playing any card that he chooses, and the other players continue by playing the next higher cards in succession until a stop is reached. The player who plays the stop card then starts a new run by playing any card that he chooses.

The Ace of Diamonds is known as Spinado, more usually truncated to Spin, and whoever holds it may play it at any time that he chooses provided that he accompanies it with the proper card, and announces that he is playing Spinado. It constitutes a stop, and he receives 3 counters from each of the other players.

During the game, the player who plays the King of Diamonds receives 2 counters from each of the other players, and if he plays the Queen of Diamonds as well he wins the Matrimony pool. The player who plays the Queen of Diamonds and the Jack of Diamonds wins the Intrigue pool, and those who play the Kings of Spades, Hearts and Clubs receive 1 counter from each of the other players.

The game is won by the player who is the first to play all his cards. He takes the counters in the Game pool and is exempt from contributing to the pools in the next deal, unless it is his turn to deal.

A player who is left with Spinado in his hand pays the winner of the game double for each card he is left with.

Spinado, therefore, should not be kept back too long. On the other hand, it is not always advisable to play it with one's first card. If, for example, a 10 is led, and the player who holds Spinado also holds the King and Jack, it is an error of judgement to play Spinado with the Jack, because if the Jack proves to be a stop there was no need for the play of Spinado, and the King is the natural stop if another player follows with the Queen.

It is better to hold up Spinado to be played with some card that is not known to be a stop.

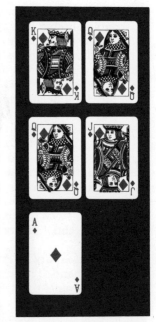

Top: **matrimony**
Centre: **intrigue**
Bottom: **spinado**

Thirty-one

Thirty-one may be played by any number of players up to fifteen. It is played with the full pack of fifty-two cards, the Aces ranking high the 2s low.

Before each deal the players contribute an agreed amount to a pool.

Three cards are dealt face downwards to each player, and three cards are placed face upwards in the centre of the table. It is known as the widow hand.

In turn each player, beginning with the one on the left of the dealer, must exchange one of his cards with a card from the widow. He cannot pass, nor can he exchange more than one card. Counting the Ace as 11, the court cards as 10 each and all the other cards at their pip values, the object of the game is to hold three cards of the same suit which will add up to 31. Next in value is a hand that contains three cards of the same rank. Failing either, the pool is won by the player who holds the highest total in any one suit.

Widow   Hand

The exchange of cards with the widow-hand continues until a player has obtained a 31-hand. When a player holds such a hand he exposes it on the table, claims the pool, and the deal passes. At any stage of the game, however, a player who thinks he has a hand good enough to win, may rap the table. The other players now have the right, in turn, either to stand pat with the cards that they hold, or exchange one more card with the widow. The players then expose their cards and the one who holds the best hand wins the pool.

The player might be advised to exchange his Five of Diamonds with the Seven of Hearts and rap, since 25 is not a bad score

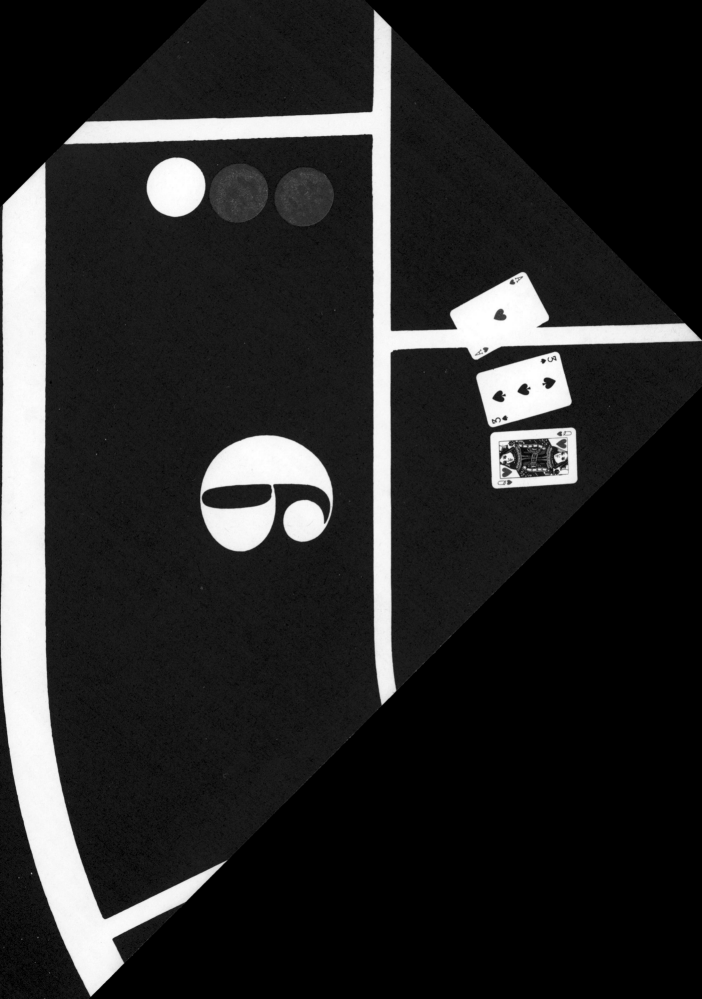

Banking Games

Baccarat

Baccarat, more correctly Baccarat Banque, is a game of chance that is played in casinos everywhere.

The game may be played by any number up to thirty or more. The banker sits midway down one of the sides of a long, oval table (see Plate 18), and the players sit in equal numbers on both sides of him. Those for whom there is no room to sit, stand behind them.

Six packs of cards are shuffled together, in Las Vegas eight packs are used, cut and placed in an open-ended box, known as a shoe designed to release only one card at a time. The court cards rank in value at 10 points each; all other cards at their pip values.

The banker, who is also the dealer, puts his stake on the table in front of him, and any player who wishes to bet against the whole of it, calls 'Banco'. If two or more call, the one nearest to the banker's left makes the bet. If no-one calls, the players combine their bets to equal the stake put up by the banker.

The banker then gives a card face downwards to the player on his right, a card to the player on his left and a card to himself. He repeats the operation so that the three of them have two cards each.

The object of the game is to form in two or three cards a combination counting as nearly as possible to 9. In counting the total, ten is disregarded; if, for example, a player's two cards total 15 it counts as a point of 5.

The banker looks at his two cards and if he has a point of 8 or 9 he shows his cards and wins the hand. If he has not got a point of 8 or 9, he announces that he will give and the player on his right looks at his cards. If he has a point of 8 or 9 he shows his cards and announces his natural. If he has not got a point of 8 or 9 he may ask for one more card which the banker gives to him face upwards. The player on the left of the banker goes through the same performance, and then the banker may, if he chooses, take one more card. Finally, the banker wins or loses to each player according to whose point is nearer to 9; equality neither wins nor loses.

To illustrate. The banker holds 10 ♠ and A ♥, making a point of 1, and he, therefore, must give. The right-hand player holds 5 ♣ and 3 ♣. He faces his cards, announces his natural point of 8, and must win. The left-hand player holds 9 ♠ and 4 ♣, making a point of 3. He must draw and the banker gives him 8 ♦, reducing his point to 1. For the moment, however, the left-handed player does not announce his point. The banker faces his cards, and, as he holds no more than a point of 1, he draws a card. It is the 8 ♣, which raises his point to 9.

The banker, therefore, wins from the left-hand player, but loses to the right-hand player because though the banker has a point of 9, against the point of 8 held by the right-hand player, a natural beats any point made by the addition of a drawn card.

The rules of play are strict. They should never be deviated from because the player who is holding the cards is playing for all on his side of the table. If he deviates from the rules, and thereby loses the hand, he is liable to make good all losses incurred through his error. A player must not look at his cards until the banker has either announced that he holds a natural or that he will give cards. When a player looks at his cards, if he holds a natural he must expose his cards and declare his natural at once. If a player does not hold a natural, he must draw a card if he holds a point of 4 or less, stand if he holds a point of 6 or 7, and use his discretion to draw or stand only if he holds a point of 5.

The layout of the staking table used in baccarat and *chemin de fer*

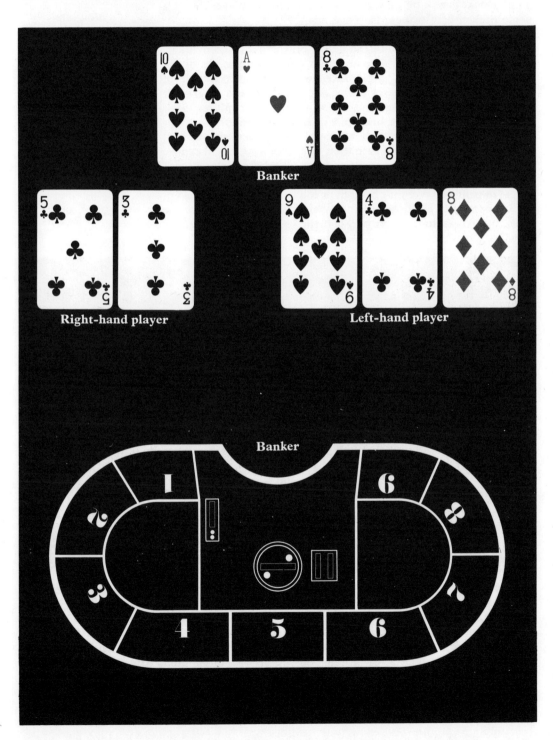

Banker

Right-hand player   Left-hand player

Blind Hookey

Blind Hookey may be played by any number of players with a single pack of fifty-two cards.

After the pack has been shuffled by one player and cut by another to the banker, it is passed to the player on the left of the banker, who removes a few cards (not less than four) from the top of the pack, and places them in a pile face downwards on the table in front of him. He then passes the pack to his left-hand neighbour who does the same thing, and so on until all the players (the banker last) have placed a small pile of cards in front of them.

Without looking at the cards, all the players (except the banker) stake to an agreed limit and turn their piles face upwards to expose the bottom card. The banker wins from all whose exposed card is lower than or equal with his and loses to all whose card is higher. By agreement, the Ace may be high or low.

Play continues with the same banker if he wins more than he loses, but passes to the next player if the banker loses more than he wins.

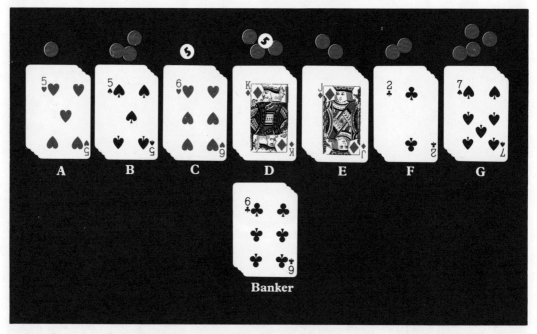

Another way of playing the game is for the banker to cut the pack into three piles. The players place their stakes on either of two piles, and the third pile is taken by the banker. The three piles are turned face upwards and the players receive from the banker or lose to him according to whether the bottom cards of their piles are higher or lower than the bottom card of his pile.

The banker wins from A, B, C and F and loses to D, E and G. Overall he loses 3 units and, therefore, the bank passes to the next player

Chemin de Fer

Chemin de Fer, nearly always called Chemmy, is the same game as baccarat (see page 220) modified for social play, because in all games of chance the banker has an advantage to a greater or lesser degree, and his advantage at *chemin de fer* is nothing like what it is at baccarat because he plays against one hand instead of against two.

For all practical purposes the difference between baccarat and *chemin de fer* is that at the latter game the bank passes in rotation round the table, the banker holding the bank until he loses a coup when it is passed to the player on his left; and the banker deals only one hand, not two, to the players, the hand being held by the one who has made the largest bet.

As the banker plays against only one hand, he may not use his judgement whether to draw or stand. The rules for play are precise and strict:

1. If his point is 8 or 9 he declares a natural.
2. If his point is 7 he stands whether the player draws any card or stands.
3. If his point is 6 he draws if the player draws a 6 or a 5, but stands if the player draws any other card or stands.
4. If he holds a point of 5 he draws if the player draws a 7, 6, 5, 4, 3, or stands, but stands if he draws any other card.
5. If he holds a point of 3 or 4 he draws if the player draws a 7, 6, 5, 4, 3, 2, or Ace or if he stands, but stands if he draws any other card.
6. If he holds a point of 0, 1 or 2 he draws whether the player draws any card or stands.

Banker's point is 6. Player has drawn a 6, so banker must draw

Banker's point is only 4, but as player has drawn a 9 he must stand

Easy Go

Easy Go is a very simple game of chance played by any number up to nine with a single pack of fifty-two cards.

The banker deals five cards face upwards to every player, except himself. He now faces a card and any player who holds a card of the same rank pays into a pool 2 units if it is the same colour and 1 unit if it is different. In all the banker faces five cards in turn, and for the second card the players pay into the pool 3 units if the cards are of the same colour and 2 if they are different; for the third card they contribute 5 units if the cards are of the same colour and 4 if they are different; for the fourth card they contribute 9 units if the cards are of the same colour and 8 if they are different; for the fifth card they contribute 17 units if the cards are of the same colour and 16 if they are different.

There is now a second show of five cards by the banker, but this time the players take out of the pool at the same rate as they paid into it.

After this, anything left in the pool is taken by the banker, but if there is not enough in the pool to meet the requirements of the players he must make it good.

The bank passes clockwise round the table.

Overall result of this game of easy go:
A wins 1 unit;
B wins 5 units;
C wins 3 units;
D wins 2 units;
E loses 3 units;
banker loses 8 units

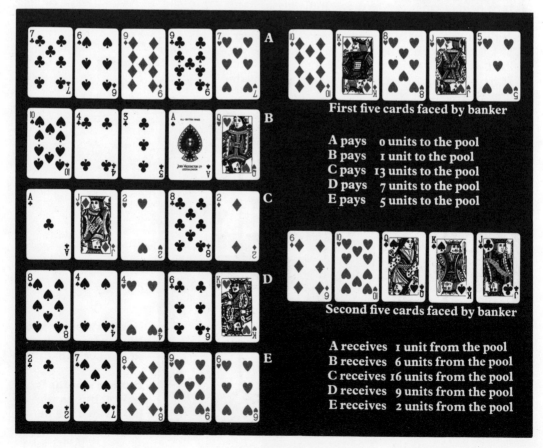

First five cards faced by banker

A pays   0 units to the pool
B pays   1 unit to the pool
C pays   13 units to the pool
D pays   7 units to the pool
E pays   5 units to the pool

Second five cards faced by banker

A receives   1 unit from the pool
B receives   6 units from the pool
C receives 16 units from the pool
D receives   9 units from the pool
E receives   2 units from the pool

Hoggenheimer

Hoggenheimer, or English Roulette, is played with a pack of cards from which the 2s, 3s, 4s, 5s and 6s have been removed, and the Joker (or one of the rejected cards) added.

After the pack has been shuffled and cut, the banker deals the cards, face downwards, in four rows of eight cards each, and places aside, also face downwards, the thirty-third card. Great care must be taken when dealing that no-one sees the face of any of the cards.

The top row is for Spades, from Ace to 7; the second row for Hearts, from Ace to 7; the third row for Diamonds, from Ace to 7; the bottom row for Clubs, from Ace to 7.

The players now stake their money. They may stake on a single card being turned up (even chance), or two touching cards being turned up (2 to 1 chance), or all four cards in a column or any group of four touching cards being turned up (4 to 1 chance), or all eight cards in a row being turned up (8 to 1 chance).

When the players have placed their bets, the banker picks up the thirty-third card and shows it. If it is the Joker he wins all the money on the table and there is a redeal. If, as is more likely, it is another card, he places it in its appropriate place in the layout, exposes the card that it replaces and transfers this card to its appropriate place in the layout; and so on until the game is brought to an end when the banker exposes the Joker.

The banker then collects the money on those chances that have not materialised in full, and pays out on those chances that have.

Hoggenheimer in progress. Stake 1 is on 10 ♠ being turned up; Stake 2 on 9, 8 ♠; Stake 3 on all four Queens; Stake 4 on 10 ♦, 9 ♦, 10 ♣, 9 ♣; Stake 5 on all Clubs; Stake 6 on 7 ♥ and 7 ♦

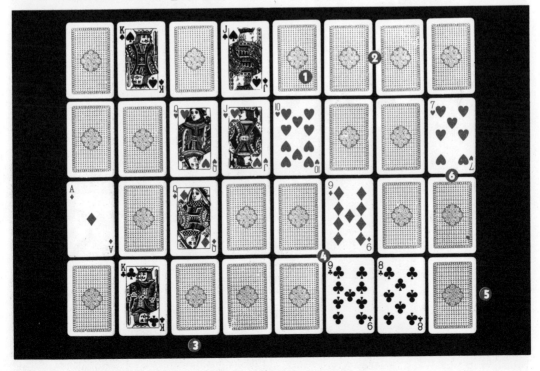

Lansquenet

Lansquenet, of German origin, is a game of pure chance that derives its name from the seventeenth-century German mercenary (*landsknecht*) with whom the game is said to have been popular.

Any number may play. The banker places the two top cards of the pack (hand cards) face upwards on the table. He then deals a card face upwards to himself, and one face upwards to the players. If either card is of the same rank as one of the hand cards it is put with them and another card dealt in its place.

The players place their bets, and the banker covers them. He then draws cards from the pack, face upwards, one at a time. If he draws a card of the same rank as the players' card he wins the bets on it; if he draws a card of the same rank as his own card he loses all the bets on the other card; and if he draws a card that matches neither card nor the two hand cards it is placed on the table and the players may bet on it.

When the players' card is matched the banker withdraws both cards and deals another card to the players. Cards that match the hand cards are placed with them. The game ends when the pack is exhausted unless the banker matches his own card first.

First card drawn from pack: Q ♠. The card is placed on the table and players may bet on it. Second card drawn: 8 ♦. The card is added to the hand card pile. Third card drawn: K ♥. The banker wins the two units staked on K ♦

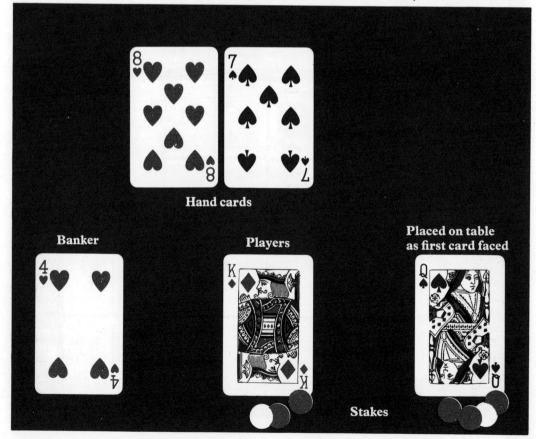

Hand cards

Banker

Players

Placed on table as first card faced

Stakes

Monte Bank

In principle Monte Bank is a game of chance that is very similar to lansquenet (opposite).

It is played by any number of persons, with a pack of cards from which the 8s 9s and 10s have been removed.

After the cards have been shuffled and the pack cut by one of the players, the banker draws the two cards from the bottom of the pack and places them face upwards on the table (the bottom layout), and then the two cards from the top of the pack and places them face upwards on the table (the top layout).

The players place their bets up to an agreed maximum on whichever layout they choose. The banker then turns the pack face upwards and if the exposed bottom card (known as the gate) is of the same suit as any of the four cards in the layouts, he pays all bets on that layout, and collects all bets on a layout that shows no card of the same suit as the gate.

The layouts and gate are then discarded, and the game is continued with new layouts and gate. The bank passes after five coups.

Stakes

Top layout

Bottom layout

Gate

Banker pays four units to players who stake on the top layout and collects the three units on the bottom layout. If the gate had been a Diamond, all players would have won; if a club all would have lost

Racing

Racing is played with the standard pack of fifty-two cards. The four Aces are placed in a row on the table. The remainder of the pack is shuffled and cut, and the banker draws the top seven cards from the pack and lays them in a vertical column immediately below the Aces, so that the lay out takes the form of a T (see illustration).

The banker deals the remaining cards one at a time, and each time that the card of a suit is dealt the Ace of the same suit is moved one card forward, the winner being the Ace that is first to pass the seventh card. A game in progress is shown on Plate 19.

Players place their stakes on whichever Ace they choose. The race ends when the first Ace passes the seventh card.

Racing layout. The banker might offer evens on a suit if there are no cards in the layout, 2-1 if there is one card (as with Clubs and Hearts here), 3-1 if there are two cards (Diamonds here), 5-1 if there are three cards (Spades here) and 10-1 if there are four cards. If there are five or more cards of a suit in the layout, it is impossible for that suit to win, and there must be a redeal

Slippery Sam

Slippery Sam or Shoot, as it is sometimes called, may be played by any number from two upwards, but the game is best for from six to eight players. It is probably the only banking game which favours the player rather than the banker, because the player has the advantage of seeing his cards before he bets and, therefore, can calculate whether the odds are in his favour or against him. Provided he bets with intelligence he should come out a winner.

The game is played with the standard 52-card pack, the cards ranking from Ace (high) to 2 (low).

The banker places an agreed sum in a pool and then deals three cards, one at a time, face downwards, to each player. The remainder of the pack (the stock) he places face downwards on the table in front of him and topples it over to make it easier to slide off the top card.

The player on the left of the dealer, after looking at his cards, bets that at least one of them will be in the same suit as, and higher than, the top card of the stock. He may bet all that is in the pool or any part of it, but he may not bet less than an agreed minimum. When he has made his bet, the banker slides the top card off the stock and exposes it. If the player has won his bet he exposes his card and takes his winnings out of the pool. If he has lost his bet he pays the amount that he betted into the pool and does not expose his card. The four cards are then thrown into a discard pile, and the opportunity to bet passes to the next player.

Meanwhile: a player must not look at his cards until it is his turn to bet; if the pool is exhausted the bank immediately passes to the next player, otherwise the banker holds the bank for three full deals round the table, and then he may either pass the bank to the player on his left or hold the bank for one more, but only one more, deal round the table.

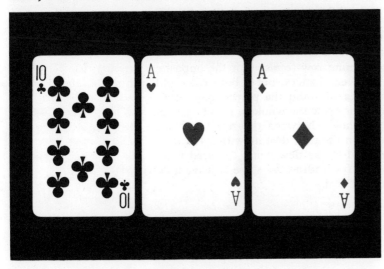

Since the player wins if a red card or a Club lower than the 10 is exposed, and loses only if a Spade or the Ace, King, Queen or Jack of Clubs is exposed, he has 32 chances of winning and 17 of losing: he should stake heavily

Trente et Quarante

Trente et Quarante, or *Rouge et Noir*, is a game of pure chance and, like baccarat (see page 220) is essentially a casino game. It is played on a long table, each end marked as in the accompanying diagram. The banker sits midway down one of the sides, the players sit, and some stand behind them, at each end.

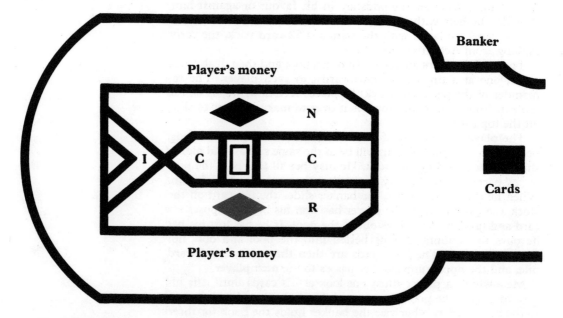

Six packs of cards are shuffled together, cut, and—with the Ace counting as 1, the court cards 10 each, and other cards their pip values—the banker deals a row of cards until the total exceeds 30. He then deals a second row immediately below it in a similar manner. The top row is *noir* (black) the lower *rouge* (red) and whichever row adds up to the lesser total wins. Apart from these two chances the players can bet on whether the first card dealt will be the same colour as the winning row (*couleur*) or the opposite colour (*inverse*). All four are even chances, but if both rows add up to 31 it is a *refait* (drawn game) and the player may either halve his stake with the bank, or allow the whole of it to be put in prison. He has the right to choose between the red and black prisons, and if his stake wins on the next deal he withdraws it.

All other identical totals end in the deal being declared void, and leave the player at liberty to withdraw his stake or leave it on the table to win or lose the next deal.

Vingt-et-Un

Vingt-et-Un, or Twenty-one, is a leading game in the casinos of America where it is known as Black Jack. Although it is a game of chance, in which the odds on winning are heavily in favour of the banker, in Great Britain it is far more of a social pastime and, under the name of Pontoon (almost certainly an easy corruption of punting) it was exceptionally popular in the trenches during the war of 1914–1918.

The game is played with a standard 52-card pack, by any number of players up to ten: if more than ten take part two packs of cards shuffled together should be used.

The banker deals one card face downwards to each player and to himself, and the players, after looking at their cards, stake any amount up to the agreed maximum.

The object of the game is to obtain a total of 21, or as near to it as possible, but without exceeding it. For this purpose an Ace counts 11 or 1 (at the option of the holder) a court card 10, and any other card its pip value.

When the players have made their bets, the banker looks at his card, and has the right to double. In this event the players must double their bets.

The banker then deals another card, face downwards, to all the players and to himself. If a player holds a pair he may announce his intention to split. He stakes the same amount as his original bet on both cards, and the banker deals a second card to each. The player plays both hands separately. The banker may not split pairs.

If the banker holds a natural (an Ace and a court card or a 10) he turns the two cards face upwards and receives from the players double what they have staked, except that if a player also holds a natural he loses only his original stake. The hands are thrown in, and the banker deals another hand.

If the banker does not hold a natural, but a player does, the banker pays him double his stake, and, after the deal has been completed, the bank passes to him. The bank, however, does not pass on a split natural. If two or more players hold naturals, the one nearest to the banker's left takes the bank.

When all naturals (if any) have been declared and settled, the banker asks each player in turn (beginning with the one on his left) whether he wants more cards or not. The player has three options. He may *Stand*; that is he elects to take no more cards. He may *Buy*; that is he increases his stake for the advantage of receiving a card face downwards. He may *Twist*; that is he does not increase his stake and receives a card face upwards. The rules to be observed are:

1. A player may not stand if he holds a count of 15 or less.
2. A player may not buy for more than his original stake.
3. If a player has twisted a third card he may not buy a fourth or fifth, though a player who has bought a third card may twist subsequent cards.
4. A player may not increase, though he may decrease, the amount

for which he bought a previous card.

5. If a player has received four cards he may not buy a fifth if the total of his four cards is 11 or less.

Five cards is the most that a player may hold, and if they total 21 or less the banker pays him double, unless the banker also holds five cards that total 21 or less when the banker wins.

The player who makes a total of 21 with three 7s, receives from the banker triple his stake. The banker does not have this privilege.

When the total of a player's cards exceeds 21 he turns his cards face upwards and the banker wins all that he has staked.

When all the players have received cards, the banker turns his two cards face upwards and deals himself as few or as many cards as he chooses. If when doing so he exceeds a total of 21 he pays the players their stakes. At any time, however, he may elect to stand and agree to pay those players who have a higher total and receive from those who have a lower or equal total.

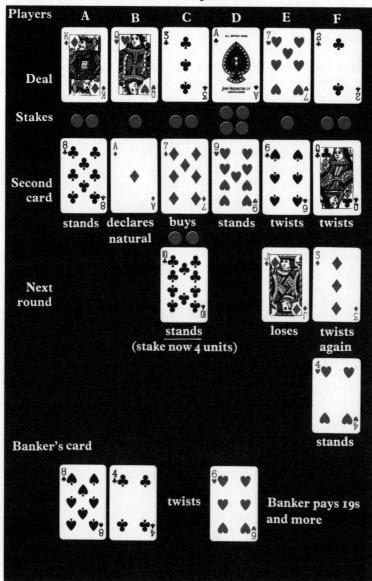

Banker pays B
(double his stake),
D and F
Banker wins from A,
C and E
Banker loses 1 unit
on deal

Card Terms

All pastimes have a vocabulary that is peculiarly their own. That of card playing is probably the most extensive, because there are so many different games and most are of obscure origin. This list, therefore, is by no means complete and comprehensive; rather it includes only the words and expressions that are used in this book and, due to limitation of space, the author has omitted those that are self-explanatory and those that most readers may be expected to know.

ABOVE THE LINE. In games of the bridge family, bonus scores and penalty scores are recorded above a horizontal line across the scoresheet. C/f BELOW THE LINE.

ABUNDANCE (ABONDANCE). In games of the solo whist family, a declaration to win nine tricks.

ALONE. In euchre, the right of the player who has named the trump suit to play without his partner.

ANTE. A compulsory bet made before the deal.

ASSIST. In euchre, a declaration made by the dealer's partner to accept the suit of the turn-up card as the trump suit.

BANCO. A bet equal to the amount staked by the banker.

BASTO. The Ace of Clubs in ombre.

BEG. In games of the all fours family, a rejection by the non-dealer of the suit of the turn-up card as the trump suit.

BELOW THE LINE. In games of the bridge family, scores for tricks bid and won are recorded below a horizontal line across the scoresheet. C/f ABOVE THE LINE.

BETE. In pinocle, failure to make the contract. C/f DOUBLE BETE and SINGLE BETE.

BEZIQUE. In games of the bezique family, the Queen of Spades (or Queen of Clubs if Spades or Diamonds are trumps) and Jack of Diamonds (or Jack of Hearts if Spades or Diamonds are trumps).

BLACK MARIA. The Queen of Spades in games of the black maria family.

BLITZ. In gin rummy, winning a game against an opponent who has failed to score.

BOODLE CARDS. In games of the newmarket family, the Ace, King, Queen and Jack, each of a different suit, from another pack, placed in a layout and on which bets are staked.

BOOK. In games of the bridge and whist families, the first six tricks won by a side, that do not count in the scoring.

BOSTON. A contract to win five tricks in games of the boston whist family.

BOTTOM LAYOUT. In monte bank, the two cards from the bottom of the pack placed by the banker face upwards on the table. C/f TOP LAYOUT.

BOWER. The Jack of a suit in euchre. C/f LEFT BOWER and RIGHT BOWER.

BOX. In gim rummy, the score for winning a hand.

BRAGGERS. In brag, the Ace of Diamonds, the Jack of Clubs and the 9 of Diamonds that serve as wild cards.

BRISQUE. Any Ace or 10 in games of the bezique family.

BUILD. (1) In casino, the play of a card to a card in the layout to make up a total that may be taken with another card in the hand. (2) In games of patience, the play of a card of the same suit on the next one above or below it in rank.

BUY. To increase a bet for the advantage of drawing a card face downwards.

BURY A CARD. In pinocle, discarding face downwards a card from hand.

CACHETTE. The widow-hand in quinto.

CALYPSO. In calypso, a complete suit, from Ace to 2, in a player's trump suit.

CANASTA. In games of the canasta family, a meld of seven or more cards. C/f MIXED CANASTA and NATURAL CANASTA.

CAPOT. In piquet, the winning by one player of all twelve tricks.

CARDS. In piquet, the score for winning the majority of tricks.

CARTE BLANCHE. A hand that contains no court card.

CASH. To lead and win a trick with an established card.

CASINO. C/f GREAT CASINO and LITTLE CASINO.

CENTRE. In games of patience, that part of the table to which the foundation cards are played.

CHECK. In poker, a nominal bet that reserves the right to call or raise if another player bets.

CODILLE. In ombre, if one opponent wins more tricks than ombre.

COMBINE. In casino, to pick up cards from the layout of the total pip value of a card in hand.

COMET. A wild card, usually a 9, in games of the comet family.

COMMON MARRIAGE. In games of the bezique family, the meld of the King and Queen of the same plain suit. C/f ROYAL MARRIAGE.

COUP. A winning play or bet.

COURT CARD. Any King, Queen and Jack.

CRIB. In cribbage, an extra hand formed by the discards of the players.

DIS. In pinocle, the 9 of the trump suit.

DISCARD. The play of a card that is not of the same suit as that of the led-card nor a trump.

DOUBLE BETE. In pinocle, the penalty suffered by the bidder whose score for melds and cards taken in tricks fails to equal his contract. C/f SINGLE BETE.

DOUBLETON. An original holding of two cards of a suit.

DUMMY. In games of the bridge family, the partner of the declarer, and the cards he exposes on the table.

ELDER HAND. The non-dealer in piquet and other games for two players. C/f YOUNGER HAND.

EUCHRE. In euchre, failure to win at least three tricks.

FACE CARD. Same as COURT CARD q.v.

FIFTEEN. In cribbage, the play of a card which, with those already played, adds up to fifteen.

FINESSE. An attempt to win a trick with a card that is not the best held nor in sequence with it.

FISH. To draw a card from the stock.

FLUSH. A hand with all cards of the same suit.

FOLLOW SUIT. To play a card of the same suit as that of the led-card.

FOUNDATION. In games of patience, a card played to the centre on which a complete suit or sequence must be built.

GATE. In monte bank, the bottom card of the pack.

GIFT. In games of the all fours family, the point scored by the dealer if he begs and the dealer decides to play.

GIN. In gin rummy, a hand in which all the cards are melded.

GO. In cribbage, the announcement that a player cannot play without exceeding thirty-one.

GO DOWN. Same as KNOCK (1) *q.v.*

GOULASH. In towie, a redeal of the four hands unshuffled and with each hand arranged in suits.

GRAND MISÈRE. In games of the boston whist family, a contract to lose all thirteen tricks. C/f LITTLE MISÈRE.

GRAND SLAM. In games of the bridge and whist families, the winning of all thirteen tricks. C/f SMALL SLAM.

GRAND SPREAD. In games of the boston whist family, a contract to lose all thirteen tricks with the cards exposed on the table. C/f LITTLE SPREAD.

GREAT CASINO. In casino, the 10 of Diamonds. C/f LITTLE CASINO.

HAND CARDS. In lansquenet, the two top cards of the pack exposed face upwards on the table.

HEEL. Same as TALON *q.v.*

HIGH. In games of the all fours family, the score for being dealt the highest trump in play. C/f LOW.

HIS HEELS. In cribbage, a Jack turned up as the start.

HIS NOB. In cribbage, the Jack, either in hand or crib, of the same suit as the start.

HOLE CARD. In stud poker, the first card dealt, face downwards, to a player.

HONOURS. (1) In games of the bridge family, the Ace, King, Queen, Jack and 10 of a suit. (2) In whist, the Ace, King, Queen and Jack of a suit.

HUITIÈME. In piquet, a sequence of eight cards.

INTRIGUE. In pope joan, the Queen and Jack of the trump suit played by the same player.

JACK. In games of the all fours family, the score for winning the Jack of the trump suit.

JACKPOT. In poker, a deal in which a player must hold at least a pair of Jacks to open.

JASZ. In klaberjass, the Jack of the trump suit.

JINX. In spoil five, an undertaking, by the player who has won three tricks, to win the remaining two.

JOKER. An extra card supplied with the standard 52-card pack used in some games as a wild card.

KITTY. Same as POOL *q.v.*

KNOCK. (1) In games of the rummy family, signification by a player that all his cards are melded. (2) In poker, signification by a player that no further bet will be made by him.

LAYOUT. Cards laid out on the table in a prescribed pattern either for the purpose of placing bets or to be moved in accordance with the rules of the game.

LEFT BOWER. In euchre, the Jack of the same colour as the Jack of the trump suit. C/f RIGHT BOWER.

LEFT PEDRO. In cinch, the 5 of the same colour as the 5 of the trump suit. C/f RIGHT PEDRO.

LITTLE CASINO. In casino, the 2 of Spades. C/f GREAT CASINO.

LITTLE MISÈRE. In games of the boston whist family, a contract to lose twelve tricks after discarding a card that is not shown.

C/f GRAND MISÈRE.

LITTLE SPREAD. In games of the boston whist family, a contract to lose twelve tricks after discarding a card which is not shown and the remaining cards exposed on the table. C/f GRAND SPREAD.

LOO. In loo, failure to win a trick.

LOW. In games of the all fours family, the score made by the player who is dealt the lowest trump in play. C/f HIGH.

LURCH. In cribbage, winning a game before the opponent has gone half-way round the scoring board.

MAKER. The player who names the trump suit.

MANILLE. In ombre, the 7 of Hearts or of Diamonds if either suit is trumps, the 2 of Spades or of Clubs if either suit is trumps.

MARCH. In euchre, winning all five tricks by one side or one player.

MARRIAGE. C/f COMMON MARRIAGE and ROYAL MARRIAGE.

MATADOR. In ombre, the collective name for the three top trumps— SPADILLE, MANILLE AND BASTO.

MATRIMONY. In pope joan, the King and Queen of the trump suit played by the same player.

MELD. A matched set of three or more of a kind or a sequence of three or more of the same suit in consecutive order of rank.

MENEL. In klaberjass, the 9 of the trump suit.

MISÈRE. A contract not to win a trick. C/f GRAND MISÈRE and LITTLE MISÈRE.

MISERY. Same as MISÈRE q.v.

MISS. The widow-hand in loo.

MIXED CANASTA. In canasta, a meld of seven or more cards of which one, two or three cards are wild. C/f NATURAL CANASTA.

MUGGINS. In cribbage, an announcement that enables a player to take points that his opponent has overlooked.

NAP. A declaration in nap(oleon) to win all five tricks.

NATURAL CANASTA. In canasta, a meld of seven or more cards of which none is a wild card. C/f MIXED CANASTA.

NULLO. Same as MISÈRE q.v.

OMBRE. The player in ombre who plays against the other two players in partnership against him.

OPTIONAL CARD. In colonel, the top card of the stock turned face upwards.

ORDER UP. In euchre, the declaration of an opponent of the deal accepting the suit of the turn-up card as the trump suit.

PAIR. (1) In casino, the play of a card and taking up as a trick all the other cards of the same rank in the layout. (2) In cribbage, playing a card of the same rank as the previous one played.

PAIR-ROYAL. (1) In brag, three cards of equal rank. (2) In cribbage, playing a third card of the same rank as a pair.

PAM. The Jack of Clubs in loo.

PARTIE. A game in piquet.

PEDRO. C/f LEFT PEDRO and RIGHT PEDRO.

PEG. In cribbage, a marker used for scoring on a board.

PICCOLISSIMO. In boston whist, a contract to make exactly one trick.

PINOCLE. The Queen of Spades and Jack of Diamonds in pinocle.

PITCH. In auction pitch, the opening lead that determines the trump suit.

PIQUE. In piquet, the winning of 30 points in hand and play before an opponent scores. C/f REPIQUE.

PLAIN SUIT. A suit other than the trump suit.

POINT. In piquet, the number of cards held in the longest suit.

POLIGNAC. The Jack of Spades in polignac.

POOL. The collective amount of players' stakes and fines.

POPE. The 9 of Diamonds in pope joan.

POT. In poker, a game in which all the players put up an ante.

PROPOSE. In écarté, a request by the non-dealer that cards may be exchanged for others from the stock.

PUESTA. In ombre, if ombre and one or both of his opponents win the same number of tricks.

PUNTO. In ombre, the Ace of whichever red suit is trumps.

QUART. In piquet, a sequence of four cards.

QUATORZE. In piquet, any four cards of the same rank higher than the 9.

QUINT. (1) In piquet, a sequence of five cards. (2) In quinto, the 5 of every suit, and every pair of cards in a suit that totals five.

QUINT ROYAL. The Joker in quinto.

RAISE. In poker, to increase a bet by putting up more than is necessary to equal the previous player.

REFAIT. A drawn game in *trente et quarante*.

REFUSE. (1) In games of the all fours family, the rejection by the dealer of a proposal by the non-dealer to make another suit trumps. (2) In écarté, the rejection by the dealer of the non-dealer's proposal that cards may be exchanged for others from the stock.

REPIQUE. In piquet, the winning of 30 points in hand alone before opponent scores. C/f PIQUE.

REVOKE. Failure to follow suit when able to or to play a card in accordance with the laws of the game.

RIGHT BOWER. In euchre, the Jack of the trump suit. C/f LEFT BOWER.

RIGHT PEDRO. In cinch, the 5 of the trump suit. C/f LEFT PEDRO.

ROB THE PACK. In cinch, the privilege accorded to the dealer of selecting cards from the stock.

ROUND. A division of dealing, betting or playing in which each player participates once.

ROUND THE CORNER. A sequence of cards in which the highest is considered adjacent to the lowest.

ROYAL MARRIAGE. In games of the bezique family, the meld of the King and Queen of the trump suit. C/f COMMON MARRIAGE.

RUBBER. Three successive games between the same sides or players: winning two of the three games.

RUBICON. Failure of the loser of a game to reach a specified minimum total of points.

RUFF. To play a trump card on the lead of a card of a side suit.

RUMMY. In games of the rummy family, the declaration by a player of all his cards in one turn.

RUN. Same as SEQUENCE *q.v.*

RUN THE CARDS. In games of the all fours family, to deal more cards and a fresh turn up after a beg has been accepted.

SACARDO. In ombre, if ombre wins more tricks than either of his opponents individually.

SCHMEISS. In klaberjass, an offer to play with the turn-up card as the trump suit or throw in the hand, as the opponent prefers.

SEPTIÈME. In piquet, a sequence of seven cards.

SEQUENCE. Two or more cards of adjacent rank.

SIDE SUIT. Same as PLAIN SUIT *q.v.*

SINGLE BETE. In pinocle, the concession of defeat and payment of a forfeit, without playing. C/f DOUBLE BETE.

SINGLETON. An original holding of only one card of a suit.

SINK. In piquet, to omit announcing a scoring combination.

SIXIÈME. In piquet, a sequence of six cards.

SLAM. C/f GRAND SLAM and SMALL SLAM.

SMALL SLAM. In games of the bridge and whist families, winning twelve tricks. C/f GRAND SLAM.

SMUDGE. In auction pitch, a bid to win all four tricks.

SOLO. In games of the solo whist family, a bid to win five tricks.

SPADILLE. The Ace of Spades in ombre.

SPINADO. The Ace of Diamonds in spinado.

SPOIL. When no player wins three tricks in spoil five.

SPREAD. C/f GRAND SPREAD and LITTLE SPREAD.

STAND. (1) In games of the all fours family, to accept the suit of the turn up card as the trump suit. (2) In *vingt-et-un*, to elect to take no further cards.

START. In cribbage, the top card of the cut turned face upwards by the dealer.

STOCK. The undealt part of the pack which may be used later in the deal.

STRADDLE. In poker, a compulsory bet of twice the ante.

SWEEP. In casino, taking in all the cards in the layout.

TABLANETTE. An announcement in tablanette that a player is able to take all the cards on the table.

TAKE IT. In klaberjass, to accept as the trump suit the suit of the turn up card.

TALON. In piquet and some games of patience, cards laid aside in one or more packets for later use in the same deal.

TOP LAYOUT. In monte bank, the two top cards of the pack placed by the banker face upwards on the table. C/f BOTTOM LAYOUT.

TRAIL. In casino, the play of a card to the layout by a player who can neither pass, combine, build nor call.

TRIO. In piquet, three cards of the same suit higher than the 9.

TURN UP. A card faced after the deal to determine, or propose, the trump suit.

TWIST. In *vingt-et-un*, a request to be dealt a card face upwards.

UP CARD. (1) In gin rummy, the card turned up after each player has been dealt ten cards. (2) In stud poker, a card dealt face upwards.

VOID. Having no cards of a specified suit.

VOLE. In ecarté, winning all five tricks.

VULNERABLE. In games of the bridge family, said of a side that has won a game and is subject to bigger penalties and bonuses.

WAIVE. The privilege, in some games of patience, to lift a card and play the one under it.

WHISTER. A partner in boston de fontainebleau.

WIDOW. Extra cards dealt to the table usually at the same time as the hands are dealt to the players.

WILD CARD. A card that the rules of the game permit the holder to specify as representing any card.

YOUNGER HAND. The dealer in piquet and other games for two players. C/f ELDER HAND.

Index